W9-CFC-225

The Pointe Book

shoes, training & technique

second edition

The Pointe Book

shoes, training & technique

second edition

Janice Barringer
Sarah Schlesinger

Princeton Book Company, Publishers

Copyright © 1998 and 2004 by Princeton Book Company, Publishers.

All rights reserved. Published 2004

Princeton Book Company, Publishers
PO Box 831
Hightstown, NJ 08520-0831

Book design by Lisa Denham. Cover design by Lisa Denham and
John McMenamin.

Printed in the United States of America

Library of Congress Cataloging-in-Publication Data
Barringer, Janice.
   The pointe book: shoes, training & technique / Janice Barringer,
Sarah Schlesinger.—2nd ed.
       p. cm.
   ISBN 0-87127-261-X
   1. Ballet dancing. 2. Ballet shoes. I. Schlesinger, Sarah. II. Title.

   GV1788.B37 2004
   794.8—dc22
                                        2004050366

Contents

Introduction
by David Howard

One of my earliest and fondest memories is a visit to a Christmas magic show. Soon after, when I saw pointe dancing for the first time, I assumed that it was also a feat of magic.

No doubt those audiences that saw pointe dancing at its inception in the early 1800s shared my childlike perspective; seeing Marie Taglioni and her contemporaries ascend to the tips of their toes must have seemed a mythical, magical accomplishment.

Since that first, entrancing glimpse of pointe work, I have spent a large portion of my life becoming intimately acquainted with the reality behind the illusion. Yet in spite of my daily exposure to the mechanics of this process, I am still swept away by the element of magic with which magnificent dancers like Gelsey Kirkland, Sylvie Guillem, Cynthia Harvey, Amanda McKerrow, Tamara Rojo, and Natalia Makarova have transformed the art of dancing on pointe.

However, I am also more and more cognizant that the freedom to create such magic is rooted in a command of craft. For many years, pointe dancing and the shoes that make it possible have remained needlessly obscured in a mist of myth and rumor. Often this aura of superstition gets in the way of a sensible approach to pointe as an essential element of the classical ballet technique. In *The Pointe Book,* Janice Barringer and Sarah Schlesinger have created a comprehensive resource of great value for everyone interested in this aspect of ballet, including professional dancers, teachers, students, parents, and audience members.

The authors' goal has been to demystify the mechanics of pointe shoes and pointe dancing. They have been assisted in this mission by hundreds of dancers, teachers, choreographers, school administrators, and medical

specialists around the world. In the tradition of the dance profession, these experts have willingly shared their knowledge to help make the next generation of dancers even stronger than their own.

This outpouring of response has afforded the book a special richness that provides the reader with a new level of awareness of an often misunderstood tool of our trade. Revelations abound on every subject from determining pointe readiness to prolonging shoe life. The result is a complete and long-overdue examination of the most fascinating component of our art form.

After considering the many facets of pointe shoes and pointe dancing covered in this volume, it becomes evident that the key word in the phrase *pointe work* is *work*. Pointe dancing is not an entity unto itself; introduced at the right time for each individual dancer, it is an extension of training. We are also reminded that pointe dancing is not an inevitability for a ballet student; not everyone is suited to its peculiar demands.

The Pointe Book is an exhaustive guide to many available options, offering intriguing insights into the technical path that we hope leads to artistry. It helps us realize that although pointe dancing has sprung from a classical tradition, it cannot remain in the Dark Ages. The world of the pointe dancer has been forever changed by expanding technique, technological advances in shoemaking, increased understanding of kinesiology, and medical attention to the special needs of dancers. In the beginning of the twenty-first century we find that the surfaces we dance upon have changed from the traditional hardwood floors to vinyl or Marley-type surfaces. Even the air dancers breathe is different. Open windows in studios and rehearsal halls have often been closed to accommodate air conditioning or other ways to artificially circulate air. How all of this will affect dancers and pointe dancing remains to be seen.

The future promises to be equally volatile. The pointe shoe will continue to change to suit the dancer's evolving needs. Perhaps a future edition of this book will have to include tips on pointe dancing in space. Will the trick then be to stay on the ground in a weightless environment? One can only speculate!

In the meantime, secretly armed with the knowledge that we find in *The Pointe Book,* we can continue to mystify the occupants of our planet. For me, the illusion of a ballerina defying gravity in satin slippers will forever remain proof positive of the existence of magic!

Preface

Our goal in writing *The Pointe Book* has been to create a resource for students and professional dancers and their teachers that present a full spectrum of information about this essential tool of their craft.

Following a brief look at the historical evolution of pointe dancing, we consider the structure of the pointe shoe as a foundation for our examination of this unique art form. And since understanding the manner in which pointe shoes are made is a vital first step in understanding how they function, we have detailed the shoemaking process based on our observation in British and U.S. factories.

Next, we consider the fundamentals of buying, preparing, and wearing pointe shoes. We review the international pointe shoe marketplace by profiling major pointe shoe manufacturers around the world and providing descriptions of their products and services. A detailed list of the varied characteristics of pointe shoes will help guide the reader in making the decision as to which shoes provide the features needed for each dancer. A fitting chart comparing U.S. street shoe sizes with each style of pointe shoe will help unravel the confusion associated with a field that has no coordination or standard.

In the area of pointe readiness, we present an array of contemporary views on when students should go on pointe. Then we examine the way major ballet schools in the United States and around the world integrate pointe work into their teaching systems. Sample classes for beginning, intermediate, and advanced pointe students are provided.

Pointe-related injuries are a fact of life for most pointe dancers, and we address this issue with a look at minor and major injuries of the foot and ankle. Finally, we present the thoughts and feelings of professional dancers about their pointe shoes.

Since our initial meeting in 1975 as a dancer (Janice Barringer) and

pointe shoe fitter (Sarah Schlesinger) contemplating the mysteries of a 2½A *Nicolini*, we have been fascinated with the idea of gathering together the available wisdom on pointe shoes. We finally had the opportunity to begin work on this project in 1988, and we quickly realized that very little had been written on the subject. It immediately became obvious that our information had to be gathered from dancers, teachers, students, choreographers, company directors, shoe manufacturers, and medical professionals. Between January 1988 and September 1989, our quest for this information took us from Florida to California and from London to Stockholm. In 1998, and again in 2003, new information was gathered after numerous new products, theories and medical experts in the field of dance burst upon the ballet scene. During this time we interviewed or consulted the exceptional group of individuals whose knowledge and ideas on this subject became the cornerstone of this book.

Dance Shoe Specialists

Victoria Antonova, Import/Export Dept., Vozrozhdenie, Russia

Irene Ashley, President of Grishko, North America

Michele Attfield, Freed of London Ltd., London

Glenn Baruch, President, Leo's Dancewear Inc., Chicago, IL

Carol Beevers, Footwear Specialist/Store Manager, The National Ballet of Canada, Toronto

Edith Bloom, Retired Sales Representative, Capezio Ballet Makers, Sarasota, FL

Mary Price Boday, The Dance Works, Distributor for Schachtner, Peoria, IL

Gine Chant-Grostern, Owner, E. Porselli retail store, London

Michael Clifford, Shoe Supervisor, Royal Birmingham Ballet, Birmingham, England

Charlotte Davis, Marketing Manager, The National Ballet of Canada, Toronto

Franc Raoul Duvall, Sansha USA, New York

Aleksandra Efimova, President, Russian Pointe Shoes, Ann Arbor, MI

Xijun Fu, Owner, Fuzi International, Olympia, WA

Frank Giacoia, Shoemaker, Capezio Ballet Makers, Totowa, NJ

Chan Hon Goh, Owner, Principal Pointe Shoes and Diamond Pointe, Toronto

Brice Gouguet, Manager, Gamba

Tim Heathcote, Footwear Brand Manager, Bloch, Australia

Julie Hegge, Shoe Coordinator, English National Ballet, London

Vanessa Hile, Bloch, Australia

Marie Johansson, Store Manager, Sansha, New York

Marlena Juniman, Vice President, Prima Soft Pointe Shoes

Bernard D. Kohler, former Managing Director, Freed of London Ltd., Bloch

Dan Leva, Product Development Manager, Capezio Ballet Makers, Totowa, NJ

Yvette Lin, Sales Manager, special orders, Freed of London, New York

Bob Martin, Dance Workshop Ltd., London

Eliza Minden, Owner, Gaynor Minden Pointe Shoes

Hiromi Okamoto, Chacott, Japan

Fernando Oliveira, Chacott Iberica and Evolution Pirouette, CA

Antonella Pagano, Marketing, Advertising & Promotion, Angelo Luzio, Canada

Anne Polajenko, Public Relations and Pointe Shoe Specialists, So'Dança Pointe Shoes, Deerfield Beach, FL

Shinji Saeki, President, Freed of London Ltd., London

Philippe Saint-Paul, USA General Manager, Sansha, New York

Alan Schofield, Representative, E Porselli Ltd., London

Sophie Simpson, PA to Michele Attfield, Freed of London, London

Estelle Sommers, Capezio Dance-Theatre Shops, New York

Mark Suffolk, Founder, Suffolk Pointe Shoe Company, Ltd., England

Rosa Swanger, Miguelito, Mexico City, Mexico

Diana Teplitsky-Kessler, Teplov Ballet Shoes, South Africa

Donald Terlizzi, Capezio Ballet Makers, Totowa, NJ

Paul Terlizzi, Capezio Ballet Makers, Totowa, NJ

Shinobu Uchino, Staff, Sylvia Co. Ltd., Japan

Julienne Viola, Director and General Manager of USA Operation, Freed of London, New York

Judith Weiss, Director of Ballet Sales and Fittings for the Capezio Retail Group, New York

Yasmin Wilkenfeld, Executive Vice President, Bloch International, Australia

David Wilkinfeld, Managing Director, Bloch International, Australia

Dancers, Dance Teachers, and Company Directors

Nina Ananiashvili, Principal Dancer, American Ballet Theatre and international guest artist

Christine Beckley, former teacher, Royal Ballet School, White Lodge, London

Michelle Benash, Juilliard School, New York

Claude Bessy, former Director, Paris Opéra Ballet School, Paris

Nancy Bielski, company teacher, American Ballet Theatre, New York; Faculty, STEPS, New York

Susanna Bjurström, Administrator, Royal Swedish Ballet School, Stockholm

Helene Braezeale, former Associate Dean of Fine Arts, Towson State University, Towson, MD

Leslie Browne, Faculty, STEPS, New York

Regina Bustillos, personal assistant to Helgi Tomasson, San Francisco Ballet

Diana Byer, Artistic Director, New York Theatre Ballet, New York

Adrienne Canterna, Gold Medal Winner, International Ballet Competition, Jackson, MS

Sandra Carlino, Director, Cumberland Dance Company, Enola, PA

Martha Chapman, Faculty, STEPS, New York

Nansi Clement, ballet teacher, New York

Kerrison Cooke, former Director, English National Ballet School, London

Clara Cravey, Principal, Houston Ballet School, Houston, TX

Alexandra Danilova, former faculty, School of American Ballet, New York

Sasha Dmochowski, Soloist, American Ballet Theatre, New York

Daniel Duell, Artistic Director, The School of Ballet Chicago, Chicago, IL

Alessandra Ferri, Principal Dancer, American Ballet Theatre, New York and international guest artist

Jim Fletcher, Public Affairs Director, English National Ballet, London

Martin Fredmann, Artistic Director and CEO, Colorado Ballet, Denver, CO

Jennifer Gelfand, former Principal Dancer, Boston Ballet, MA

Linda Gelinas, Dance Captain, Metropolitan Opera, New York

Nick Giordano, Dance Nicola, Montreal

Nathalie Gleboff, Executive Director, School of American Ballet, New York

Lorraine Graves, former dancer and Ballet Mistress, Dance Theatre of Harlem, New York

Nils-Åke Häggborn, Balettchef, Royal Swedish Ballet, Stockholm, Sweden

David Howard, internationally renowned ballet teacher and international guest teacher

Rodney Irwin, ballet teacher, Ruth Page Foundation School, Chicago, IL

Margret Kaufmann Pankov, Ballet Mistress, Les Grands Ballets Canadiens, Montreal

Darci Kistler, Principal Dancer, New York City Ballet, New York

Patricia Klekovic, ballet teacher, Ruth Page Foundation School, Chicago, IL

Joanna Kneeland, former ballet teacher, Las Vegas, NV

Natalie Krassovska, Ballet Teacher, Dallas, TX

Sherri LeBlanc, Soloist, San Francisco Ballet

Diana Levy, Ballet Mistress, Metropolitan Opera, New York

Delores Lipinski, ballet teacher, Ruth Page Foundation School, Chicago, IL

Larry Long, Director, Ruth Page Foundation School, Chicago, IL

Mikhail Messerer, international guest teacher

Sulamith Messerer, ballet teacher, Royal Ballet, London

Rosemary Miles, faculty, Atlanta Ballet, Atlanta, GA

Eugene Mills, former Associate Professor and Ballet Director, Western Michigan University, Kalamazoo, MI

Sandra Organ, former dancer, Houston Ballet; Faculty, Ben Stevenson Academy, Houston, TX

Marianne Orlando, former teacher, Royal Swedish Ballet School, Stockholm, Sweden

Vanessa Palmer, Principal Dancer, Royal Ballet, London

Michelle Proulx, shoe supervisor, Les Grands Ballets Canadiens, Montreal

Nicole Rhodes, Principal Dancer, Australian Ballet, Melbourne

Jenifer Ringer, Principal Dancer, New York City Ballet, New York

Sandra Robinson, Associate Professor, University of South Florida, Tampa, FL

Jo Rowan, Chairman, Department of Dance, Oklahoma City University, Oklahoma City, OK

Edith Royal, former dance teacher, Winter Park, FL

Victoria Schneider, faculty, Harid Conservatory, Miami, FL

Richard Sias, former Associate Professor, Florida State University, Tallahassee, FL

Larissa Sklyanskaya, former faculty, San Francisco Ballet School

Christine Spizzo, Former ABT Soloist and faculty member of North Carolina School of the Arts, Winston-Salem, NC

Marina Stavitskaya, Faculty, School of American Ballet, New York

Edward Stewart, former Artistic Director, Ballet Theatre of Maryland, Annapolis, MD

Gailene Stock, Director of The Royal Ballet School, London

Gösta Svalberg, former Director, Royal Swedish Ballet School, Stockholm, Sweden

Allysen Swenson, former ballet teacher, Houston Ballet School, Houston, TX

Kate Thomas, School Director, STEPS, New York

Victor Trevino, Artistic Director, Les Ballets Grandiva, New York

Amanda Turner, Faculty, STEPS, New York

Ashley Tuttle, Principal Dancer, American Ballet Theatre and lead in Broadway's *Movin' Out*

Françoise Vaussenat, Director of Studies, École Nationale de Ballet Contemporain, Montreal

William Martin Viscount, freelance choreographer and teacher, Fort Worth, TX

Jocelyn Vollmar, ballet teacher, San Francisco Ballet School, San Francisco

Katie Wade, Director, School of English National Ballet, London

Gretchen Ward Warren, Associate Professor, University of South Florida, Tampa, FL

Vincent Warren, Conservateur, Bibliothèque de la Danse de l'École Nationale de Ballet Contemporain, Montreal

Glenn White, former special assistant to Artistic Director Gerald Arpino, Joffrey Ballet, Chicago, IL

Anton Wilson, former member, Ballet Trockadero de Monte Carlo, Severna Park, MD

Steven Wistrich, Artistic Director of Company and School, City Ballet of San Diego, CA

Elizabeth Rowe Wistrich, choreographer and teacher, City Ballet of San Diego, CA

Health Specialists

Dr. Steven Baff, Podiatrist, New York

Dr. Richard T. Braver, D.P.M., Sports Adviser to Fairleigh Dickinson University (NJ); Medical Adviser to Runner's World Magazine; Consultant for Dr. Scholl's Foot Health

Michelina Cassella, Director of Physical Therapy Service, Sports Medicine Clinic, Children's Hospital, Boston, MA

Sean Gallagher, Director of Authentic Pilates, New York

Dr. Louis Galli, Podiatric Foot and Ankle Associates, New York

Dr. James G. Garrick, M.D., Center for Sports Medicine and Dance Medicine, St. Francis Hospital, San Francisco, CA

Dr. William G. Hamilton, Physician to The New York City Ballet, New York

Shirley Hancock, former Principal Physiotherapist, Royal
   Ballet School, The Royal Academy of Dancing, and the
   Remedial Dance Clinic, London
Liz Henry, Assistant Director, Westside Dance Physical
   Therapy, New York
Katy Keller, former Assistant Director, Westside Dance
   Physical Therapy, New York; Physical Therapist, Juilliard
   School of Music, New York
Romana Kryzanowska, former Director of Pilates Studio,
   New York
Marijeanne Liederbach, Principal, PT Plus, New York
Dr. Janiz A. Minshew, Chiropractor, New York
Marika Molnar, Director, Westside Dance Physical Therapy;
   Physical Therapist to The New York City Ballet, New York
Dr. Tom Novella, Podiatrist, New York
Dr. Nathan Novick, retired Chiropractor, New York
Dr. Donald Rose, Director, Harkness Center for Dance
   Injury, New York
Dr. Lillie Rosenthal, Kathryn and Gilbert Miller Health
   Care Institute for Performing Artists, New York
Dr. Alan S. Woodle, D.P.M., Company Podiatrist, Pacific
   Northwest Ballet Company, Seattle, WA

In addition to these formal interviews, we have gathered extensive information through telephone calls, e-mails, and written correspondence/surveys from dancers, teachers, students, dance store owners, shoe fitters, and shoemakers throughout the world.

It would be impossible to thank all of these contributors by name, but they are represented on every page because their concerns evolved into the questions that we have chosen to address.

We are especially grateful to David Howard and Robert Cornfield for their encouragement and advice. Special thanks to Jennifer Katz for tape transcription services, Audrey Daniels, Vincent Warren, and Nick Giordano for their translation services, Mikhail Messerer for his invaluable assistance and generosity, Samantha and Pat from Gamba Timestep Ltd., Miss Pat at Anello and Davide, Marilynn and Jim Dale, Robert and Vivien Altfeld, Gradimir and Margret Pankov, Patricia Renzetti and Martin Fredmann, Rosalie O'Connor, Virginia Johnson, Keith

Longmore, Sian Pritchard, all the manufacturers who painstakingly supplied detailed information for Chapter 9, teachers and directors of the schools mentioned in Chapter 11 who supplied updated information, Nancy Bielski for her invaluable advice, and Cherry Dowsley, Mary Miller, Leslie Bradley, Heidi Menocal, Anne Parshall, and David Miller of Ballet Theatre of Annapolis.

Today our approach to pointe dancing has been shaped by centuries of experimentation. During our travels to gather material for this book, we have found little agreement about any detail of the process, ranging from how a dancer ties ribbons to when students should begin pointe work. In summarizing what we have learned, we have attempted to reflect this diversity of opinion.

The one truth that united everyone who shared his knowledge and experience with us was a belief in the importance of keeping this unique art form alive. For that reason, creating this book has been an exceptionally rewarding experience for us. We hope readers will find it both useful and provocative.

With the exception of most of Chapters 1 and 12, every section of the book has been rewritten to include new information, while retaining material that will never go out of date. Some chapters are only slightly amended, while others have major changes. Chapters 4, 6, 7, and 9 are completely new.

Janice Barringer and Sarah Schlesinger, 2004

1

A Brief History of Pointe Dancing

The First Performances on Pointe

While there is little agreement among dance historians about the precise date and location of the first performance on pointe by a ballerina, there is no doubt that the introduction of dancing sur les pointes had a profound effect on ballet technique. The ability to rise to the tips of her toes afforded the ballerina the opportunity for virtuosity on a new plane. With the appearance of pointe shoes, the female dancer's technique expanded, enabling her to create the illusion of incredible lightness and to project an increased sense of daring.

Although dancers may have risen on their toes since ancient times, the first documented performances on pointe appear to have taken place in England and France between 1815 and 1830, 240 years after Catherine de Medici commissioned the first ballet in 1581. During the intervening years, a number of developments in the evolution of the female dancer's technique paved the way for the appearance of pointe dancing.

The Development of Pointe Dancing in the Seventeenth and Eighteenth Centuries

When King Louis XIV of France ordered the founding of the Royal Academy of Dance in 1661, the dancers initially performed on ballroom floors. When they were raised up on a stage, the audience had a different view of them and their feet became more important. As the stages grew larger, choreographers became more concerned with sideways movement and created the concept of turned-out legs. The height of the proscenium inspired a new movement vocabulary of elevated steps.

Men dressed as women took the female roles until 1681, when four young ladies danced in a ballet for the first time. These early ballerinas wore shoes with heels, constricted bodices, voluminous skirts, unwieldy headpieces, and enveloping shawls. Their costumes both reflected and

1

dictated the nature of their technique, which was limited to gracefully executed sliding, walking, and running in intricate floor patterns.

During the first half of the eighteenth century, dance technique experienced rapid development, and the dancer's dress was adjusted to accommodate these new physical demands. In 1726, Marie Camargo made her debut at the Paris Opéra Ballet and introduced the *entrechat*. To display these rapid changes of her feet from fifth position front to back and front again, she had to wear a shorter skirt. While initially she danced in the commonly accepted heeled shoes worn by her contemporaries, she soon abandoned them for a flatter shoe that provided an improved springboard for her complicated jumps. Camargo also devised an undergarment to wear beneath her petticoats, from which tights later evolved.

In 1734, Marie Sallé, a French dancer and rival of Camargo's, appeared at the Drury Lane Theatre in London, performing in a ballet called *Pygmalion* for the first time. She replaced her usually cumbersome style of costume with a simple muslin dress that followed the lines of her body, and wore her hair flowing loosely down her back instead of binding it up in an ornate headpiece.

The French Revolution swept away the remains of unwieldy costuming, and dancers began to appear in *maillot*—tights named after a costumer at the Paris Opéra. Flat ballet slippers tied with ribbons became standard footwear. These short-soled slippers with pleats under the toes were developed in response to the need for a more flexible shoe. The new slippers facilitated the fully extended pointing of the foot, as well as jumps and turns. They were the foundation upon which the first pointe shoes were built.

During the Revolution, many dancers and choreographers left the Paris Opéra to perform in England and other parts of Europe. One of these emigrants was Charles Didelot, who had introduced the concept of a flying machine in a production at Lyons in 1795. Didelot's contraption enabled dancers to stand briefly on their toes before being whisked upward, creating the illusion of lightness as they portrayed the ethereal, unreal characters of classical ballets.

Didelot's flying machine was enthusiastically received in London in 1796. As theatrical dancing evolved, women had become more athletic, and the audience adored watching them perform such feats as sailing across the stage aided by hidden wires. When the dancers landed on their toes, their fans cheered with delight. This favorable response encouraged choreographers to seek ways for their stars to linger in an elevated position.

Pointe Dancing in the Nineteenth Century

During the early 1800s, ballerinas were schooled in an increasingly challenging technical vocabulary including multiple *pirouettes*, jumps, and leaps. The attempt to dance on pointe without the support of wires was a logical extension of this growing emphasis on technical skill. Dancers discovered that by rising higher and higher on half pointe, they were able to balance on the ends of their fully stretched toes.

A print of ballerina Maria del Caro dated 1804 shows her nearly on the tips of her toes. On the basis of reviews and prints, Geneviève Gosselin, who died at the peak of her career in 1818, is thought to have danced on pointe in a production of Didelot's *Flore et Zephire* in 1815. Prints dated 1821 have been found showing Fanny Bias in the role of Flore, and she appears to be on pointe.

The Russian ballet master Adam Flushkovsky declared that he had seen Avdotia Istomina dancing on the "very tip of her toe" in St. Petersburg in the years between 1816 and 1820. On the London stage, an unfortunate dancer named Mademoiselle Julia is reported to have lost her balance while standing on pointe in 1827, and to have fallen to a chorus of critical scorn.

These earliest appearances on pointe probably involved little more than briefly held poses on the tips of the toes to give an illusion of weightlessness. They represented isolated *tours de force*, and were not yet part of the fabric of dance technique.

In 1832, Marie Taglioni appeared on pointe in the first performance of *La Sylphide*. Her performance not only ushered in the Romantic Age, but also introduced the use of pointe dancing as an essential choreographic element. Romantic ballet as represented by *La Sylphide* did not evolve in isolation, however, but rather as one aspect of a movement that involved every form of art in the early nineteenth century. It was part of a revolt against the eighteenth-century tradition of stressing classic perfection over feeling and meaning.

Ballet was an art form ruled by such traditional conventions when Taglioni demonstrated that pointe shoes could be used as an aesthetic element to convey a sense of character that was essentially Romantic. She used pointe to bring a new poetic quality to ballet that was consistent with stylistic developments in scene design and dance music.

While there are no films or notations of Taglioni's performance, dance historian Walter Terry suggests that August Bournonville's later choreography of *La Sylphide* was probably very similar to the original Taglioni version. There are no extended pointe segments, but *relevés* on both feet, *arabesques, attitudes,* and *bourrées* were probably performed on pointe. The elements of technique that could be executed on pointe were obviously limited by the nature of early pointe shoes. However narrow her technique, Taglioni's opening-night performance in *La Sylphide* caused one member of her audience to write, "Hers is a totally new style of dancing, graceful beyond all comparison, wonderful lightness, an absence of all violent effort. She seems to float and bound like a sylph across the floor."[1]

Pointe shoes similar to those worn by Taglioni in the 1800s have been preserved by private collectors. Her cobbler was Janssen of Paris, and several pairs of shoes bearing his stamp can be seen in the Haydn Museum in Eisenstadt, Austria. Upon examination they appear to be nothing more than soft satin slippers, heavily darned at the tip. They had no box to protect the toe, and featured a flexible leather sole that supported the foot. Darning along the sides and over the toe kept the slippers in shape. They were essentially a one-sized tube of satin and leather that bound and squeezed the toes into a uniformly narrow pointe that had little relevance to the shape of the wearer's foot.

In order to work in such soft shoes, early pointe dancers probably padded the toes for added protection. Stitched ribbons and starch were the only other primitive attempts at reinforcement, leaving the dancers to rely on the strength of their feet and ankles. Wearing these slippers, a cloudlike costume, and wings, Taglioni created the image of the ballerina as a vision of perfection. Her performance pulled together the elements of a style that had been evolving for decades and quickly spread to England, Italy, Denmark, Germany, Russia, and the United States.

In 1832, Amalia Brugnoli danced on pointe in London, causing a critic to observe that her staccato work on the tops of her toes was unequaled by anything except Paganini's (violin) bow. Pauline Montessu performed a slow turn on pointe in 1833, and Angelica Saint-Romain astonished the public by performing *capriccios* on the tips of her toes.

4

Three other great Romantic ballerinas made their debuts following Taglioni's triumph: Fanny Elssler in 1833, Carlotta Grisi in 1836, and Fanny Cerrito in 1840. Fanny Elssler was particularly skilled in pointe technique. When she visited the United States, it was said that her admirers drank champagne from her slippers. A similar myth claims that some of Taglioni's Russian fans bought a pair of her shoes for three hundred rubles, cooked them, and had them for supper.

Pointe Dancing at the Turn of the Nineteenth Century

Ballerinas influenced by the theories of Italian dance master Carlo Blasis again expanded the technique with exuberant new physical pyrotechnics in the late 1800s. For example, Pierina Legnani introduced thirty-two *fouettés* in a performance of *Swan Lake* in 1892. Dancing on pointe became a means of expressing fire and strength as well as fantasy. This expanded technical vocabulary gave the ballerina supremacy over the male dancer, which lasted until Nijinsky took Paris by storm in 1909.

Inspired by the feats of dancers like Legnani, the Russians invited Enrico Cecchetti to teach them the Italian technique, which they subsequently combined with elements of their own technique and French technique into what we now know as the Russian style. In addition to Italian technique, the Russians also embraced Italian pointe shoes. The shoes worn by Legnani were less pointed than the shoes worn by Taglioni and had a flatter, sturdier base. They also had stronger soles and a box that was molded with more substantial layers of fabric.

Pointe shoes created by the Italian shoemaker Nicolini were imported to Russia for use by the Russian Imperial Ballet until shipments were suspended during the Russian Revolution. These shoes had no nails and were lined with white kid leather. Since only their tips were stiffened or blocked, they were soundless on stage. Russian dancers used various techniques to stiffen the toes, such as cutting up old pasteboard suitcases for support.

By the time of the great classical ballets of Petipa and Ivanov, pointe work in the Russian ballet had become a series of intricate steps performed entirely on the toes. When *Sleeping Beauty* premiered in 1890, the dancers performing the fairy variations wore pointe shoes with a blocked toe made of newspaper and floured paste, which was reinforced by a light cardboard insole stretching between the tips of the toes and the instep.

As pointe dancing spread, variations in technique began to emerge. For instance, while the Italians tended to rise to pointe with a sprightly spring, the Russians rolled smoothly. The French rise was a cross between a spring and a roll.

In spite of the fact that her shoes weighed only one-half ounce more than the unblocked shoes of Taglioni's days, Anna Pavlova added a new dimension to pointe dancing in her portrayal of *The Dying Swan*. She was constantly on pointe in *bourrée*, a feat that had previously been thought impossible. Pavlova was rumored to have a secret process for preparing her slippers; after having a student break them in, she ripped out the cardboard and the fabric and leather liners and replaced them with a mysterious inner sole of her own design. She was reported to wear shoes with very wide platforms, which afforded her superior balance. However, she supposedly took special care to have the platforms touched up in photographs to look narrower and more delicate, creating the illusion that she balanced on "nothing."

Pointe Dancing in the Twentieth Century

The ballets created between 1909 and 1929 by Michel Fokine, Léonide Massine, and George Balanchine for the Ballets Russes, under the direction of Serge Diaghilev, brought pointe dancing into the twentieth century. For the first time, the ballet audience saw ballerinas performing backward *bourrées*, slow *balancés*, and traveling *relevés* in *arabesque* on pointe.

These advances were followed by further feats of skill performed on pointe by the "baby ballerinas" of the new Ballets Russes in 1931. Teenage ballerinas Irina Baronova and Tamara Toumanova performed sixty-four *fouettés* on pointe, six unsupported *pirouettes*, and extended balances to the delight of cheering audiences. The company rechoreographed the classics to incorporate these new "tricks" on pointe.

In the 1920s, one of the most popular stars on Broadway was Marilyn Miller, a toe dancer. Harriet Hoctor, another Broadway favorite in the 1920s and 1930s, stunned audiences at the Hippodrome in London by tapping up and down an escalator on her toes in shoes supported by steel shanks. Other Hoctor tricks included executing a backbend while doing *bourrées* on pointe, zooming through a circle of *piqué* turns at breakneck speed, and tapping out the meter of Edgar Allan Poe's poem *The Raven* with the tips of her shoes. Other revue dancers wore steel reinforcements to allow them to perform the Charleston on pointe.

In this "trick" pointe dancing tradition, Gloria Gilbert used ball bearings in the platforms of her shoes to allow her to turn at a dizzying rate while performing backbends. Toe-tap became a national craze as entrants in local amateur nights performed such feats as tapping on toe and playing the trumpet at the same time. A "showbiz" approach to pointe continued to spill over into the classical realm during the 1950s, when audiences expected ballerinas to do such tricks as sustaining *attitude* on pointe for an extended period while the conductor had the orchestra play the same phrase over and over, waiting for the choreography to resume.

During the Second World War, shoes were often in short supply owing to the upheaval throughout Europe. Alexandra Danilova recalled trying to extend the life of her shoes by darning them and coating them with a kind of shellac used to make straw hats stiff. Other dancers speak of strengthening their feet to be able to stand on pointe without shoes in order to dance in footwear that had been reduced to shreds.

By mid-century, pointe shoe boxes had become considerably harder in order to accommodate the technical demands on the dancer's foot. In the process of creating harder shoes, however, shoemakers produced pointe shoes with little flexibility, making it difficult for the dancer to have a sense of contact with the floor.

The continuing evolution of contemporary ballet technique led pointe shoe manufacturers to nonstop experimentation in succeeding decades. The result has been a wide range of pointe shoe designs, from extremely strong to ultralight, in a variety of styles and shapes that enable dancers to jump higher, move more quickly, and accomplish the increasingly difficult pointe technique utilized by choreographers such as George Balanchine. A typical pair of contemporary pointe shoes weighs about four ounces more than those worn in 1932.

Balanchine once said that if no pointe existed, he would not be a chore-ographer. The great critic Walter Terry quotes Balanchine as explaining:

> Ballet is artificial. It is like poetry, it is invented. Where words fail, poetry can succeed and the same is true of ballet: something you

cannot explain can be expressed on pointe. You can't tell a story on pointe but it can, when imaginatively used, give you an extra feeling similar to modulations in music or color intensities in light. In this sense, the pointe, even if it cannot tell a story, communicates drama. A ballerina on pointe is the maximum in dance.[2]

While pointe dancing is sure to live on in the "museum" works of the past, such as *Swan Lake* and *Giselle,* questions have been raised about its relevance to newly created works, since both choreography and the tools of the dance tend to change as the culture does.

Writing in 1986, dance critic Clive Barnes observed that the influence of modern choreography on classical ballet companies was tending to diminish the significance of the pointe shoe in new repertory. He suggested that toe dancing may be perceived as an unnatural movement, and "there is actually an aesthetic against the pointe work now, just as the cultural climate favored pointe work in the age of Romanticism."[3] Barnes wondered if pointe was an organic part of ballet technique or only a technical aid. However, works by choreographers such as Christopher Wheeldon and James Kudelka for major ballet companies around the world have clearly demonstrated that the dimension of pointe is still very much alive, and that contemporary ballet artists are indeed integrating pointe into their creative visions.

NOTES

1. Trucco, Terry. "To the Pointe," *Ballet News*, vol. 3 (March 1982), p. 21.

2. Terry, Walter. *On Pointe* (New York: Dodd Mead, 1962), p. 100.

3. Barnes, Clive. "Barnes On.....," *Ballet News*, vol. 7 (February 1986), p. 39.

For more information on the Romantic period, see Ivor Guest, *The Romantic Ballet in England* (Middletown, CT: Wesleyan University Press, 1966), and Ivor Guest, *The Romantic Ballet in Paris* (Middletown, CT: Wesleyan University Press, 1972), and refer to the Bibliography.

The Foot and the Pointe Shoemaking Process

Anatomy of the Foot

The real pointe is the foot itself and not the shoe, which is only a covering. To meet the unique demands of pointe dancing, the foot has to be strong, supple, and as sensitive as the hand. Rather than serving as a passive weight-bearer, it must assume positions and execute movements beyond its normal limits. The original nature of her foot can be either a plus or minus for a pointe dancer.

The foot is a complex structure containing twenty-six bones, with a maze of ligaments connecting them. Ligaments are bands of tissue that bind bones together. The foot is animated by muscles and tendons, the tough fibrous tissue that connects muscle to bone and originates either in the foot itself or in the lower leg. Some muscles and tendons are large and visible through the skin, while others are quite small and impossible to see.

Nerves control the foot and give it feeling. Bones, ligaments, muscles, tendons, and nerves work together to operate a structure that is extremely resilient and has a broad range of motion.

The skeleton of the foot is composed of three major parts—the *tarsus*, consisting of seven tarsal bones; the five *metatarsals*; and the fourteen *phalanges* (see figure 1). The bony point that appears in the middle of the foot is part of the fifth metatarsal. Each of the toes has three phalanges, with the exception of the big toe that has only two. The metatarsal joints at the ball of the foot connect the phalanges (phalanxes) or toe bones and the metatarsals or foot bones.

The solid back part of the foot is made up of seven tarsal bones. They are divided by cartilage, a tough elastic substance, and bound by ligaments that permit movement. The largest of the seven tarsal bones is called the *calcaneus* or heel bone.

9

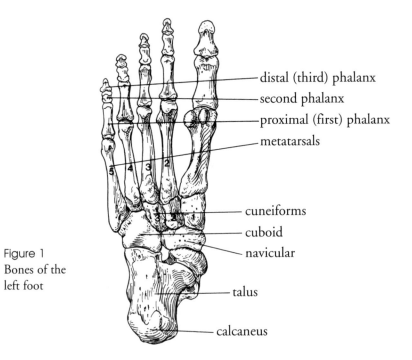

distal (third) phalanx
second phalanx
proximal (first) phalanx
metatarsals

cuneiforms
cuboid
navicular

talus

calcaneus

Figure 1
Bones of the
left foot

Above the calcaneus is the *talus* or ankle bone, which fits into a concave receptacle formed by the lower leg bones, the *tibia* and *fibula*. The talus receives the weight of the body through the tibia and then transfers it to the calcaneus.

The connection between the talus and the lower leg bones is cushioned by dense cartilage and held together by ligaments that run along the outside of the bones. There is no muscle around the ankle joint.

The part of the heel we can see and feel is an extension of the calcaneus. There is a protective bursa, or small, moist, friction-reducing envelope, between the calcaneus and the Achilles tendon. The *sustentaculum tali* offers support on the inside of the calcaneus; its edge can be felt about an inch below the ankle bone. On the outside, there is a similar projection called the *peroneal tubercle*.

The *cuboid*, found in front of the calcaneus, is situated between the calcaneus and the two outer metatarsal bones. On the inside it forms a joint with the outer *cuneiform* and *navicular*. The navicular is on the inside of the foot; it forms a joint to the rear with the talus, and to the front with the three cuneiforms. These three cuneiforms form a joint with each other and the three metatarsals in front, and with the navicular behind. The outer cuneiform also forms a joint with the cuboid.

The bones of the foot form two arches—the longitudinal arch along the inner side that is made up of the calcaneus, talus, navicular, the three cuneiforms, and the first three metatarsals; and the transverse arch which is formed by the convex arrangement of the tarsal and the metatarsal bones and which crosses the forefoot. When dancers speak of their arch, they are generally referring to the part of the sole between the ball and the heel, while the term *instep* describes the surface of the arch.

The arches are held together by long ligaments, and maintained by muscles. The spring ligament is the most important long ligament in the foot, and is attached to the sustentaculum tali and the *plantar* or sole surface of the navicular, supporting the talus.

Long and short plantar ligaments run under the foot between the bottom of the calcaneus and the three middle metatarsals. The short plantar ligament is situated under the long plantar ligament; it begins at the calcaneus and is then passed forward and slightly beyond the cuboid. The *medial* or *deltoid ligament* begins at the end of the tibia and spreads into three bands attached to the navicular, the sustentaculum tali, and the body of the talus. The *lateral ligament* is on the outside of the foot and attached to the end of the fibula. It divides into three bands that connect with the front of the talus, the calcaneus, and the body of the talus.

Movements of the Foot and Ankle Joint

The foot both bears weight and executes movements such as propulsion. Four layers of short muscles along the sole of the foot, called the intrinsic muscles, adjust the bones of the foot to the shape required for weight-bearing and hold this position. The long muscles attached to these bones and traveling up the leg are used when performing various movements.

There are eight possible movement patterns of the foot. The first two, plantar flexion or pointing the foot downward, and dorsi flexion or pointing the foot upward, take place in the ankle joint. They are limited by the shape of the bones and tightness of surrounding ligaments and tendons. *Inversion* or the raising of the inner border of the foot and *eversion* or the raising of the outer border happen in the back part of the foot between the talus and calcaneus. *Adduction*, the turning-in of the fore-foot, and *abduction*, the turning out the forefoot, take place in the mid-tarsal region between the talus, navicular, calcaneus, and cuboid bones. Finally, *supination* is the combination of adduction and inversion, while *pronation* is the combined action of abduction and eversion.

The toes stabilize the foot when it is bearing weight. Toes can move by curling downward or flexing, and by extending.

Muscular Action

Weight-bearing, propulsion, shock absorption, lifting (e.g., *relevé*), and free movement without weight-bearing (e.g., *battement frappé*) are per-formed by a series of muscles extending between the bottom of the knee and the bones of the foot as well as by the previously mentioned four layers of short intrinsic muscles on the soles of the foot. The only devi-ation from this pattern is the gastrocnemius, the large muscle at the back of the calf that originates at the lower end of the femur above the back of the knee. It acts as a knee flexor assisting the hamstrings. As it passes through the leg it joins with the soleus; these two muscles form the Achilles tendon that is inserted into the back of the calcaneus. The flex-ibility of this tendon determines the depth of *demi-plié* possible.

Four muscles turn the foot up and raise the inner or outer border: the *tibialis anterior*, the *extensor hallucis longus*, the *extensor digitorum longum*, and the *peroneus tertius*. The tibialis anterior helps maintain the arch of the foot.

Five other muscles point or plantar flex the foot: the *peroneus longus, peroneus brevis, tibialis posterior, flexor digitorum longus*, and *flexor hallucis longus*. Tibialis posterior is an important supporter of the arch, and flex-or hallucis longus flexes the big toe to the ground and assists in take-offs during propulsive movement. Tibialis anterior and tibialis posterior, as well as flexor hallucis, maintain a normal relation between the front and back of the foot.

To achieve a position on pointe, the anatomical progression is through a rise to half pointe and then to three-quarter pointe or full pointe. To achieve a rise, the trunk and pelvis move as one and come slightly for-ward with the line of gravity, to lie over the toes when the rise is com-pleted. Anatomically, the calf muscles contract, lifting the heel and hind foot against gravity. Tone must be maintained in the muscles of the leg and hip, including the gluteals, the adductors, the hamstrings, and the quadriceps. Complete control requires full strength in the intrinsic muscles of the foot as well as the calf and other leg muscles.

When dancing on pointe, the weight of the body is supported by the intrinsic muscles of the foot and the longitudinal arches, but it rests on the metatarsals. The pointe shoe is designed to protect the toes and force them to stretch out in a gentle curve, instead of buckling under the weight of the body.

Anatomy of the Traditional Pointe Shoe

Since the foot of a pointe dancer changes shape every few seconds when she is in motion, she needs a shoe that can adjust to provide comfort and support, whether she is on pointe or in a flat position. The contemporary pointe shoe does just that.

Inside the end of most contemporary pointe shoes (with the exception of shoes such as Gaynor Minden that are made with elastomeric materials) is the *box* or *block* made from densely packed layers of fabric and paper, which are shaped and dipped in glue. It is this hardened glue that makes the shoe stiff. This box of fabric and glue extends over the phalanges, encasing, protecting, and supporting the toes and giving them a small round platform on which to perch. The blocking is thickest at the tip but extends as far as halfway down the shoe in a thinner form, providing a sturdy structure under a skin or *upper* of satin, canvas, or leather. Shoe blocks come in varying degrees of hardness, and varying widths and vamp lengths.

A short outer sole made of thin leather allows for flexibility and contact with the floor. Although most of these outer soles are made in one piece, a few companies have introduced split outer soles to provide more flexibility in the shoe. A sturdy but pliable insole made of various combinations of leather and fiber reinforces the dancer's arch. A narrow supportive spine called the *shank* is usually placed between the outer sole and the inner sole. This centerpiece is the core of the shoe, extending from the middle of the heel to just under the ball of the foot, and usually shaped like a flattened spoon. The shank must be supple, but not brittle, to conform to the arch of the dancer's foot as it lifts off the floor. Typically, it has been made from leather or fabric, although recently, longer-lasting mate-

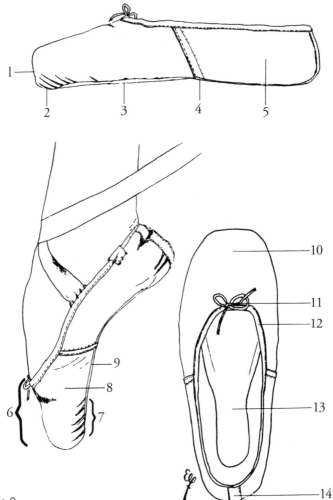

Figure 2
Anatomy of the pointe shoe: (1) platform or tip, (2) edge of the pleats or feathers, (3) outer sole, (4) waist seam, (5) quarter or heel section, (6) vamp—the top of the box that covers the toes. (Vamp length is the distance between the drawstring knot and the top edge of the box. Some European manufacturers refer to vamp length as the distance between the drawstring knot and the edge of the pleats or feathers.), (7) pleats or feathers—area underneath the box where the satin is pleated to fit under the sole, (8) wings or supports, (9) shank or narrow supporting spine, which is attached to the back of the insole, (10) stiffened box or block made of layers of glue and fabric and surrounding the toes and ball of the foot, (11) drawstring knot, (12) drawstring casing—bias tape stitched around the edge of the shoe to contain the drawstring, (13) insole, (14) back seam, which divides the quarters.

rials have been introduced by several companies. For instance, Gaynor Minden's shanks are made with an elastomeric material that makes them unbreakable. In addition, they never lose their original stiffness. In the United States we sometimes refer to the entire unit formed by the insole and its attached reinforcement as the shank. To prevent confusion, we use the term *shank* to refer only to the inner reinforcing tongue. An additional protective sock lining is usually glued over the insole.

The side and top of the shoe are covered with a cotton lining and an outer layer of satin, canvas, or leather. The upper extends over the toes, across the box or block, and under the foot to connect with the sole in carefully crafted pleats.

The descriptive terms given in figure 2 are commonly used by American and European manufacturers to describe the parts of the pointe shoe.

The Pointe Shoemaking Process

The following pointe shoemaking process describes the method for making handmade shoes. Very recently, some manufacturers have changed to mass production. The dancer must read the manufacturers' descriptions very closely to be able to determine which method is used for each model of shoe.

To more fully comprehend the unique nature of pointe shoes, we begin with a basic explanation of how they are made. While pointe dancers and their shoemakers are usually strangers to one another, they depend on each other for their livelihood.

Sulamith Messerer, the renowned former Bolshoi star who has not only taught company class for the Royal Ballet, but also teaches for prominent companies all over the world, recalled that very young ballet students at major company schools in Russia learned how pointe shoes were made. Since their pointe shoes were made by the company's own shoemakers, they were able to observe the process directly. As a result, they had a much clearer understanding of their shoes and were better able to communicate about them.

Since few American dancers have such an opportunity to observe the process for themselves, we have synthesized the steps of pointe shoe construction as we observed them in four factories in the United States and England. Pointe shoe construction varies from manufacturer to manufacturer, yet the basic process for making handmade shoes, while quite complex, is much the same (with the exception of the elastomeric and mass-produced shoes). One manufacturer estimates that it takes 137 operations performed over three days by seven people to make one pair of pointe shoes. Thus it is not surprising that no two pairs are ever alike, even when crafted by the same maker.

Traditionally, pointe shoes are made by the *turnshoe process*, which means they are *lasted* (placed on a foot-shaped form) and sewn inside out, slipped off the last, and then turned right side out for shaping, drying, and finishing. Until the 1870s, all shoes were made in this fashion, but now only pointe shoemakers and some running shoe manufacturers use the method. Pointe shoes are made on a straight last and have no right or left since this kind of "no-footed" construction gives better balance and a truer, straighter point. A straight last allows the foot to tell the shoe what to do, rather than having the shoe establish the form of the foot.

While some of the cutting and sewing phases of the process have been automated, the majority of the work on pointe shoes around the world is still done by hand. Since the pleating and shaping is still done by hand, the process remains a nineteenth-century craft. This method is being challenged by a few manufacturers, but these new shoes have not been on the market long enough to judge the long-term effects on dancers' health.

The Process

Step 1. Cutting or Clicking

The vamp section, quarter sections, and linings that form the upper of the toe shoe are cut from special patterns. After inspecting the fabric for imperfections, cutting-room employees do multicuts of yards of satin and lining material for stock shoes using a hydraulic press to cut many layers at one time. Special orders are hand-cut from individual patterns, and alterations related to the height of the vamp, sides, and back are done at this stage. Uppers are stamped with a date and lot number.

Step 2. Sewing or Closing

Seamstresses at sewing machines join the fronts and backs (vamps and quarters) of the upper, and sew the satin and cotton lining sections of the upper together. The back strap is sewn on and opened flat. At some factories, the binding and drawstring that adjust the snugness of the shoe are attached at this time. At others they are added when the shoe is near completion. When working on stock shoes, seamstresses usually work on a batch of ten of one size. Excess threads are removed at a trimming table.

Step 3. Preparing the Insole, Shank, and Outer Sole

The insole, shank, and outer sole are cut out of large pieces of leather to the shape needed by heavy mechanical presses or by hand, with knives that look like cookie cutters. Shoulder leather is frequently used. A number of makers commented on the difficulty of finding a steady supply of leather in an age of synthetics. The leather soles and insoles are then shaved to perfect the surface and to establish uniform thickness. Then, on a machine that looks like a sewing machine, a channel or groove is cut around the perimeter of the sole. Later, when the shoe is assembled, this groove becomes the stitching line. After the channel is cut, the soles may be buffed in a wringerlike device.

Step 4. Pulling Over

The upper is stretched inside out over the last, which is a foot-shaped form. At some factories the last is covered with tissue paper to make it easier to remove the shoe. Once made of wood, today most lasts are constructed of heavy plastic. As many as eight thousand lasts may be required to make a full line of pointe shoes. The shape of each last—designed to mold the shoe into a curve somewhere between the flat and arched foot—is a compromise. While a professional dancer may have her own last molded to her foot, most student dancers wear stock shoes formed on standard factory lasts in the size, shape, and style of their choice. Lasts may be wrapped with leather and tape to change their shape temporarily for a special order.

Step 5. Blocking

The shoemaker assembles the *blocking* over the lining of the upper in layers. Fabric (often burlap; the English called it hessian), paper, and special-formula glue are used to build up the inside of the box. In some processes, a burlap triangle is added to form the platform. The specifics of this part of the process differ greatly from manufacturer to manufacturer. Many place special emphasis on materials and methods that ensure the shoe will be "noiseless." Glue formulas are usually kept top secret. The combination of fabric and glue must stay malleable enough to be worked on through the day.

Step 6. The Lasting Step

The lasting step begins as the shoemaker pulls the uppers taut and uses his hands as well as various pushing and pulling instruments to mold the still soft block into its finished pointe shape—square, long, flat, oval, or curved. He inserts the pleats by hand and pushes them into position with an awl-like instrument called the bone. This step is critical because the fit and flexibility of the shoes depend on the pleating. Many shoemakers feel that pleating is the most difficult part of the process. At Capezio, pointe shoes are made with ten pleats. One disappears from view when the shoe is turned, leaving a broad central pleat with four smaller pleats on either side. After the pleats are formed, the shoemaker holds them with his thumb and ties them in place.

Step 7. Stitching and Turning

The pleats are stitched down with linen thread, and excess cloth is trimmed. The upper is stitched to the sole in the pre-cut channel. Then the shoe is turned right side out.

Step 8. Insole Insertion

The insole and attached reinforcing shank are placed inside the shoe with glue and nails. Next the shoemaker stamps and shapes the inside of the shoe, and glues on an inner sole or sock lining.

Step 9. Hammering Out

Using an enormous shoehorn, the shoemaker reinserts the last. Then he shapes the shoe from the outside, using a smooth-edge hammer to mold the block or box over the shape of the last, particularly at the toe, to get rid of any bumps or uneven edges. He deepens the pleats, scores cuts on the soles for traction, and stamps shoemaker, size, and last information on the soles.

Step 10. Drying

Finished shoes are placed on a rack to dry for two to four days. At some factories, the shoes are baked in a hot-air oven. Some manufacturers sponge finished shoes with a nonabrasive soap solution to remove excess glue and other residue.

Step 11. Inspection

Dried shoes are inspected for quality, and either stored until needed or prepared for shipment.

About the Shoemakers

Pointe shoemakers are usually trained on the job and many remain in the profession for a lifetime. They are almost always men, although women are often involved in the preparation and finishing stages of the process. Most of the makers are highly skilled craftsmen who do not necessarily have any interest in ballet or knowledge of the dancers for whom they create shoes.

In the early days of American pointe shoe manufacturing, shoemakers were recruited as they got off the ship from Italy. Many apprenticed at factories as young men and remained a lifetime. According to legend, one Capezio shoemaker was so dedicated to the company that he asked to be buried in the factory; his ashes are rumored to be there today.

While the older shoemakers used to bring their entire families into the business, fewer members of the younger generation are joining the profession. There is apprehension in the industry about the eventual loss of a willing and capable work force in an area that requires long practice, devotion to craft, and exceptional skill.

The Pointe Shoe Fitting Process

No other event in a dance student's life is anticipated with as much excitement as being fitted for a first pair of pointe shoes. Often this initial enthusiasm is replaced with disillusion at the fitting session. Not only do pointe shoes feel extremely uncomfortable on the novice's feet, but the first fitting can also be a confusing, frustrating experience for everyone involved. With careful forethought, a teacher can greatly simplify this experience for the student, the parent, the dance shop, and the school.

Teacher Involvement

If possible, the teacher should accompany the student to the first fitting, or arrange for representatives from a dance shop to visit the studio for a group fitting. If this is impossible to arrange, the teacher should be sure to provide students and their parents with a complete orientation to the fitting process. This orientation should include a discussion of how pointe shoes should fit, their cost, and the importance of not wearing them at home without the teacher's supervision. The school's preferences in ribbons, shoe padding, and use of elastic should also be explained.

In view of the rising cost of shoes, it is essential that teachers inform parents about the economic commitment involved in placing a child on pointe, and clarify the importance of an exact fit. Inevitably, parents seek to have their children fitted in shoes "to grow into." The teacher must help them understand why this concept cannot be applied to the process of buying pointe shoes.

During this time parents and students should inquire about the types of shoes that are available. Are they made of the light paste, the stronger paste, or the new elastomeric materials? This is important to know because all three types of shoes break in differently, and must be cared for in a different manner. The expectations for how long they will last will also vary enormously. As much as this is important, getting the correct fit is of primary concern.

Since the bones of the feet do not complete their final ossification—hardening and joining—until the dancer's twentieth to twenty-third year, incorrect fitting can damage the future growth pattern of a young dancer. The shoe must fit snugly; otherwise it could cause calluses and bruises on joints, or accidents to the ankles and toes. Shoes that are too large make it impossible to achieve proper support and balance.

Pressure from parents, because of the cost of pointe shoes, to have their children fitted in shoes that are too large has led some teachers to compromise their standards. In recent times parents have tried to manipulate schools and teachers more than ever before, but allowing students to pad their shoes for longer wear is unsafe and irresponsible.

If parents are not able or willing to make the necessary investment to keep their child in correctly fitting pointe shoes, it would be far more advisable and healthier for the child to remain in soft slippers. Making parents aware that advanced pointe students go through a pair of shoes in one to three weeks, and that a ballerina at the height of her profession might wear out sixty-five pairs a month, can help put the realities of starting a student on pointe in an accurate perspective.

The teacher's knowledge of the student's foot structure, overall strength, and potential for advancement should prompt a suggestion for a specific brand, style, and possible size of pointe shoe to try. The more information imparted in advance, the higher the probability that the student will be fitted correctly and not have to return to the dance shop to exchange her shoes.

With the addition of more and more brands and styles, using an experienced fitter is very desirable, since it is difficult to keep up to date with an ever-changing market. Finding a shop with skilled fitters is the most important step in the pointe shoe buying process.

A store dedicated to selling dance shoes offers the best prospect of finding experienced fitters. While children's shoe stores, general shoe stores, and department stores stock dance shoes, frequently they cannot offer the same specialized fitting services. Fitters from the Capezio flagship store in New York will come to schools and companies at their own expense, bringing shoes with them to do a personal fitting. Ordering pointe shoes by mail is always risky, but is absolutely out of the question when buying a first pair. If there is no local source where shoes can be tried on, a trip should be planned to the nearest location where this is possible.

Preparing for a Fitting

There are a number of preparatory steps a dancer can take before a pointe shoe fitting that will greatly simplify the process. She should be sure her toenails are properly cut. The nails should not be allowed to hang over the toes; they should reach only to the tips of the toes. The corners of the nails should be slightly rounded.

Dance tights of the same weight as those worn in class should be brought to fittings. If nylon socks or stockings are worn, an improper fit may result. Know the exact size and width of current ballet slippers and street shoes. Although American pointe shoes are marked from two to three sizes smaller, or one size up from a street shoe, and foreign shoes are sized on a variety of different standards, current shoe sizes can be helpful to the shoe fitter. While some shops measure the feet to determine a first size to try, trained fitters can quickly identify this size on the basis of ballet slipper and street shoe sizes.

At the Fitting

Pointe shoe fitting is not an exact science. It involves a great deal of trial and error. All fittings take time, but first fittings can be especially lengthy. Ample time needs to be allowed for the fitter to find the best shoe for a particular foot, within the limits set by the teacher's requirements. The handmade nature of many shoes means that no two pairs are ever identical, and this further complicates the process. Some shoes on the market are now machine-made, which eliminates this problem.

Some stores make advance appointments for pointe shoe fittings. Otherwise it is a good idea to call and ask for a suggestion about the best hour to come in for a fitting. Hectic times such as Saturdays at the beginning of dance semesters should be avoided.

The best time for a fitting, in terms of a dancer's feet, is after class in the late afternoon. Feet are generally smaller in the morning; as circulation increases during the day, they tend to swell.

The dancer should be sure to show the shoe fitter her bare feet before the fitting begins. Although tights are worn for the fitting itself, they can obscure important information about toe and foot shape, and alignment that the fitter needs to observe. The foot should then be covered with tights and whatever padding is going to be used in class.

Finding the Right Shoe

Pointe shoes have to feel right, in addition to looking right. Although this is very hard to discern when trying on a first pair of pointe shoes, it will become much easier as time goes on.

The goal of the fitter is to find a pair of shoes that will fit the customer's foot like a glove, providing support and helping to prevent the foot from buckling. The more information the dancer gives the fitter about the way the shoe feels, the better the chance the wearer has of getting a perfectly fitted shoe. Since pointe shoes are initially quite hard, and conform snugly to the foot, a great deal of important information about their fit is hidden inside a barrier that the fitter cannot penetrate.

While a measuring stick reading or ballet shoe size may give the fitter a place to start, most of the work on the dancer's feet must be done in a lengthy trial-and-error process. The dancer needs to have control over her feet for balance, and the ability to move freely and with ease. The need to feel the floor and be able to work on *demi-pointe* are as important in pointe shoes as in soft shoes.

Stock Shoes

Ideally, each pair of pointe shoes should be custom designed and specifically molded to a dancer's feet. Since that is not realistic for students or dancers working on a shoestring, they are relegated to wearing stock shoes. Just a generation ago that meant something very different. There were relatively few pointe shoes on the market and even fewer models. Foreign shoes were either difficult or impossible to obtain. During the Cold War, Russian shoes were actually smuggled into the United States and sold to eager dancers looking for alternatives. That meant dancers had to be very creative. After buying shoes right off the shelf, the process of recobbling began. This continues even today, when there are many more stock options, with dancers who feel their shoes need that special personal touch.

Manufacturers are constantly involved in research and development efforts to improve their stock shoe lines. This field has simply exploded recently. It seems that there are as many shoes and models as there are choices in the automobile business. Not only are there more extensive choices in length, width, hardness, strength of shank and box, and length of vamp, but now there are ¾ shanks, ¾ graduated shanks, graduated memory shanks, split outer soles, ¾ split outer soles, and various new recipes to make the shoes last longer yet make less noise. One major deficiency is that there is no shoe at this time that is both narrow and shallow enough to accommodate the unusually shallow foot. Even when a shoe is custom-made, it must be made on a last that corresponds to the foot, and shallow lasts do not seem to exist.

The Hard Shoe–Soft Shoe Debate

While most teachers want the shape of a pointe shoe to be determined by the student's foot, they may set a uniform policy about whether first shoes should be very hard, hard, medium, or soft. These terms relate to the strength of the box, which corresponds to the arch strength.

Some teachers recommend a classic, harder shoe for beginners, and gradually work toward having students wear lighter shoes as their bodies develop. They believe that a strong shoe will strengthen the foot as the dancer works in it. This is a popular choice with parents because harder, heavier boxes mean longer wear.

Other teachers suggest a softer shoe, thinking that the dancer must depend on the strength of her foot and not her shoe. They believe that a lighter shoe forces the foot to build its own strength, as once dependence on hard, stiff shoes has been established, it is often impossible to make the change to lighter slippers because it involves learning a new way of dancing on pointe.

In some cases, hard shoes or soft shoes are dictated by the nature of the dancer's foot. Many professional dancers have worn hard shoes throughout their careers. Once a dancer reaches performance level, soft shoes or hard shoes may be determined by the nature of the choreography.

Over the years, a variety of techniques has been explored in the effort to develop a longer-lasting, heavier student shoe to satisfy those who endorse a hard shoe for beginners. The earliest of these, the suede-tipped durable toe shoe remains a popular beginner's choice in many parts of the country. In recent years, some teachers and orthopedists have expressed concern that the design of these shoes is not ideal for young, growing feet because of the concentration of weight at the toe. The value of the suede tip feature, which has been a major selling point, has also been questioned. While it is designed to prevent the bottom of the point from wearing out, it may actually limit the dancer's mobility. This type of shoe, while still available, is rarely seen anymore.

Another early experiment for hardening shoes was use of the steel shank. This has almost disappeared from the market and should be avoided completely. The steel shank has no flexibility and can cause severe injury to a dancer who falls off pointe with her foot caught in this rigid vise.

An inevitable development in the quest for a hard, durable student pointe shoe has been the introduction of plastic boxes. Lacking in flexibility, such shoes have already been responsible for a variety of injuries. Author Joan Lawson found that in Australia, dancers who wore shoes with plastic boxes suffered an increased occurrence of stress fractures to the second and third metatarsal bones of the toes. Many of them had inflammation of their Achilles tendons and ankles, as well as bursae on their heels. When wearing shoes with plastic blocks, dancers cannot rise slowly through the quarter, half, and three-quarter pointe positions. They simply go up or down because the rigidity of the shoes does not allow the muscles of the feet to work properly. The newer plastic shoes have tried through technology to eliminate these problems to produce long-lasting yet safe shoes.

In other words, the jury is still out in the hard shoe–soft shoe debate. If a dancer is not given any guidelines on shoe weight from a teacher, a good choice for a beginner might be a medium-weight shoe in a shape appropriate for her individual foot.

Protective Padding

Whether protective padding is necessary or advisable is widely debated among dancers. Ideally, if the shoe has been fitted properly, toe pads and lamb's wool should not have to be stuffed in the shoe's platform. Without additional padding, a dancer's toes should just touch the edge of the inside of the platform, allowing her to feel the floor.

In the past, if a dancer decided that protective padding was needed, conventional foam rubber or fur toe pads were the only choice, and they were frowned upon by serious teachers of ballet. These pads prevented the toes from moving freely, keeping the foot from having contact with the floor, and therefore causing shoes to be fitted too large. In addition, pads made from man-made materials tended to heat up and make the feet perspire, which encouraged the formation of soft corns.

Through much experimentation, recent technology has produced more acceptable gel pads that have made pointe work less painful. Several companies carry many sizes and shapes of various cushions and toe pads that have proven to be very popular among students. Though wearing these types of pads has seemed "Dolly Dinkle" to the professional world, and been considered taboo by experienced dancers and teachers, it is slowly being accepted by some of the younger dancers in major companies.

Over the years it has been accepted to use a small amount of lamb's wool to keep shoes from rubbing blisters. This wool can be wrapped around individual sensitive toes or placed over all five toes in a thin layer before the shoe is put on. To keep the lamb's wool from slipping, some dancers place a thin padding of it over the joints of the toes before putting their feet inside their tights. The theory behind the use of lamb's wool is that it allows the toe to slip slightly against the soft fibers to avoid contact with an abrasive canvas lining. If a dancer uses lamb's wool, it should be purchased at a dance shop, since drugstore lamb's wool is of the wrong texture. In some parts of the world where it is not available, soft cotton is used as a substitute.

Many teachers believe students are better off if they develop calluses on their toes early in their pointe training. Some suggest that wrapping the knuckle of each toe in a band-aid or masking tape, and avoiding any padding inside the shoe, prevents blisters and helps develop calluses. Others feel that taping the toes prevents them from toughening, and suggest other techniques. For instance, Claude Bessy, retired director of the Paris Opéra Ballet School, encouraged her students to clean their feet in alcohol, and to avoid soaking them in water since water tends to soften the skin. She did not even like her students to go to the beach in the summer because wading in the water would soften their feet.

Another suggestion for avoiding blisters is to use a lot of talcum powder in shoes since the powder absorbs the moisture, which is largely responsible for causing blisters. Sprinkling talcum powder between the toes is a good way to prevent abrasion. However, powder should be applied over a trashcan and kept far away from the studio or stage floor, since it is very slippery.

Some dancers wear small quantities of various kinds of paper products in their shoes as padding. In fact, finding the specific type of paper can become an obsession, as it did with one dancer who felt that she had to have paper toweling from the restrooms of the Pentagon in Washington, D.C., wrapped around her toes to be able to function properly on pointe. Though paper toweling is a very popular choice with professional dancers, one has to be careful that it does not crinkle inside the shoe, which can cause blisters.

In England, a product called surgical spirit is used to deaden the top layers of the epidermis, which helps the dancer with tender feet get used to wearing pointe shoes. It cannot be used if blisters have developed. Some dancers use antiseptic liquid bandages such as New Skin, found in pharmacies. Other possible toe coverings are the top of a cotton sock, an old pair of tights, or a nylon stocking. The companies that have made the new gel pads and cushions also have a variety of tape, paper, and other products, either to pad the toes or to prevent blisters.

Too Big or Too Small Shoes

Many problems dancers experience with their feet arise from incorrectly fitted pointe shoes. The most common culprit is shoes that are too big. Pointe shoes stretch out as the dancer works in them, and she may end up sinking into a shoe that seems snug in the store. When the foot sinks into the shoe, the big toe twists. Big shoes are a frequent cause of bunions, corns on toe joints, blisters, and bruised nails.

The shoe fitter should check to be sure there is no excess room between the drawstring and the foot or at the heel. If the heel is too baggy, the dancer may pull the drawstring too tight and the shoe will dig into the Achilles tendon. Some shoes are now offering elastic drawstrings that can put too much pressure on the foot (a drawstring can be adjusted; elastic cannot). If a big shoe gives inadequate support to the arch, the shoe may collapse, causing the dancer to go over on her pointe. The platform in a big shoe may also collapse when a dancer has softened the edge of the toe by continuously sliding down into it.

On the other hand, a shoe that is too short can bring great discomfort to the Achilles tendon when the dancer is standing flat. Short shoes can cause the ends of the toes to become pressed and inflamed. Shoes that are too narrow squeeze the toes and joints, and do not allow them to work properly. When the toes press against each other, soft corns can form and toenails become ingrown.

The shoe should hold the toes snugly, but not so snugly that they are bunched together. They should be able to spread slightly sideways, and the tips of the toes should just feel the ends of the shoes when the weight is evenly distributed. The right and left edges of the dancer's feet, and her large and small toe joints, should be slightly tight against the edge of the shoe. The shoe must support the foot; any room for movement inside the shoe may leave the foot unsupported.

The toes must not be bent or pressed against the tip and should not feel sore inside the shoe. The dancer should *demi-plié* in the shoe to see if her arch has room for expansion. An arch that does not have room to expand can gradually lose its elasticity.

Dancers with longer second or third toes should be careful not to cram them into a shoe that is too short. This can cause the longer toe to bend, resulting in corns and callous formations, or possibly to disjoint from its normal structure, which can lead to an arthritic condition.

Additional Sizing Problems

Vamp Length

The length of the *vamp*, the part of the box that covers the top of the foot, must be determined by the length of the dancer's toes. A long-toed foot requires a longer vamp than a short-toed foot. The vamp should be long enough to cover the joint at the base of the big toe; otherwise the joints of the toes may pop out of the shoe. The inside edge of the binding at the center front of the foot should reach as far as, or just beyond, the third phalange of the first and second toes.

If the vamp is too short, it will cause the foot to break over the toe, making it look extremely ugly. If, on the other hand, the vamp is too long, it will throw the dancer back and prevent her from attaining a full-pointe position. It can also cause the front tendons to strain.

Box Shape

Usually students with long toes and narrow feet need a more pointed box, and those with short toes and squat feet require a squarer box. In some cases the location of the instep will determine a different choice. Those with shallow feet often do well in shoes with flatter boxes.

The Outer Sole and the Width of the Box

The end of the outer leather sole does not come to the outer edge of the heel as it does in a street shoe. This is to accommodate the drawing inward of the muscles and the stretching downward of the toes, which both narrows and shortens the foot. Therefore, the shoe must be wide enough to hold the metatarsal arch with the toes slightly spread when flat, but still narrow enough to hold the foot securely when the dancer is on pointe.

The outer edge of the binding at the heel should cover the rounded portion of the heel, so that the back of the shoe stays in place when the dancer is on pointe and the outer sole slips upward. When the dancer is on pointe, with the foot and leg fully stretched and the toes uncramped, the outer sole should reach the end of the heel.

In 2002, with Leo's leading the way, several manufacturers introduced pointe shoes with split outer soles with the purpose of making the shoe more flexible and easier to point. These shoes are recommended only for dancers with very strong feet.

One Foot Larger Than the Other

It is imperative to have both feet fitted for pointe shoes. Most people have at least a slight variation of size or width in their feet, and a shoe that is perfect on one foot may be a disaster on the other. If the dancer has a significant difference in size and/or width between her feet, she can circumvent this problem by buying two pairs of shoes in different sizes at the same time. Since pointe shoes are made on straight lasts and there are no rights or lefts, the dancer can create two mixed pairs and alternate between them. Another possible approach is to experiment with inserting a thin insole in one shoe.

Testing for Proper Fit

After pointe shoes have been placed on both feet, the student should first stand up with her feet flat on the floor. The ends of the toes should be stretched out, straight, and just touching the front wall of the shoe. If the toes are pushed back, the shoes are too small. If wrinkles appear in the box area, either the box or the entire shoe is too narrow. If a finger can be slipped between the edge of the box and the top of the foot when the foot is flat or on pointe, the shoe is probably too wide. The metatarsal arch should be held firmly and comfortably within the toe piece of the shoe.

Next, the dancer should stand in second position and *demi-plié*. This stretches the heel and toe. Assess the way the foot feels in this position. Is it touching the front? Is it bent? Since the foot naturally contracts when it goes on pointe, the shoe should be slightly tight when the foot is flat on the ground and in an expanded state. The big toe should just touch the edge of the platform, and the sides should be supported with a sensation of slight pressure but not pain.

Next the dancer should stand in first position. While keeping her right foot flat, she should cross her left foot in front of her right leg, placing the platform of the left shoe gently on the fitting surface, and pressing down on the large toe. When the foot is in this position, is it touching the front and back of the shoe? The heel of the shoe should lie smoothly over the heel of the foot. If too much material can be pinched together at the heel, the shoe is too long. Is there any extreme pressure? Can the toes move? If so, then repeat this movement, crossing the right foot over the left. The end of the leather sole should come to the end of the heel in this position. There should be adequate room through the width of the shoe. The dancer should not feel as though her feet are in a vise, but neither should there be a gap on the side of the slipper. If there is a gap, it may be from either excessive width or excessive length and width combined.

The dancer should then rise carefully to *demi-pointe*. If the shoe pops off the heel in this position, it may be too wide.

Finally, the dancer should rise to full pointe. For the first-time pointe shoe customer these procedures should be followed: (1) The student should face an adult and hold both that person's hands. (Some dance shops have barres for this purpose.) (2) The student should step directly onto pointe with her right foot and then step directly onto pointe with her left foot. She should not *relevé*. (3) The fitter should then examine the fit in pointe position, while the student remains supported by another adult or the barre. Dancers must remember that their shoes are not secured with ribbons when they try this maneuver. They should also be careful not to break a pair of shoes they may not buy.

The Problem of Returns

Before buying shoes, dancers should be sure that the store has a return policy allowing them to return or exchange the shoes, if the teacher finds them unsatisfactory. The teacher should check the shoes at the first possible opportunity, and the student should be careful not to wear them, attach ribbons or elastic, or soil them in any way, until the shoes have been approved.

The student should stand on a sheet of clean paper when trying on shoes for a size check. If the fit is not satisfactory, the teacher should be very clear about the nature of the problem. If possible, a suggested alternative should be put in writing since many beginner pointe students are unfamiliar with the terminology involved, and may not be able to communicate their teacher's wishes correctly to the fitter.

The issue of returning worn shoes that appear to have factory flaws is a problem for both dancers and shop owners. Since many of the shoes are handmade, such flaws are well within the realm of possibility. However, they are often difficult to prove once a dancer has worn her shoes, since the breaking-in process may actually create the problem. To further complicate the matter, sometimes a legitimate flaw does not appear until a shoe has been worked in for the first time.

Each shop has its own policy on handling returns. If a customer sincerely believes that a shoe has a factory flaw, she should bring it in to the dealer for examination. Usually, when a customer comes in with a reasonable complaint, a dealer is ready to solve the problem amicably. The dealer may offer to exchange the shoe at once, or ask the customer to wait until it has been returned to the factory for evaluation.

If the factory feels the complaint is justified, it gives the dealer a refund on the shoe, which will be passed along to the customer. However, if the factory rejects the request, the dealer must absorb the cost of replacing the shoe. Factory allowances might be made on shoes that have limited wear and have been incorrectly sized or shaped, made with faulty materials, or that exhibit poor workmanship.

When dealers refuse to accept a pair of worn shoes as flawed, they believe the damage was done by the dancer. The fact that some dancers abuse return policies and constantly seek to return worn shoes can make dealers especially wary. At best, returns are a no-win situation for everyone involved. If a dancer feels her dealer is responding unfairly to a return request, she can either contact the manufacturer directly or seek another dealer. The best protection is to examine shoes carefully in the store and again before sewing ribbons on them or altering them in any way.

Time for a New Pair

Beginners frequently outgrow their shoes before they wear them out. Teachers have to watch beginners carefully, and question them when they suspect a shoe may have grown too tight. Some children will complain loudly, and others will suffer in silence.

Shoes that wear out may become soft and mushy in the box and shank; sometimes the block or shank may crack or be severely bent out of shape. In any case, the shoe no longer provides the needed level of support. The new elastomeric shoes never wear out, so this will not be an issue. The condition of the satin upper is rarely a factor in shoe replacement.

Many dancers remove the ribbons from their old shoes, launder them, and put them on new shoes. Others strip the shanks and insoles, and use old pointe shoes in place of soft slippers in class. This process is endorsed by some teachers, but others feel that it is an unwise practice. Patricia Klekovic, who teaches at the Ruth Page Foundation School, explains that the argument for wearing deshanked pointe shoes is that they allow the dancer to feel as if pointe shoes are always part of her foot. On the other hand, if a dancer always wears pointe shoes, she may find it difficult to perform without them, lacking the sense of freedom gained from working in soft slippers.

Students at the Royal Ballet School in London wear soft slippers for the first years of their training and then switch to deshanked pointe shoes. Students at the Paris Opéra Ballet School also wear deshanked pointe shoes for technique class.

Proponents like deshanked shoes because they provide added support as well as resistance, so a dancer has to work harder to point her toe. Deshanked pointe shoes accustom the dancer to dancing with the added bulk of pointe shoes. Some dancers find that the ribbons on deshanked pointe shoes offer added ankle support, and caution against wearing the shoes with only elastic across the instep, since severe ankle injury can result.

Dancers and teachers who look with disfavor on the idea of wearing de-shanked pointe shoes are concerned that the foot does not have enough contact with the floor when it is always encased in such a hard shoe. They feel that the muscles supporting the metatarsals are not worked adequately since the stiffness of the deshanked shoe inhibits the full use of the foot. Opponents believe that no foot can work well and be supple if it is restricted in heavy and unworkable deshanked pointe shoes with blocked toes.

When a dancer returns to the dance shop for new pointe shoes, it is a good idea to bring her current pair with her. The wear patterns provide the fitter with useful information in making necessary adjustments in style and size. For instance, a lot of dirt on the satin at the heel of the shoe, or a split on the heel seam, may indicate a shoe that is too short.

Dancers are constantly experimenting with slight adjustments in width or length, or changes in style or brands. As progress is made on pointe, and as total body strength develops, lighter and less restrictive shoes may be appropriate. Many dancers also find that their feet grow wider as they continue to dance on pointe.

NOTES

1. Lawson, Joan. "Shoes and Injuries," *The Dancing Times* (September 1983), pp. 946–47. Production changes since 1983 might change the significance of these early findings.

Pointe Shoe
Size Charts

This list has been compiled by the authors and approved by the pointe shoe companies to be used only as a guide in this very perplexing field.

Tim Heathcote of Bloch says they have a policy that any pointe shoes purchased should be done so under the strict instruction and guidance of the dance teacher. The pointe shoe needs to be fitted correctly by a qualified fitter, and then checked by the teacher. There are so many factors involved in fitting a pointe shoe that a street shoe size really has no bearing at all. Therefore, Bloch cannot translate sizes, and does not appear on the list below.

Judy Weiss of Capezio would like to remind dancers that the information below just helps the fitter get started.

U. S. Street Shoe Sizes Compared to Pointe Shoe Sizes

Company/Model	Ratio to U.S. street shoe size
ANGELO LUZO NO3z	2 sizes smaller than street shoe
ANGELO LUZO NO5z	2 sizes smaller
ANGELO LUZO N71z	2 sizes smaller
ANGELO LUZO N31z	2 sizes smaller
ANGELO LUZO N51z	2 sizes smaller
ANGELO LUZO S66m	2 sizes smaller
ANGELO LUZO N83z	2 sizes smaller
CAPEZIO PLIÉ I (196)	½ size bigger
CAPEZIO PLIÉ II (197)	½ size bigger
CAPEZIO TENDU I (198)	½ size bigger
CAPEZIO TENDU II (199)	½ size bigger
CAPEZIO GLISSÉ (102/102A)	½ size bigger

CAPEZIO *PAVLOWA* (P102)	3 sizes smaller
CAPEZIO *NICOLINI* (N156)	3 sizes smaller
CAPEZIO *CONTEMPORA* (176/176X)	3 sizes smaller
CAPEZIO *INFINITA* (183)	2½ sizes smaller
CAPEZIO *AERIAL* (191)	2½ sizes smaller
CAPEZIO *PRELUDE* (#190)	2½ sizes smaller
FREED *CLASSICS* (SBT102)	2½ sizes smaller
FREED *CLASSIC WING BLOCK* (SBTWB)	2½ sizes smaller
FREED *STUDIOS* (STU)	2½ sizes smaller
FREED *STUDIOS II* (STU II)	2½ sizes smaller
GAMBA G93	2 to 2½ sizes smaller
GAMBA G97	2 to 2½ sizes smaller
GAYNOR MINDEN	approximately ½ to 1 size bigger

(Do not fit tight because the specially lined satin does not stretch out nearly as much as many other pointe shoes.)

GRISHKO *2007*	2½ sizes smaller
LEO'S *0051 SPLIT SOLE*	same or ½ size smaller
LEO'S *PAS DE DEUX POINTE 1*	2 sizes smaller and 1 width larger
MARK SUFFOLK *SOLO*	2½ sizes smaller
SO' DANÇA (Cecilia Kerche)	2½ to 3 sizes smaller

(Size depends on how snug the dancer likes to wear her shoes and how much padding is used inside.)

Fitting Charts

Angelo Luzio

U.S. street shoe size	Pointe shoe size
3	1
3.5	1.5
4	2
4.5	2.5
5	3
5.5	3.5
6	4
6.5	4.5
7	5
7.5	5.5
8	6

Angelo Luzio (cont'd)

U.S. street shoe size	Pointe shoe size
8.5	6.5
9	7
9.5	7.5
10	8

Chacott

The *Veronese II* is in centimeter sizes; the *Coppelia II* uses continental sizes.

U.S. street shoe size	*Veronese II* pointe shoe size	*Coppelia II* pointe shoe size
3		
3.5		30
4	21	31
4.5	21.5	32
5	22	33
5.5	22.5	34
6	23	35
6.5	23.5	36
7	24	37
7.5	24.5	38
8	25	39
8.5	25.5	40
9		41

Evolution Pirouette, exclusive distributor for Chacott Iberica in the United States, has a special fitting system that can be done via Internet or fax. EPFIT, or InterFax System, involves drawing an outline of the foot on a sheet of paper, taking several measurements, answering a series of questions that relate to the dancer's foot and pointe shoe needs, and specifying brand and style of pointe shoes previously worn.

Fuzi

U.S. street shoe size	Pointe shoe size
5	33
5.5	33.5
6	34
6.5	34.5-35
7	35.5
7.5	36
8	36.5
8.5	37.5-38
9	38.5-39
9.5	39.5-40

Fuzi width fitting chart

U.S. street shoe size	Pointe shoe size
N	A
M	B
W	C, D, E

Grishko

U.S. street shoe size	Pointe shoe size
3	1
3	——
3½	——
4	——
4½	1.5 or 2
5	2 or 2.5
5½	2.5 or 3
6	3
6½	3.5
7	4
7½	4.5
8	5
8½	5.5
9	6
9½	6.5
10	7
10½	7.5

Leo's Dancewear

U.S. street shoe size	Pas de deux "Pointe 1"	Split-Sole Pointe
3	1	3
3.5	1.5	3.5
4	2	4
4.5	2.5	4.5
5	3	5
5.5	3.5	5.5
6	4	6
6.5	4.5	6.5
7	5	7
7.5	5.5	7.5
8	6	8
8.5	6.5	8.5
9	7	9
9.5	n/a	9.5
10	n/a	10

Prima Soft

U.S. street shoe size	Gala and Volé	Prima Russe	Silhouette & Royale
5½	35	35-36	36
6	3½	35-36	36
6½	3½	36	36
7	4	37	37
7½	4½	37-37.5	37-37.5
8	5	37.5-38	37.5-38
8½	5½	38	38
9	6	39	39
9½	6½	39	39
10	7	40	40
10½	7½	40	40
11	8	41	41
11½	8	41	41
12	8	41	41

Principal

U.S. street shoe size	Pointe shoe size
1	30.5-31
2	31.5-32
3	32.5-33
4	33.5-34
5	34.5-35
6	35.5-36
7	36.5-37
8	37.5-38
9	38.5-39
10	39.5-40
11	40.5-41

Russian Pointe

U.S. street shoe size	Pointe shoe size
2	29
2.5	30
3	31
3.5	31.5
4	32
4.5	33
5	34
5.5	34.5
6	35
6.5	36
7	37
7.5	37.5
8	38
8.5	39
9	40
9.5	41

Sansha

Sansha notes that these sizes are approximate. They add that the proper fitting of a pointe shoe depends on many different things, and that pointe shoes should be fitted by a professional.

U.S. street shoe size	Pointe shoe size
1	1
2	2
3	3
4	4
5	5
6	6
7	7
8	8
9	9
10	10
11	11

Sylvia

U.S. street shoe size	Pointe shoe size
4.5	21.5
5	22
5.5	22.5
6	23
6.5	23.5
7	24
7.5	24.5
8	25
8.5	25.5
9	26
9.5	26.5
10	27

5 Preparing and Caring for Pointe Shoes

The preparation of dance shoes is a process that is highly personal to each dancer and shrouded in the mystique of several hundred years of dance history. Each dancer develops a system of preparing her shoes that grows out of vanity, personal taste, and the demands of her anatomy. The following guide to preparing pointe shoes is a basic orientation to the process that incorporates traditional techniques and practical concerns. It has been written with the dancer who is still paying for her own shoes in mind.

Darning Shoes

Although darning has gone out of style in our mechanized society, it remains a special tradition that is actually quite practical. Darning shoes offers improved traction and can also extend the wear obtainable from a pair of pointe shoes because it prevents the satin from fraying.

Darning shoes requires a large, curved darning or embroidery needle and cotton embroidery thread the same color as the pointe shoes. A thimble and a pair of pliers are helpful for pulling the needle through the boxing in the toe.

The darning covers the entire toe of the slipper underneath the shoe and the tip of the end. Some experienced darners suggest sewing over the ridge of the toe block to avoid having the satin rip away from the block. Before starting to darn a pair of shoes, the dancer should put them on and slightly soil the satin by putting one pointe at a time on the floor and turning them from one side to another. This soil spot indicates the area to be darned.

The dancer starts as close to the sole as possible and stitches a series of bars of thread back and forth across the pleats, adjacent to the sole, until they reach as far as indicated by the soil. The needle should be stuck into the satin deeply, and the fabric should be picked up with each stitch.

Beginning at the sole again, the dancer blanket-stitches over each bar of thread. Then she connects the rows by pushing the needle through the loops of the row below, continuing until all the bars are covered.

After the darning is finished, it can be covered with a thin layer of colorless shellac and the slippers hung up to dry for several days. As the shoes are worn, wear patterns in the satin on the sides of the toe and under the big and little toe joints may appear. As this happens, these areas can also be darned. Some dancers also use darning as a technique for changing the shape of their shoes. A quick alternative to conventional darning involves cutting the satin away from the toe platform and stitching around the edge of the cut.

In England and Sweden, dancers also crochet toe caps, which they sew onto the tips of their shoes. Some English pointe shoe manufacturers include crocheted toe caps in their product lines. When the caps are attached, they must be completely stitched onto the shoe, or the cap will stretch and come loose, possibly causing the foot to slip.

Sewing on Ribbons

After the teacher has approved the fit of a new pair of pointe shoes, ribbons can be sewn on. Pointe shoes require about two to two-and-a-half yards of ribbon, either 5/8-inch or 7/8-inch wide. The actual length varies according to the size of the dancer's ankle. A variety of ribbons are on the market, including those that are satin on one side and grosgrain on the other. The rougher, grosgrain side is placed toward the leg, and helps grip the tights and hold the shoe in place.

The entire length of ribbon is folded in half, and the two ends are placed together. It is then cut into two equal pieces. If the dancer is going to sew her ribbons on in four pieces, she should fold each piece of ribbon in half and cut again. There will now be four pieces of ribbon that are each approximately twenty-two inches long. Some dancers prefer to sew one piece of ribbon forty-four inches long to each shoe, attaching the center of the ribbon to the inside of the sole under the heel.

Christine Spizzo used one length of ribbon on each shoe when she danced for American Ballet Theatre. She ran the ribbon under the heel and sewed it on either side. When it was time for a new pair of shoes, she took off the ribbon and reused it, using the holes made by the needle as a guide for sewing again. This method saved time and also gave her the security of knowing the ribbons would not pull loose.

Some dancers like to sew about five inches of cloth tape to their ribbons to give them added strength and keep them from slipping. This tape needs to be a little narrower than the ribbons, and is attached from the point where the ribbon is sewn to the shoe to the point where the ribbons first cross. The easiest way to attach the tape is to baste it to the ribbons before sewing them onto the shoes.

To attach ribbons, the dancer folds the back seam of the shoe against the sole and toward the front. The ribbons are then placed inside the shoe in the angles made by folding the heel forward. Their raw edges should be facing the lining of the shoe. A light pencil mark is drawn on the shoe lining on either side of the ribbon to use as a sewing guide.

Ribbons are usually sewn tilting slightly forward so they will lie flat on the instep. The location of the instep may dictate sewing them farther forward or backward. Some dancers do not sew the ribbons at any angle but prefer to sew them on straight.

In the case of a sickled foot, a dancer can experiment with sewing one ribbon slightly forward and the other stitched slightly backward of the pencil mark.

About one inch of the ribbon should be folded under before sewing it to the shoes, in order to make the attachment strong and to avoid raveling. Some dancers make one 5/8-inch fold and then fold the ribbon over again. Place the folded end between the pencil marks. The fold should be even with the bias tape edging of the shoe. The ribbons should be pinned to the shoes and tested before sewing.

If the placement seems correct, sew small whip stitches around the two sides and bottom of the ribbon using a double strand of thread or heavy dental floss. Advocates of dental floss find it stronger and easier to thread through a needle. Go through all thicknesses of the ribbon, but only through the white canvas shoe lining. Ideally, stitches should not show through the exterior satin.

When sewing across the top of the ribbons, use a running stitch. Avoid sewing ribbons to the upper binding and drawstring around the top of the shoe or it will be difficult to adjust the drawstring as the shoe takes the shape of the foot. Avoid finishing the stitches with a large knot since this could bruise the skin. The ends of the ribbons should be clipped on the bias to prevent fraying. If nylon ribbon is used, raveling can be prevented by running the ends very quickly through a match flame, which will melt the fibers.

If a dancer has extra fabric at her heel because of a broad front foot, a high instep, and a narrow heel, she may be able to help the problem by sewing her ribbons on at a slightly more acute angle than usual toward the front of the shoe. Those dealing only with narrow heels may want to try sewing their ribbons slightly farther back than normal.

For performance, some dancers sew their ribbons with the shiny side of the satin in, to reflect less light. This is also said to tie a tighter knot. Some teachers have their students wear ribbons on ballet slippers during their pre-pointe years to get used to working with them.

Elastic

Elastic can be used on pointe shoes as a ribbon insert, across the vamps, or on the backs of the heels to keep the shoes on the feet.

Dancers often sew elastic into their ribbons so the ribbons adjust to the changing size of the ankle. This allows a dancer to have a more normal *demi-plié* while wearing pointe shoes.

To insert elastic in ribbons, sew the ribbons on the shoe as described above. Then mark each ribbon where it touches the back of the ankle-bone. Cut the ribbons straight across, melt the ends in a match flame, and sew a two to three inch length of three-quarter inch elastic to the ribbon. This can be done by hand or machine. Then sew the remaining ribbon to the other end of the elastic. After this has been done on all four ribbons, tie them as you normally would, and cut off any extra ribbon.

Elastic can also be attached to the base of the ribbons at the spot where they are sewn to the shoes. This is helpful because it gives when the dancer jumps. When using this technique, the ribbons must be sewn on sloping forward.

A wide piece of elastic can be sewn across the vamp of a shoe for added support if a dancer has weak ankles and highly developed arches. It must not be too tight, however, or it can stop circulation. In England, dancers are able to buy an elastic cloth through Frederick Freed Ltd. that is similar in texture to the elasticized fabric that girdles are made of in the United States. Dancers then cut the cloth to any desired width and configuration, and sew it into the shoe covering the instep. Until recently, when Gaynor Minden introduced vamp elastic, it had been difficult to find elastic or elastic cloth in the United States. Freed dealers also have access to this valuable aid.

Whether to wear elastic on the heels of pointe shoes remains controversial. Although it is a common practice to wear an elastic loop around the ankle or to run ribbons through an elastic loop on the back of the heel, many teachers with British training believe that a shoe requiring elastic is a badly fitted shoe. They feel that elastic in any form is dangerous for the soft tissue at the ankle, restricting the bend of the Achilles tendon and inhibiting the blood flow through the important veins of the foot and leg. As a result the Achilles tendon and bones of the heel can become inflamed. Teachers who oppose elastic contend that if ribbons are correctly attached, the slight pull forward should hold the shoe on firmly at the heel after the ribbons have been wrapped across the instep and around the ankle.

If elastic is used at the heel, it should be between 3/8-inch to 5/8-inch wide and sewn to the outside of the shoe so it cannot rub the heel. A length that will fit snugly from the back of the heel, around the ankle, and back to the heel again should be measured. The elastic should fit snugly, but not too tightly. It can be attached to the shoes with a whipstitch, starting at the top edge of the shoe, down the right side, across the bottom and up the left side of the elastic. The elastic should be sewn at a slight angle at the back of the shoe and not secured to the casing. When the shoes are worn, the foot is slipped through the elastic and into the shoe before the ribbons are tied.

Tying on the Shoes

Shoes should be pulled on the feet with both hands. Using only one hand tends to twist the shoe around the foot. Ribbons should be tied carefully to allow the shoe to remain correctly positioned on the foot.

There are a variety of techniques for tying ribbons. In the first, the shoes should be tied while the dancer is kneeling on one knee and leaning back slightly. The knee of the free leg is bent, with the foot placed flat on the floor. If the shoes are tied with the toe on pointe or the leg straight, the ankle may not be allowed enough room for flexibility, and it will be difficult to move the foot fully on pointe and *demi-pointe*. Some dancers find that flexing the foot while tying their ribbons keeps them from tying the shoes too tightly.

One ribbon should be extended forward of the foot, crossed over it, and allowed to lie flat in the center of the foot, in line with the anklebones. Then the same ribbon is brought around to the back of the ankle and to the front again, so it lies flat on the center front of the leg at a point slightly above the first cross. Then the ribbon is taken to the side of the leg and held firmly.

The second ribbon is brought forward and crossed over the first ribbon so that it lies flat in the center front of the leg. It is taken around the ankle and knotted with the first ribbon in the hollow between the anklebone and Achilles tendon. The ribbons are tied in a small, tight double knot that is tucked under or between the ribbons, so no ends are visible. If the ends of the ribbons are visible on the shoes of students at the Royal Ballet School, the offending ends are disparagingly called "pigs ears." The knot should not be tied over the Achilles tendon or the shinbone, to avoid pressure, which can lead to inflammation.

In another technique, both ribbons are crossed over the instep. They are wrapped around the foot, crossing the Achilles tendon, and brought back across the instep. The ribbon, which is on the outside of the foot, is brought across the Achilles tendon to meet the ribbon on the inside of the foot. A knot is tied between the inside anklebone and the Achilles tendon. It should fit into the hollow on the side of the foot.

Excess ribbon is folded and tucked from the top under the ribbons, which are wrapped around the ankle. The ribbons which cross the ankle should lie on top of each other rather than winding up the lower leg.

Ribbons that are tied too tightly can keep the calf muscles from working properly and inhibit the foot from making contact with the floor. They can also impair circulation and cause damage to muscles, tendons, and ligaments in the feet and ankles.

The Drawstring

The drawstring in the front of the shoe should be tightened until the shoe feels snug and secure on the foot. It should be tightened only when the foot is in the pointe position. Never pull it by one end. Some teachers suggest tying the drawstring in a small bow and tucking the ends in. Others feel that this can induce scar tissue and bruising when the knot presses on the fine blood vessels and causes constriction. They prefer to pull the drawstring gently to the tightness required, knot it, and cut off the excess. In either case, the drawstring should not be cut until the shoes have been worked in several times. Then, any necessary adjustments can be made, and the drawstring can be tied in a double knot.

Some shoes are manufactured with elastic drawstrings, which can press on the Achilles tendon if pulled too tightly. Even conventional drawstrings can dig into the heel and stop the stretch of the Achilles tendon. Tight drawstrings can dig into the tendon sheath, causing inflammation, or press on either of the two bursae at the heel area, causing bursitis. To avoid this, the drawstring can be stitched in place one-half inch on either side of the heel. This will hold the drawstring in place over the heel without pressure, while allowing it to be tightened as needed over the front of the foot. It will also prevent the development of Achilles tendinitis, bursitis, or heel lumps, which can result when the up-and-down motion of *relevé* causes the tendon to stretch in a constricted shoe.

Other Techniques for Keeping Shoes On

In addition to traditional ways of attaching and adjusting ribbons, elastic, and drawstrings, dancers have developed a number of other methods to fasten the shoe securely to the foot. A customary practice, which is also reputed to bring luck, is to spit on the knot as it is made when the ribbons are tied. Some dancers take a stitch through the knot as well.

At the Houston Ballet, dancers use clear Johnson & Johnson surgical tape and wrap it around their knotted ribbons. There is also tape that is made especially for this purpose being sold by companies that make products specifically for dancers. This secures the ribbons but still allows a quick change of shoes since it can be slipped off.

Slipping heels are remedied by dabbing a few drops of water-soluble glue between the heel of the tights and the heel of the slipper. Alicia Markova is reported to have glued her whole foot into her shoes. Another technique is to rub the heels of tights in crushed rock rosin before putting shoes on.

Some dancers dunk the heel of the shoe, foot and all, into a bucket of water before class or performance. Others wet their tights before putting on the shoe and then wet the shoe after pulling it on. In either method, as the water dries, the wet shoe clings to the foot, shrinking in the process. Those who argue in favor of water point out that rosin can be abrasive to the foot, while water is not. However, water can destroy the resiliency of most types of shanks and dissolve some glues, possibly causing the shoe to lose its shape.

Making Shoes Slip-Proof

Darning shoes or cutting the satin off the tips helps cut down on traction problems. Some dancers rub the satin off the tops of their new shoes by scraping them on gravelly pavements or driveways. A carpenter's knife or Exacto knife is useful for roughing up the bottom of a pointe shoe to gain traction, or the sole can be scored with a scissor point or sandpaper.

A box of rock rosin is kept in many studios to provide protection from slipping. Rosin is a sticky, rocklike substance made from pine tree sap. Dancers apply it to their shoes to increase friction with the floor. A rosin box is placed in a studio corner or in the dressing room, and dancers simply grind their toes into the rosin as needed. A rasp is often kept with the rosin box to score the soles of shoes for added traction. Excess rosin can be removed from shoes with a wire nailbrush.

In emergencies, dancers have sprinkled powdered detergent and cleansers (such as Ajax, Comet, or new blue Cheer) on a stage or studio floor that has a nonporous surface such as tile. Once they have been spread evenly, they must be energetically rubbed in and then the excess swept away. While they do retard slippage, these substances often create problems for dancers, orchestra members, and audience patrons who subsequently inhale them. It presents a problem if there is floor-work in the choreography. Coca Cola and Sweet 'N Low are also used to de-gloss a slippery floor when nothing else is available.

In extreme circumstances, dancers who must dance on very slippery surfaces can have 1/8-inch thick rubber soles put on their pointe shoes by a shoemaker. The rubber may cover the platforms, the pleats (which are particularly slippery), and the entire sole, or it may be in two pieces, leaving the middle of the sole uncovered. The Capezio store in New York on Broadway and 51st Street provides this service as well as Vasili Shoe Repair, 850 Eighth Avenue, which is only one block away on 51st Street (telephone 212-581-2491). Former ABT soloist Christine Spizzo danced for ten years in *Phantom of the Opera* on Broadway. She said the dancers in the show had to wear rubber on their shoes because the stage floor was painted with high gloss black enamel paint. One advantage to this was that the rubber gave the shoes a longer life.

Other nonslip measures include spraying shoe tips and soles with glue products. While a number of dancers recommend Scotch 77 spray adhesive, David Howard advocates rubber cement. He has developed a method of preparing pointe shoes for dancers who must perform on slippery surfaces. He scrapes down the edges of pointe shoe soles to "get rid of the ridges." Then he paints the soles and tips with five or six coats of Contact rubber cement. After the cement has dried, rosin is then applied to the soles. This treatment lasts long enough to see a dancer safely through one performance.

Breaking in the Shoes

Dancers generally feel the need to break in new pointe shoes, which means to mold them to their feet and make them more comfortable. They are seeking a workable compromise between the original rigidity of the shoe, needed for support, and the right amount of give needed for fluid motion. Since heat and perspiration from the feet can further soften the shoe, breaking in is a tricky business. Students should not attempt to break in their first shoes on their own.

Traditionally-Made Pointe Shoes
(Paste and paper toe boxes)

Breaking in shoes is more complicated than it used to be because first there must be an understanding of what materials have been used to make the shoes. In the very recent past, boxes were made with a paste that would break down with use and with water. The amount of paste used, how far it came up on the sides (wings), and the thickness and material of the shank determined just what breaking-in routine was needed for each type of foot.

Today many shoes are still made with the same *English Paste*, the most fragile or delicate type of shoes. Freed's *Classic Deep Vamp* is an example of these shoes. They require much care when being broken in. They are made of sugar, flour, and water with each company using their own secret recipe to produce the desired result. These shoes are susceptible to changes in weather and humidity, as well as sweat and water damage. The boxes of these types of shoes should be allowed to dry for several hours after wearing.

Box-Softening Techniques

Some dancers like to wear a pair of new pointe shoes around the house the night before working in them for the first time, walking around in them, and rising from quarter- to demi- and three-quarter pointe to mold them to their feet. If a dancer is experienced on pointe, she can rise to full pointe several times on each shoe and turn the toes back and forth. The shoe can also be worked with the hands to mold them slightly. The insole can be eased by lightly pressing it back and forth at the instep level between the palms. It should take very little force since most of these shoes are made with a laminated cardboard or leather board shank material that responds well to gentle manipulation. The box can be pressed gently with the heel of the hand or it can be flattened by placing the shoes flat on the floor and carefully stepping on the box with the heel of the foot.

Another popular box-softening technique involves the use of rubbing alcohol or water. A cotton ball is lightly soaked and rubbed across the box of the shoe at the place it should bend on *demi-pointe*. Pouring these liquids directly on the shoe, however, could weaken it and make it unwearable. Shoes that are softened with water or alcohol must be allowed to dry completely before wearing or storing. Those dancers who prefer alcohol to water for breaking in shoes feel that water takes too long to dry and can cause the shoes to shrink. In addition, alcohol on the box is thought to offer protection from blisters. Alcohol is sometimes used to make a noisy shoe quieter. Noise can also be reduced by hammering the shoes or banging them against a wall. A piece of suede is sometimes glued to the tip of the shoe for the same reason.

Many dancers indulge in more extreme tactics to break in their shoes, including banging them in doors, whamming them with hammers, and having large men jump up and down on them. Manufacturers estimate that these tactics can reduce shoe life by fifty percent; the strength of the box is lost if the shoe gets smashed too hard, wet too much, or overly heated. That is true of the English paste shoes, but not necessarily with shoes made with *Modern Paste.*

Some Capezio, Repetto, Bloch, and other shoes are also made with layers of paste, but use a glue that is less water-soluble and more durable. The part of this type of shoe that is quite difficult to break in is the wings: that is the stiffening in the box that extends up the sides of the shoe. They will take a little extra time, but gently manipulating them with the fingers will probably give the desired flexibility. These shoes are more durable than the other paste shoes, but they can still crack and separate from the sole if mistreated. The shanks used in these shoes are usually less affected by water and humidity.

Technologically Innovative Pointe Shoes (Elastomeric toe box and shank)

The latest development in pointe shoes has been shoes like Gaynor Minden and others whose boxes are made from molded, injected, or heat-formed plastic and rubber-based materials. They are often referred to as "space age" pointe shoes. These shoes have extremely durable boxes that change very little with wear, and each has its own unique breaking-in requirements. Gaynor Minden says that their shoes need no breaking in at all. When buying these shoes, it is best to follow the manufacturer's instructions. If you have more questions, access the company via telephone or the website to obtain the customer service number. Most of these shoes have several choices of shank strength, vamp height, wing length, and overall box strength to give the dancer multiple choices.

Altering the Shank

Some dancers, because of inflexible ankles and insteps, find it very difficult to break in the shanks of their shoes. They may resort to cutting off the inside shank near the heel where the sole of the foot bends. This is usually done with a utility or an Exacto knife. The process involves cutting the shank carefully, layer by layer, until the small section at the back of the heel can be removed, along with the nail that has held it to the shoe. The edge of the remaining shank has to be beveled with the knife and tapered toward the heel for comfort. If the bottom sole of the shoe is difficult to balance on, the edges can also be cut with a utility knife, and tapered toward the satin.

Stock Shoes: New Options

In recent years, many manufacturers have added new elements to their stock shoes. One of these is three-quarter shanks and another is flatter outside soles, which make it easier to balance on the flat foot. While several three-quarter shanks are offered in stock shoes, many companies offer it as a special order. The most current design, which was first introduced by Leo's with a few other companies following suit, is a split outside sole.

Although these many new options should make the hours of painstakingly tailoring shoes seem unnecessary, many dancers still insist upon modifications to meet their very personal needs.

Other Alterations

Shoes that are being used in performance may need to be altered in a variety of other ways. If the satin is too shiny, it can be dulled by applying a light shade of pancake make-up, such as Max Factor Natural #1, with a sponge and a small amount of water to both the shoes and ribbons. The shoes must be dried thoroughly before wearing. Pancaking shoes can tighten them up and hide smudges. However, George Balanchine did not want his dancers to use pancake on their shoes because he liked their feet to be "obvious."

While pointe shoes can be ordered in various colors, dancers can dye their own satin pointe shoes without too much difficulty. A brand of dye called Evangeline, that is used by the bridal industry, does an excellent job and can be painted on with a brush. Evangeline can be found at a shoemaker's shop or through a company that sells shoemaking supplies. A bridal shop might be a good source of information on where to buy Evangeline dye in your area.

Powdered Rit or Tintex dye can also be used to change pointe shoe color. While using liquid Rit or Tintex might seem an easier approach, it tends to streak, and does not do an acceptable job. Instead, mix powdered dye with rubbing alcohol, starting with a small amount of dye, and add granules until you get the color you want. You can test colors on old pointe shoe ribbons. Paint the dye on with a brush. Since you are not using heat, the dye granules do not dissolve and you will have to brush them off after the shoes are dry.

A bump on the top of a pair of new shoes can be gotten out by wetting it and beating it flat with a hammer or a rolling pin, or beating it on the floor. Shoes with vamps that are too long can be modified to make them more flexible by carefully ripping the stitches around the vamp with a seam ripper, trimming the satin to the proper length and sewing the drawstring back on by hand or machine.

Shoes may also be altered to accommodate a temporary foot problem. For instance, Sandra Organ, formerly of the Houston Ballet, cut a hole out of the satin of her shoe over a bad blister to give it air. Dancers may slit the shoe over a bunion and stitch around the slit to keep it from raveling. This slit looks like a big buttonhole and provides enough give to take the pressure off the bunion.

The Cost of Pointe Shoes: Extending Their Life

While major ballet companies order hundreds of pairs of shoes for their principal dancers each year, most student and professional pointe dancers find themselves laboring under much more limited footwear budgets. The artistic director of both the South Carolina Ballet and Ballet Savannah, William Starrett, tries to give his dancers about one pair of shoes every two weeks. The amount depends on the dancer's position and the length of her contract. They have a pointe shoe fund drive every year, which raises between eight thousand and ten thousand dollars. This helps defray the cost, but definitely does not cover it entirely. The director of New York Theatre Ballet, Diana Byer, says the company spends about eight hundred to one thousand dollars per dancer per year for shoes. When they go out on a six-week tour, she sends them with five pairs each. As they need more, they contact her. She does not like to send them out with many pairs because she is afraid they will start wearing one pair per performance; since they are a small company, they simply cannot afford it. Pointe shoe prices have risen dramatically during the past ten years, and steadily increasing costs of production do not indicate a change in this pattern in the immediate future. Although the cost of pointe shoes seems exorbitant to the dancer, manufacturers actually make limited profits because the pointe shoemaking process is so labor-intensive. To put the matter in a broader perspective, it is very difficult to find handmade street shoes of any kind on the market today, and those that are available often cost hundreds of dollars a pair.

Because shoes break down so quickly, making dancing on pointe prohibitively expensive, in recent years pointe shoe companies have come out with shoes that are more durable and longer lasting. The ballet world had previously thought that dancers needed handcrafted shoes made of natural, flexible materials. For manufacturers to turn to automation or plastics as a means of controlling prices was unacceptable for years. But after much testing, several major manufacturers have done just that. Even Freed has introduced its student shoes, Studios I and II, which are not handmade, but are still made with natural materials. The machine-made, elastomeric shoes with "space-age" engineering are known to be extremely comfortable and long lasting and have an added feature of not having to be broken in. They have become very popular all over the world. Nevertheless, the majority of professional dancers working with major companies are still wearing the traditional, handmade paste shoes.

Various changes in ownership have taken place in the pointe shoe industry in recent years. When Selva decided to close, no buyer was found to continue manufacturing their pointe shoes, largely because of the economic infeasibility of the process. Capezio bought the Selva name and retired the line, with the exception of some specialized products like tap shoes. In 1987, Frederick Freed Ltd. was purchased by Chacott, a Japanese pointe shoe manufacturer, and now Repetto is owned by Gamba. The fact that only other pointe shoemakers exhibit any interest in these companies when they go on the market is evidence of their limited profit potential. For many companies, pointe shoes are a labor of love, largely subsidized by sales in more profitable types of dancewear and footwear. Although the new machine-made shoes and longer-lasting materials are beginning to change that scenario somewhat, dancers still use a variety of techniques to extend the life of their shoes.

Alternating Shoes

Pointe shoes have no right or left. While some dancers like to have each shoe take the shape of one foot or the other, others prefer to alternate their shoes. If a pair of shoes starts out identically shaped, they can be changed from one foot to the other on a daily basis to keep them on balance. Quite a few dancers have found that alternating shoes can actually double the life of a pair of shoes by avoiding consistent wear on the same spot by the big toe. Alternating also helps dancers identify foot-use problems such as a tendency to roll in their shoes.

However, dancers whose feet are not similar to one another will have difficulty alternating shoes. For instance, those with toes of uneven lengths may find that their shoes take the shape of their feet with just one wearing, making alternating impossible.

Caring for Shoes

The following instructions are meant for paste shoes.

Since as much as a half pint of sweat can be produced by a dancer's feet during an hour-long class, pointe shoes become damp during each wearing. In response to this condition, the dancer needs to smooth out any wrinkles that may have formed, and stretch and arch shoes carefully.

After taking shoes off, and before putting them away in a dance bag, stuff a plastic bag into the box of the shoe and fill it tightly with paper. Plastic lasts, which are available in some dance shops, can be inserted in the shoes as they dry and used as shoe trees to prevent the pointe shoes from becoming misshapen. After smoothing out the wrinkles, allow the shoes to dry in an airy, nonhumid environment. Hang the shoes over a heater, put them in front of an electric fan, or place them in the oven with the heat turned off but with the pilot light on; leave the ribbons hanging out the oven door to avoid forgetting that pointe shoes are inside. In humid climates, shoes can also be placed in a refrigerator, since the air is dry.

Drying out can take up to three days. After the shoes have dried, arch them gently, collapse the heel, fold one side over the other, wind the ribbon flat around them and put them away.

Buying two pairs of shoes at a time, and allowing each pair to rest and dry between wearings, seems to make them more durable. Alternate shoes for each class, and change after an hour of wear at a long rehearsal. Wearing the same pair of shoes for each class and rehearsal, and stuffing them into a dance bag, sopping wet, rapidly destroys them. Alternating shoes can extend total life by up to fifty percent.

If a dancer takes three classes a week, she needs three pairs of shoes to allow each pair the required three days to dry. In the long run, this approach prevents the shoes from going soft prematurely, and results in extended wear from each pair. Wearing dry shoes is also much healthier for the feet.

Shoes worn for class and rehearsal may begin to show signs of wear that are only cosmetic and do not require that particular pair to be discarded. For instance, if the satin on the toe tears, cut it off. If the canvas insole that covers the shank comes loose and bunches up, pull it out. A dancer can often continue to dance on shoes with loosened shank nails and frayed side seams.

Shoes can be cleaned with commercial pointe shoe cleaners or cleaners designed to be used on silk and satin shoes. Mild, nonabrasive soap and water can also be used, unless the shoes are made with water-soluble glue.

If pointe shoes are kept for long periods of time, it is important to keep them in a climate-controlled environment. When Christine Spizzo stored her shoes for a long period of time, she discovered that they had been eaten by a type of weevil (a small beetle). Therefore, she now keeps them in a very cold place in the winter, and in a dehumidified room in the summer. She says they must never be subjected to high humidity.

Rehardening

Even with careful treatment, the most typical box (and up until recently, the only kind) made with the paste that breaks down quickly will become softer and softer until it can no longer provide adequate support. Once this disintegration takes place, many dancers try to revitalize the blocks of their shoes to make them last longer. Before reblocking, pointe shoes should be stuffed with paper or a plastic last as soon as they are taken off, and allowed to dry out in a warm place.

One reblocking technique involves pouring several applications of a liquid shellac into the toe of the dry shoe and letting it soak into the block between applications. Allow the shoes to dry thoroughly before wearing.

Another technique involves applying commercial liquid floor wax with an old toothbrush to the outside of the tip, pleats, and box of the shoe. The wax is only applied where hardness is desired. The boxes are then stuffed with paper, and the ribbons are folded inside the shoes. The shoes are put on a baking sheet in a cold oven and baked for three minutes at two hundred and fifty degrees. It is important not to preheat the oven. Turn off the heat after three minutes and leave the shoes inside the oven overnight.

The Houston Ballet uses a hot box, which is a wooden box about four feet tall and two-and-a-half feet wide. A door extends the entire length of the box. Inside are drawers with wire bottoms to allow heat to circulate. Light bulbs are used as the heating elements and surround the drawers. A dancer pours Future floor wax in a pair of shoes, allows it to soak in, and then dabs out the excess before placing the shoes in the hot box. Houston dancers report getting several additional wearings from a pair of shoes by using this method. You can duplicate the hot box by turning a regular oven to two hundred degrees, placing your shoes in the oven, leaving the temperature set to two hundred for ten minutes, then turning off the oven and leaving the shoes in until the oven cools. When trying any of the methods involving an oven, be sure to heed the warning of Sandra Organ; she noticed that her shoes smelled like garlic bagels the day after she dried them in an oven she had recently used for making croutons.

Dancers have tried block strengthening with a variety of shellac-like substances and floor waxes. One product frequently mentioned around the country is Pratt and Lambert's Fabulon, a clear floor finish. In recent years Super Glue, Crazy Glue, or Jet Glue are most often mentioned by dancers for hardening both the box, tip, and shank.

When Christine Spizzo danced for ABT, she said the company dancers used Bull's Eye spray shellac to extend the life of their shoes. She warns that it must be done in a well-ventilated room. Now, as a teacher at the North Carolina School of the Arts, she notes that Jet Glue seems to be the most commonly used hardener.

When first interviewed for this book, Jennifer Gelfand had recently won a gold medal at the International Ballet Competition in Jackson, Mississippi. Later, she joined the Boston Ballet and danced for many years as a principal. She liked to drip Crazy Glue inside the tips of her shoes. She said, "They stay hard for three-and-a-half weeks, even when I use them every day." She also used the spray shellac Zinsser to stiffen the arches. It can be bought in a hardware store and takes about twenty minutes to dry.

In the fall of 2003 Jennifer retired from dancing.

Recycling Shanks

Some dancers remove the shanks from an old pair of pointe shoes they are discarding or converting into flat shoes, and place them under the inner soles as a reinforcement for a pair of shoes that are getting soft.

NOTE

Virtually every dancer and teacher interviewed for this book is a contributor to this chapter. We like to think of it as a wonderful dressing-room jam session, with all of them sitting around after a class sharing this wisdom with the rest of us.

 # Shoe Accessories

A plethora of accessories has recently appeared on the market to make pointe work less painful, more comfortable, and to aid in dealing with bunions, corns, long second toes, or other abnormalities. These products are also intended to extend the life of the shoes and to assist in a better fit. A variety of ribbons and elastic are also available. Companies and the products they carry are listed below.

BUNHEADS DANCE ACCESSORIES
53 Church Street
Saratoga Springs, NY 12866
Telephone: (518) 581-0521
E-mail: info@bunheads.com
www.bunheads.com

Bunheads, Inc. was created in an effort to provide innovative, quality dance accessories for the serious dancer. Founded by a former soloist with the New York City Ballet, the company has more than thirty years' experience of sweat, sewing, blisters, bumps, and bruises, and understands the small things that can help make the dancer's life a little easier.

Ouch Pouch® These toe pads are made of a thin layer of gel material inside a smooth fabric pouch. Cushioning covers the ball of the foot as well as the toes; soft seams flatten on pointe. The toe pads can be cut to size. Hand wash and air dry only.

Ouch Pouch Jr.® These are good for smaller or wider feet, or for those who only want the toes cushioned.

Jelly Toes® This elasticized fabric tube is lined with a gel pad. It should be cut to size and placed over any of the toes, and is intended to reduce the pressure that can cause blisters and corns.

Jelly Tips® This elasticized fabric tube is sonic-welded at one end, and is coated on the inside with gel to help alleviate the pressure that causes bruised toenails. It is especially effective on longer toes, and should be cut to the length needed for protection. It should be short enough so that circulation is not impaired.

Space Pack® Place the Spacemaker between the first two toes to align the big toe with the big toe joint, helping to alleviate pressure and to reduce inflammation of the bursa. Spacers are less stocky than Spacemakers. Place them between any of the other toes to help prevent nails from cutting into adjacent toes and to take pressure off soft corns.

The Big Tip® A larger version of Jelly Tips, but it is specifically designed for the big toe. It should be cut to length so that circulation is not compromised.

The Really Big Tip® Another, larger version of Jelly Tips designed for larger toes. There are two sizes and two items per packet.

Bunion Buster® Designed for bunion relief. It is an elastic fabric tube with a gel coating on the inside for the big toe and bunion area. It helps alleviate friction and take pressure off the joint. Cut along the length of the tube and place it over the big toe so that the Buster covers the bunion area.

Jelly Tube® This is a smaller version of Bunion Buster to protect the small toe and bunionette area on the side of the foot. Cut along the tube's length and place it over the pinky toe so that the gel covers the aforementioned area.

Sticky Strips® These are easy-to-use doubled-sided tape strips to keep the heels of pointe shoes on. There are thirty-six strips per packet.

Shank Tacks® Each container holds fifty tacks that provide extra support and reinforcement for soft or broken shanks. They are especially recommended for dancers with greatly arched feet.

Flexers® Many female dancers develop Achilles tendinitis owing to the nature of pointe work. Too often, ribbons that are tied too tightly restrict the ankles and create excessive pressure on the tendons. Flexers are designed to help alleviate the pressure that causes this irritation. Pieces of elastic sewn onto ribbons stretch with the movement of the ankle, enabling the dancer to rise from *plié,* through *demi-pointe,* and onto pointe with minimal constriction and no bagginess. They are available in two colors and each set has four Flexer ribbons.

Knot Keepers® These invisible adhesive strips help keep ribbons securely tucked in place.

Rolled Ribbon, Packaged Ribbon, Bolt Elastic, and Pre-Cut Ribbon and Elastic and Rock Rosin are also available.

DANZTECH, INC.

Eckhard Kuennemann or Janet Kuennemann
624 Third Avenue
Salt Lake City, UT 84103
Telephone/Fax: (801) 363-5813
E-mail: danztech@ix.netcom.com
www.danztech.com

DanzTech was founded in 1987 by Janet and Eckhard Kuennemann to develop and provide impact-absorbing padding for toes. Janet's extensive experience as a performer and instructor of ballet has given her first-hand knowledge of its rigors and subsequent pain and injuries. With Eckhard's professional background in physics and computer simulation, the founding team is the perfect partnering of science and art. DanzTech's mission is to provide impact protection for the toes and foot care products in general.

Toe Savers ™ Primas Z-Flo, a soft, feather-light fluid that forms a pillow around painful pressure points. A mini gel pad is incorporated into the toe area to provide impact protection. This product features a wrap-around seam design with soft, absorbent lining, a padding-free compartment in the vamp area, and hypoallergenic components.

Toe Savers ™ Minis This product includes a compact pad that works alone or in combination with other forms of padding. It is made of Gelastic®, a soft, yet durable hypoallergenic gel that is designed to soothe, while providing impact protection for the toes. It can be washed, air dried, and repowdered with baby powder.

Toe Savers ™ Elite Toe Pads This Mini Gelastic® pad has been incorporated into the toe pad as a cushy bumper pad to provide extra impact protection.

Toe Savers ™ Blister-Aid Kit This contains several Gelastic® blister pads of various sizes, and five yards of 3M Coban™ athletic wrap to hold the pads in place. It sticks only to itself, not to the skin, tights, or shoes.

Toe Savers ™ SoftSpacers Kit The kit includes four small spacer pads, two large spacer pads, and two wedge pads.

EUROTARD
1328 Union Hill Rd
Alpharetta, GA 30004
Telephone: (770) 475-3045
Fax: (770) 664-7208
Sales E-mail: sales@eurotard.com
Customer Service E-mail: help@eurotard.com

Eurotard makes dance clothing as well as a full range of dance-related articles.

Pointe Comfort These shoe pads are designed for the experienced dancer, and are constructed of orthotically tested Visco Elastic Polymers. There is one size only.

Ultra Lite Pointe Comfort Eurotard's new Ultra Lite is specifically designed for the training and development of pointe work. This thinner product is designed so that the dancer can feel the floor.

GAYNOR MINDEN
140 West 16th Street
New York, NY 10011
Telephone: (800) 637-9240, (212) 929-0087
E-mail: fitters@dancer.com
www.dancer.com

Totally Toes Pointe Shoe Fitting Kit This includes Dynamic Box Liners, gel crescents, gel ovals, and mushroom-shaped micro-pads. Sizes are small, medium, and large.

Pointe Shoe Adjustable Toe Separators Sizes: one size fits most.

Pointe Shoe Heel Grippers Sizes: one size fits most.

Vamp Elastic Sew this product into the front of the shoe to prevent the over-arched foot from "popping out."

Sockliners This product is designed to reduce excess material at the heel and sides of the shoe.

Toe Wrap This is the same soft, light, stretchy, resilient tape that surgeons use.

Tip Tops Platform Protector Kit This includes DucoCement and four moleskin covers for protecting the tips of pointe shoes.

PILLOWS FOR POINTE INC.
231 Commack Road, Suite 85
Commack, NY 11725
Telephone/Fax: (800) 269-3844

Pillows for Pointe Inc. has been serving the dancer since 1992. Products are geared to the ballerina and sold in dance shops.

Lamb's Wool Curl Toe Pillows Sizes small, medium, and large. The soft seam eliminates the bulky side seam found on other toe pads.

Gellows Reversible Toe Pads These come in sizes S/M and M/L, with a nonsilicone polymer on one side and a knitted seamless fabric liner on the other.

Loose Lamb's Wool One ounce of pure Australian wool.

Cedar Chip Sachets Sachets designed to keep the inside of shoes smelling fresh, to absorb moisture, help retain shape, and to make shoes last longer. They come in pairs.

The Dance Shoe Pillowcase Holds two pairs of pointe shoes. It is lightweight mesh and machine washable.

Powdered Rosin Two ounces of refined powdered rosin, prepackaged inside a resealable plastic bag.

Rock Rosin The personal container size.

Rock Rosin Studio The studio-size pail.

Ballet Pink Ribbon and **European Pink Ribbon** Three yards each of 7/8-inch-wide single-face satin ribbon.

POINTE BLEUE
943 Harrison Street
San Francisco, CA 94107
Phone: (866) TOE-TAPE
www.pointebleue.com

Pointe Bleue makes a dance gauge tape that has advantages over the adhesive, sports, and masking tapes that are used by dancers for protection from chafing and blisters. It is pliant, conforms to the shape of the toe, and allows freedom of movement while protecting the skin. It comes in both 0.5- and 0.75-inch widths, and is therefore suitable for dancers of all ages and sizes. The tape is composed of cotton gauze, natural rubber latex, and natural dye. It breathes and is not affected by perspiration. It also adheres only to itself—not to skin, hair, or clothing. The tape is painless to remove and leaves no gummy residue. Pointe Bleue tape comes in rolls of thirty yards.

Other Sources

Most major dance shoe manufacturers sell some form of pointe shoe pads, cushions, lamb's wool, and rosin. Check their websites for details.

7 The Shoe Master

While preparing this book, author Janice Barringer interviewed Michael Clifford, shoe supervisor of the Birmingham Royal Ballet in Birmingham, England, for his insights into a ballet company's use of shoes. His title is more commonly known as the shoe master. Michael was trained in technical backstage theater. His first job with the company was as a wardrobe assistant; but twelve years ago, when the shoe supervisor fell ill, he stepped in and got the show on.

Janice Barringer: Are you in charge of what everybody wears?

Michael Clifford: Yes. The job breaks down into two kinds of shoe-buying and fitting. There is the *stock*, which consists of pointe shoes and boys' and girls' "flatties" which is an ongoing roller coaster!—just keeping the dancers' shoes up-to-date, because their feet change. I'm in constant communication with the manufacturers three, four, or five times a year. If we have a problem, we try and get the people who make the shoes in to see the dancers and sort it out as quickly as possible, especially if it's to do with pointe shoes that are made in the U.K.

The other part of the job is *character shoes*: ballet boots, boots, and shoes. *Sleeping Beauty* is a prime example of a ballet in which everybody wears shoes and boots. They go from pointe shoes to boots to shoes, and all the shoes are bespoke [the English word for custom-made or made-to-order]. When we were doing fittings for *Sleeping Beauty,* the girls were saying they were a bit loose for *Mazurka.* I just thought that it was better looser, because I know that later they would fit. The girls will go from *fairies* or *waltz* in pointe shoes into *hunt* where there is a quick change. By this time their feet are very swollen and big sloppy boots are usually a relief!"

JB: Those beautiful leather boots are expensive. Do all the dancers have their own?

MC: Yes, I don't have anybody sharing.

JB: Which companies do you deal with? Are you willing to go anywhere for the dancers?

MC: When I first took over the job, all the girls were in Freed of London shoes. There was no exception; it was the director's choice. When we started getting principal dancers from abroad, it was easier to allow the dancers to stick with the shoes with which they came. The first group was from Stuttgart, and those dancers wore Karl Heinz Martin. So I just carried on ordering their stock. There was a bit of a language barrier, but I managed to get through that. The next were dancers from Australia who wore Bloch. Now there is a mixture of pointe shoe makers used in the company. I try to get the girls to stick to pointe shoes made in England, but it is not a hard-and-fast rule.

JB: But some people can't change. Other shoes don't work for them.

MC: Some ballet companies abroad won't let them order the shoes they want. If they have ordered shoes and there are fifty pairs left, YOU WILL USE THOSE FIFTY PAIRS until they are gone. Here, Freed of London is on our doorstep, so we have a shorter manufacturing period from placing the order to receiving it.

JB: Do you determine how many pairs of shoes is reasonable? What happens if you go over that number?

MC: It's really at my discretion. We try to budget for ten pairs per month, per girl in the *corps de ballet*, possibly stretching it to between twelve and fifteen pairs per month for soloists. And then, for principals—it's whatever they need. Then again, if a soloist is also doing a lot of principal work, I can stretch it. The girls will never take more shoes than they need. They will only wear and sew as many shoes as they need. They simply just go through their shoes—they're not selling them, they're using them!

JB: Do the dancers wear shiny or pancaked shoes?

MC: The decision is made by the choreographer or designer. A rule of thumb is that if it is a traditional classical ballet, it will call for shiny shoes. In *Sleeping Beauty*, all the shoes are shiny. For other ballets, shoes can be pancaked (to a matte finish)—then they can last a bit longer because we just touch them up with pancake.

Swan Lake is a little unusual: in Acts I and III, shiny shoes are *de rigueur* while pancaked shoes are used for Acts II and IV. *Giselle* and *Coppélia* use many pointe shoes because the shoes cannot be touched up with pancake when they get dirty. Some of the dancers go through many pairs of shoes because each costume has a different color tights, and the shoes must match the tights. If they are in bare legs, they use pancake on the shoes to match the skin tone.

JB: What are the stresses of your job?

MC: I get all the "pre-stress"—usually the girls start preparing their shoes a month in advance, so I get all the stress before they go on stage. After that I don't hear anything! The stress moves on to the wig master who is responsible for doing their hair.

As the "shoe master," Michael's life is never dull. When he was first starting the job, mysteriously all of the hinges kept falling off the doors of the theater. It took a while to realize that the girls were closing their brand new shoes in them to flatten the boxes. Now, he says, most theaters have stronger hinges. Another story involves hearing a strange noise. He didn't know what it was or where it was coming from. More thorough investigation led to the discovery that the girls had taken stage weights to their dressing rooms and were hammering their shoes on them. He had thought it was the plumbing.

JB: Please tell me more interesting things dancers do to their shoes.

MC: One of our principals takes ages to prepare her shoes—she shaves the sole to the absolute minimum. Quite often she shaves them so much that the shoe falls completely apart. She brings them to me to be glued back together.

There was a fad for a while when all the girls cut their shanks way down; but now they are moving back to full soles, which pleases me as well as the Pilates teacher. We feel it is healthier and also helps the dancers to work their feet. They haven't been forced to do it, but on their own they are slowly moving back to full soles.

The company orders 5,000 meters of pink satin ribbon a year. Then each dancer gets 50 meters apiece. It is shiny on one side and matte on the other and dyes really well. The elastic used on pointe shoes is from Schrek Klaus in Germany. It looks weak, but it is rubbered on one side so it doesn't slide, and it is slightly see-through. They also order vamp elastic that is used by girls with big arches.

One company dancer goes over on her arch so much that Freed makes a tilting block for her. In the other extreme, some girls need to be pushed over so the blocks are made to tilt the other way.

JB: What about shellac?

MC: Since so many dancers shellac their shoes, I order it in five-liter containers from a big warehouse that supplies carpenters. When we go out on tour, I put a liter bottle in each dressing room. It's amusing to watch them completely bash everything out of their shoes and then put shellac in to make them harder.

When it is put into traditionally made pointe shoes, shellac soaks in. K.H. Martin shoes have plastic inside the tip, so no matter how much shellac you use, it doesn't soak in. Gaynor Minden shoes are the same. When shellac is used, the shoes have to dry out. They need dry heat. When the girls receive their shoes, they have already been dried for forty-eight hours at the factory. Still, I usually recommend that they put the shoes somewhere with dry heat to help with the continuation of the drying. You need to get rid of the moisture. If you dance on shoes as soon as they arrive from the factory, they don't last as long because they are still slightly damp. That's why I have a lot of stock and I rotate it. I put down the date it arrives, and put the latest arrivals at the top. When the dancers reach for the shoes in the pigeonholes, they are the ones that arrived a couple of months before.

Profiles of Pointe Shoemakers and Sellers

American Makers

Capezio Ballet Makers

1 Campus Drive	Canada Fax: (800) 835-1276
Totowa, NJ 07512	Int'l Ph: (973) 595-7094
Telephone: (201) 595-9000	Int'l Fax: (973) 595-9120
Fax: (201) 595-9120	Europe Ph: 44-1603-405522
U.S. Ph: (800) 533-1887	Europe Fax: 44-1603-78890
U. S. Fax: (800) 522-1222	Puerto Rico Ph: (800) 595 9022
Canada Ph: (800) 595-9022	www.capeziodance.com

Capezio is the largest manufacturer of pointe shoes. In addition to its dance products, the company creates special shoes for everyone from the Pope to dancers in Broadway shows and midgets in the circus.

In 1887, when Cecchetti was making his debut in St. Petersburg, an Italian cobbler named Salvatore Capezio opened a small shop across the street from the old Metropolitan Opera House in New York. Five years later, he became the Met's official shoemaker, making both costume shoes for the singers and dance footwear for the *corps de ballet*. Then, in 1915, Anna Pavlova endorsed his shoes; and at the Paris Exposition in 1925, Capezio dance slippers won the gold medal.

Capezio took up the challenge of making shoes for dancers. He was constantly dissecting ballet and pointe slippers, and experimenting with new ways of constructing them. During his lifetime, he built up his business from a tiny shoeshop in Manhattan's West 40s to an important manufacturing entity, with retail agencies in every major city. He died in January 1940, at the age of seventy.

After Capezio's death, leadership of the company passed to Ben Sommers. The founder of the Capezio Foundation and a prime mover in the development of American dance, Sommers had, at the age of fourteen, begun working for Capezio as an errand boy and shipping clerk. He was hired by Jimmy Salvaggio, later known as Jimmy Selva.

In recalling those early years, Ben Sommers remembers that the Capezio *fabbrica* where the shoemakers worked in the 1920s consisted of two or three houses on West 39th and West 40th Streets. The factory included a cutting room, stitching room, and shoemaking room. At that time, shoes were stitched by hand. (The Goodyear stitching machine had yet to be introduced.) After Jimmy Selva left Capezio in 1925 to form his own business, Ben Sommers became more involved with both the dance and theatrical aspects of the Capezio enterprise. Following Mr. Capezio's death, he served as president of the company from 1940 until 1976. Today the CEO of Capezio-BalletMakers is Paul Terlizzi, a fourth-generation member of the Capezio family.

Capezio offers a full line of pointe shoes designed to provide dancers and dance students with a wide variety of choices in the areas of shank and box strength, as well as basic shape. Capezio's goal in creating these choices is to make it unnecessary for customers to order custom-made shoes. Capezio's owners feel that the two major strengths of their shoes are that they are consistently made and are long-lasting.

Since proper fitting of a pointe shoe is of prime importance, Judith H. Weiss, Capezio's Director of Ballet Sales and Fittings, and her assistant, Brandon Currie, travel the entire country offering their expertise. Judy says they invite themselves and pay for everything. They go to ballet schools and ballet companies, visiting whoever wants to be fitted. They send all the shoes ahead so they will be there when they arrive. "This is our second year of doing it and we have been really, really successful!" they say.

For more than thirty years, Judy has been creating custom pointe shoes for lead ballerinas. Her expertise was the foundation for Capezio's latest shoe development. The *Prelude* is made for dancers with a moderate to wide forefoot, and toes that taper. It features a long vamp with a three-quarter shank to enhance stability and provide support, while preventing the foot from rolling over. Dancers with average or high arches will prefer the design of this shank. The platform is formed to maintain the tapered shape in the interior of the shoe, while creating a wider, very flat shape on the exterior of the toe box. The shape of this toe box is flattering whether standing flat, in *demi-pointe,* or on full pointe.

The *Glissé* (#102/102A)is designed with new construction techniques. It has a broader, feathered, hand-molded toe box, with a higher platform and a U-shaped vamp that allows the dancer to roll straight from flat to pointe with more support. In addition, there is an elastic drawstring and a hard (#3), skived shank. The color is European pink and the sizes are 4 to 10 and M, W, and WW widths. In the spring of 2004 the *Glissé ES* (#102ES/102ESA) was introduced. The shoe is built on the foundation of the Glissé, has a harder (#5) skived shank, an elastic drawstring, and a broader feathered, hand-molded toe box that has a higher platform. The U-shaped vamp allows the dancer to roll straight from flat to pointe. It comes in European pink, sizes 4–10 and M, W, and WW widths.

Style numbers 196/197, the *Plié I* and *Plié II,* both offer a vamp that extends beyond the toe box for better support. They also have a hard (#3) shank and side wings. *Plié II* has a broader box and wider platform than the *Plié I,* and it offers WW width. The color is European pink.

Tendu I and *Tendu II (#198/199)* have a medium (#2) shank and break in quickly.The *Tendu II* has a broader box and wider platform, and offers WW width. European pink is the color.

The *Contempora* (#176) has a broad, feathered, medium-strength box and a wide platform, a pre-arched, medium (#2) shank. The vamp is half an inch longer, and the heel height is quarter of an inch lower. It also has a shorter sole. The color is European pink.

One of the older shoes in the line, the *Pavlowa* (P103) has a Russian-style, feathered, tapered box. It also has a flat platform, a pre-arched, hard #3 shank, and a strong box. The vamp is quarter of an inch longer, the heel height is quarter of an inch shorter, and the sole is also shorter. The color is European pink.

Capezio pointe shoes may be custom-ordered in any size and width, vamp height, side and heel height, and length and strength of the box. Sock linings are available in cotton or suede, and drawstrings are available in cotton and elastic. In addition to European pink, drawstrings can be made up in black, caramel, ivory, pink, red, and white. They can also be manufactured in leather at an additional charge. The special make-up department (SMU) can be reached at (800) 533-1887.

Fuzi International

1901 53rd Avenue SE	E-mail: fu@fuzi.net
Olympia, WA 98501	www.fuzi.net
Phone and Fax: (360) 786-0226	

Xijun Fu, the owner and designer of Fuzi shoes, was trained at the Beijing Dance Academy. He danced with the Central Ballet of China and the Santiago Ballet in Chile; and was the artistic director of the Lexington Ballet and Kentucky Ballet Theatre for six years. Later, as a guest artist with companies in South America, Canada, and the United States, he wore shoes of his own design. Other dancers were so impressed that they asked him to make shoes for them. Those requests have resulted in yet another choice for dancers.

The *Fuzi* shoe offers three models. One has a full red board shank, one a three-quarter shank, and one a split sole. The box is made with four layers of thin canvas and special glue. Lengths range from 33 (U.S. street size five) to 40 (U.S. street size 9.5) and there are five widths—A,B,C,D, and E. The shoes can be ordered on-line and usually take only about a week to arrive.

Gaynor Minden

140 West 16th Street	http://www.dancer.com
New York, NY 10011	European Office
Telephone: (212) 929-0087	Telephone: 44 01273 429 429
Fax: (212) 929-4907	Fax: 44 01273 429 420
E-mail: fitters@dancer.com	

Inventing revolutionary pointe shoes took Eliza Minden eight years of research and development, but it made possible a leap into the technology of the 21st century—elastomerics: materials usually found in space capsules, race cars, underwater exploration equipment, and other forms of materials intended to make pointe shoes longer-lasting and pain-free. The shoe has anti-shock poron[®1], four thousand linings, ultra-thin cellular urethane foam to absorb impact and suppress noise, a pleatless toe box yielding greater platform space, and a side closure for the drawstring.

Since introducing its first, stiff model in limited sizes in 1993, Gaynor Minden has expanded its pointe shoe line. It now includes five shank stiffnesses, three box shapes, two vamps, three heels, and three widths.

There are also the *Sleekfit* styles for dancers with narrow heels and wide metatarsals; all in all, Gaynor Minden has 2,853 size/style options. They are all stock shoes; no special orders needed.

The shanks come in *Hard, ExtraFlex, Supple, FeatherFlex,* and *Pianissimo.* All are injection-molded elastomeric, and all are designed to be unbreakable and never to lose their original stiffness.

The three box choices are (#2) narrow and tapered, (#3) medium, and (#4) wide. Midfoot selections are narrow, medium, and wide. Vamps come in regular or deep, and heel choices are regular, high, or sleek.

The *Sleekfit* line was developed because so many ballet dancers have wide metatarsals, but not a correspondingly wide heel, and thus standard shoe size grading is not applicable. Gaynor Minden's sizing runs about a half to a full size up from American street shoe sizing. Their size 8, for example, will probably fit a street shoe size 7. Gaynor Minden does not fit the shoes tight, and the specially lined satin does not stretch out as much as other conventionally lined satin.

Special orders are still accepted for modifications to vamps, heels, sides, linings and so on. White shoes are offered as well as the classic pink.

Leo's Dancewear, Inc.

1900 N. Narragansett	Fax: (312) 889-7593
Chicago, IL 60639	E-mail: nfo@leosdancewear.com
Telephone: (312) 889-7700	www.leosdancewear.com

Begun by Leo Harris in 1924, today Leo's is managed by the family's second and third generations. The company's pointe shoes are sold in retail outlets throughout the United States.

Pointe shoes are cut at Leo's every two weeks, and one employee oversees the complete manufacture of a pair of shoes. However, because the company's shoemaking process is extremely uniform, one maker can complete work that was begun by another, if necessary.

The latest groundbreaking shoe on the market is style 0051, the *Split Sole Pointe Shoe.* Leo's was the first company to develop this flexible shoe and has a patent pending. "The absence of an outer mid-sole greatly reduces resistance in pointing this shoe," says Leo's president, Glen Baruck. It has a pliant, full-length red board shank, a scored split outer sole, and a feathered box. The broad toe box has a flat, stable platform and is very quiet. There is a nonslip suede sock lining or a soft cotton lining, and an elastic drawstring.

The 0051 comes in sizes 3-10, widths B, C, D, and E, with satin ribbons included.

Leo's other pointe shoe is the Style 041 *Pas de Deux Pointe 1*. This shoe has a suede toe and a fully lined upper. It comes in pink, sizes 1-9L, 13S-9L, and widths B, C, D, and E.

In the spring of 2004 two new models were introduced: *Inspiration* and *Inspiration* ¾. Both models have full, leather, scored outer soles, and the toe box features a flat platform, a broader shape, and is designed to be very quiet. The shoes come in B, C, D, and E widths, and include ribbons. The difference in the two shoes is the shank. The *Inspiration* has a full red board and a medium-weight shank, while the *Inspiration* ¾ has a three-quarter fiberboard shank. This three-quarter shank is not just cut off at the back of the shoe, but goes from medium weight in the front, tapering down in the middle, until there is almost nothing in the rear quarter of the shoe. This provides the additional flexibility of a three-quarter shank shoe, but with additional comfort, since the dancer does not feel the sudden drop of the shank.

Liberts

4920 Northpark Loop	Fax: (719) 592-1526
Colorado Springs, CO 80918	E-mail: feedback@liberts.com
Telephone: (800) 624-6480	www.liberts.com

This is a wholesale company catering to studio owners, teachers, businesses, or colleges. If a catalog is desired, proof of business must be mailed or faxed to Liberts. Information may be obtained by calling the toll-free number or by going to the website. Along with many other dance-related articles, four Capezio shoes are carried, as well as two made expressly for Liberts.

The *200* is a suede toe pointe shoe which features a strong shank, and provides good support. Pink ribbon is included. This shoe is fitted 2½ to 3 sizes smaller than street shoe size, and comes in child C width and adult C to E widths.

The *400* style is a Brazilian shoe with a broad box for dancers at all levels. It has a suede toe, a scored leather sole, drawstring, and cotton lining. It comes in European pink satin. The sizes correspond to U.S. street shoe size. Ribbon is also included.

Prima Soft

213 Old York Road	www.prima-soft.com
Jenkintown, PA 19046	Wholesale: (215) 886-2255
Telephone: (215) 572-5177	Wholesale orders and
Fax: (215) 886-9226	information:
E-mail: prima@prima-soft.com	(800) 431-6005

When they open new accounts across the country and in Europe, the first thing president David Juniman and vice president Marlena Juniman tell their customers is not to bend or flex their pointe shoes. People are astonished because, after all, that is what dancers have been doing for more than a century! Having been a consultant for major pointe shoe manufacturers and importers, Marlena always tried to have them change the way the shoes were made, to get the dancers "off the vamps and into the boxes." Since the company has gone to the expense of making new lasts, they have been able to achieve just that. With this new design, it is no longer necessary to slam shoes in doorways or to hammer and pound them; they break in naturally as they are worn.

The shoes are made of natural materials with graduated shanks that provide excellent support, and mold naturally to the foot. The way the box is shaped has also been changed. The *Perfect Placement Toe Box* is "to get the dancer on the floor and off the vamp." Five different styles are offered.

The Gala (#701) is a versatile shoe that fits a multitude of foot types. It is available in a natural or hard graduated shank; the hard is recommended for "banana feet" that "go over" in other pointe shoes. It has an elastic drawstring and the *Perfect Placement Box*. This shoe is quiet and good for the beginning dancer as well as the professional.

The Prima Russe (#702) has a "V" vamp with no drawstring. It is available in a flex or regular graduated shank, with a shorter *Perfect Placement Box*, which is excellent for the squarer foot with shorter toes, or feet that taper only slightly. The graduated flex shank works well for beginning dancers or those with a lower arch, and is also recommended for professionals who like a lighter shoe. The regular graduated shank offers more support and is longer-lasting. This shoe also comes in a custom extra-wide width.

The Silhouette (#703) is a shoe for the longer-toed dancer with a flexible arch. The *Perfect Placement Box* aligns the toes straight down into the toe box creating a center of balance needed for the flexible, high-arched foot. It is available in one graduated shank strength, and can also be special ordered in extra-hard. There is no drawstring and it has a "V" vamp.

The Royale (#709) is a "V" vamp shoe for the dancer who likes the feel of an American shoe, but also likes the style of Russian shoes. Like all other models of Prima Soft, it has a *Perfect Placement Box* and a graduated shank. This shoe fits narrow, medium, or wide feet, and also works well for people with shallow feet. It is available in one shank strength. A new, extra-wide width-size is now available in XXXX, and can even be made in XXXXX.

Prima Soft's newest shoe, *The Volé* (#710), has a graduated memory shank that comes back to shape each time the dancer goes from pointe to flat. It also has an elastic drawstring and the *Perfect Placement Box*. Although it comes in one shank strength, harder shanks may be specially ordered in quantities of six.

British Makers

Dance Workshop Ltd.

Unit B4 Phoenix Industrial Estate Rosslyn Cresent, Harrow	Middlesex HA1 2SP, UK Telephone: 44 20 8424 2200 E-mail: Bob@dwinnovation.com

Dance Workshop Ltd. was formed in July 1995 by Bob and Pat Martin, with financial support from Derek Gandolfi. After working for Gamba for thirty-five years, Bob decided to move on and form his own company. His lifetime ambition is to develop what he calls the "ultimate" pointe shoe.

Bob Martin had already developed the famous *Turning Pointe* with his friend Rodney Freed, but he wanted to go farther. His shoes, which are sold worldwide by the recommendation of dancer to dancer, are custom-made for each dancer. Dancers send him an old shoe of the correct length, and then discuss their special requirements via e-mail, fax, or phone. Even though he makes bespoke (custom-made) pointe shoes, Bob never meets (in person) ninety percent of his customers.

The sizes range from 8 to 13, with half and quarter sizes throughout. Fittings are N (narow), X (medium), XX (wide), and XXX (extra wide).

Bob Martin has made shoes for Royal Ballet ballerinas Antoinette Sibley and Lesley Collier; now Dance Workshop continues to make shoes for world-famous dancers and companies.

Freed of London

94 St. Martin's Lane	Freed of London
London WC2N 4AT, UK	21-01 43rd Avenue
Telephone: 440 20 7240 0432	Long Island City, NY 11101
Fax: 440 20 7240 3061	Telephone: (866) MYFREED
E-mail: shop@freed.co.uk	Fax: (718) 729-8086
www.freedoflondon.com	info@freedusa.com: general questions

Frederick Freed, founder of Frederick Freed Ltd., was the son of a sample shoemaker who opened his own shoe repair shop in England. Although young Frederick initially thought of becoming an engineer, at the age of sixteen, during World War I, he began making ballet shoes at a firm in London's West End. As Freed explained on his eightieth birthday in 1979, "I went into a room where I saw rolls of satin and bits of leather, and you know the old saying: if you see a girl you fall in love with, it clicks right away and you don't want to know anyone else."

After observing veteran makers use seven to nine nails to pleat the toes of the shoes they were constructing, Freed invented a method of lasting-up that required only three nails. He developed a special sensitivity to the needs of dance customers, and his intense interest led him to open his own shop. Frederick Freed Ltd. was established in 1928, when Freed, his wife, and an assistant left Gamba to open a retail store in St. Martin's Lane, where they sewed shoes in the basement.

As his business prospered, Freed realized that many dancers stopped dancing because the traditional shoes of his day had a fixed width, and were too narrow for some customers. So he began to concentrate on providing custom shoes, a skill and a service that remain Freed's special province. Today, Freed's shoes are exported all around the world.

After the death of Frederick Freed and his longtime friend and colleague Sam Thompson, who succeeded him as chairman of the board, the company was purchased by Chacott Ltd. of Japan, a firm which also specializes in the manufacture of pointe shoes. While concerned with increasing productivity and service standards, the directors of Chacott have stated their firm's intention to maintain the unique integrity of the Freed line.

Bernard D. Kohler, managing director of Frederick Freed, Ltd. for well over forty years, was a key figure in guiding the company into this new era. Now that he has retired, Michele Attfield, a trained dancer and a director of the company, is the main spokesperson. Although they both see Freed's approach to serving the needs of individual dancers as starting with a basic stock shoe design and varying it to fit personal specifications, the company has recently introduced four new models.

The Freed stock shoe, the *Classic Deep Vamp* SBTDV, is a satin block pointe shoe, which is all-satin and has a sturdy arch. Stock widths are medium, wide (X), extra wide (XX), and extra extra wide (XXX). Narrow can also be ordered. Sizes range from 10½ small to 9 large. Both regular and deep vamps are available from stock.

Freed's stock shoe has a standard blocking, a basic insole, and average-sized vamp sides and back. It is made in a heavy, cotton-backed corset satin. The glue used in Freed shoes is made of natural starches. A special paper is used for building the block.

The *Wing Block* SBTWB incorporates a supportive wing block, and has a "V"-cut deep vamp to lend support to the metatarsal. This model comes in sizes 2.5 to 7, with widths M, X, XX, and XXX. No maker requests are allowed.[2]

The *Student Block Toe* was developed for the students at the Royal Ballet School. It is a lighter-weight shoe with a flexible insole, suitable for younger dancers.

First launched for the young dancer, but now also worn by advanced students and professionals, both *Studio* and *Studio II* are made with the same biodegradable ingredients as all other Freed Pointe Shoes, but with new technology, allowing every pair to be identical. Both styles have extra-durable platforms, pleating underneath for improved contact with the floor, and a suede sock for greater comfort and better grip. *Studio II* has a wider platform and lower profile than *Studio I.*

Studio I and *Studio II* come in four widths, C, D, E, and EE, and with a choice of two insoles. The lengths are 2.5 to 8. Every pair comes with its own mesh shoe bag and ribbons.

Freed special-order shoes offer several custom features. For example, wings can be strengthened with newspaper, a stronger fabric, or with layers of glue. Vamp lengths and styles can be altered, and insoles can be varied in at least fifteen different ways, in terms of materials and construction. They can also be cut from different strengths of board, the thinnest of which closely resembles poster board. The insole favored by Margot Fonteyn is called the *Phillips insole*. Flexible and suitable for a dancer with a high arch, it is named after Miss Phillips, the first dancer who ordered such an insole. Fonteyn's *Phillips insole* was only a half-inch wide in the middle. Insoles can be cut wider for broader support, and made with or without a supporting shank (also called the *centerpiece*). Shanks are three-fourths as long as the insoles, and can vary in terms of materials, shape, and size. They are attached to the insole with glue and three nails. Freed makes the last nail in the insole easy to remove, since many dancers like to do so. (There are supplemental charges for custom changes.)

Whereas all Freed makers use the same patterns and processes, each has the artistic freedom to impose his own technique and style on the work, whether stock or custom shoe. For instance, pleating style varies from maker to maker. Each craftsman finds his own style, and determines whether his pleats will be narrow or wide, short or long.

Each maker has a personal symbol, which is used when the maker begins to construct a pair of shoes. Initially the symbols were the letters of the alphabet, but Freed became concerned that dancers were confusing the letters with widths. Consequently, they adopted other symbols such as a circle, dot, square, split triangle, castle, the ace of spades, and dead spider. Although Freed meant the symbols only as a means of internal identification, dancers began using them to order their shoes. To avoid confusion, a symbol belonging to a retired shoemaker is not reintroduced for five or six years.

Although it is quite difficult to serve a dancer by mail or telephone, Freed will work with a dancer thousands of miles away to help find a satisfactory maker. They try to second-guess the dancer's physical needs and professional pressures, and translate them into structural and cosmetic shoe changes.

Perhaps the ideal pointe shoe-fitting situation exists when Freed, with the aid of the school's faculty, fits the students at the Royal Ballet School. Starting with the earliest days of a Royal Ballet student's training, Freed analyzes the student's feet and adjusts her shoes as she progresses. Fitters are able to suggest makers for individual students, since the latter are well aware of the special aspects of each craftsman's style. This relationship often continues throughout a dancer's career.

In addition to the Royal Ballet honor, Freed is now the official shoe of American Ballet Theatre.

Gamba of Covent Garden Limited

3 Garrick Street, Covent Garden	E-mail:
London WC2E 9BF, UK	RetailStore@GambaDance.com
Telephone: 44 20 7437 0704	www.GambaDance.com
Fax: 44 20 7497 0754	

Luigi Gamba, founder of the firm, arrived in London at the age of fourteen. After a stint as a waiter at the Savoy Hotel, which catered to a theatrical clientele, he opened a shoe shop. By 1912, he was making "our special Toe Ballet Shoes, the same make as the original shoes supplied to the famous Milan School." Prior to this, all pointe shoes worn in England were imported from Italy. Gamba shoemaker Alfred Furse was the first Englishman to make pointe shoes for Anna Pavlova. Today, Gamba's theatrical division makes shoes for international companies of such major productions as *Les Miserables* and *Phantom of the Opera.* Gamba has eight shops in the United Kingdom, with a flagship store on Garrick Street in Covent Garden.

The innovative *Turning Pointe,* which took seven years to develop, was considered Gamba's "prize" product. The new *Pro-Pointe* has been created by Rodney Freed to surpass it. It has a sleek profile and smooth finish, which is achieved by the innovative use of elastic binding. It comes in NE (narrow), ME (medium), WE (wide), and XW (extra wide), all with elastic binding. The sizes range from child 13 to adult 8, with half sizes starting from size 1. These shoes are made-to-order only.

The Gamba *G93* has a flat box and a square platform with a high vamp, sides, and back. Its flexible carbon fiber shank can be bent a thousand times without alteration. Resistant to heat and humidity, the shoe is designed to be consistent throughout its life. It is available in a medium shank only. Sizes are the same as the *Pro-Pointe*, and the widths are N, X, XX, and XXX. Ribbons are included.

The newer *G97* design features flexible wings and a flat outer sole edge to prevent rocking. The flat box and high vamp give better support and the wide platform is designed for better balance. It offers two different blunt cut three-quarter shank strengths which are medium and hard. Ribbons are also included.

Designed to meet the needs of the advanced and professional dancer, the *GPP* is made-to-order only. Widths are NN, N, M, W, and WX, and the sizes range from child 13 to adult 8, with half sizes starting from size 1.

Mark Suffolk Pointe Shoe Co., Ltd.

Unit 16, Churchill Works	Telephone/Fax:
Highfield Street, Earl Shilton	44 1455 442767
Leicester LLE9 7HS, UK	E-Mail:
	mark@suffolkpointe.fsnet.co.uk

Mark Suffolk founded the Suffolk Pointe Shoe Company in 2000, having had almost twenty years' experience in pointe shoemaking, designing, and fitting. He was responsible for the design of several very successful shoe styles, and is instrumental in creating a whole new approach to the process of pointe shoe design and development. With the help of his wife, Lynne, he runs a workshop that employs a skilled, dedicated team. There is a dance shop within the factory where dancers from all over the UK come for fittings.

Since the importance of a correctly fitted pointe shoe is crucial, Mark decided from the outset that he would offer a greater range of width fittings, more than is available from any other manufacturer. There are primarily five width fittings: N (narrow), X, XX, XXX, and XXXX, with the addition, if required, of a further four fittings that fall between these widths. The size range available is children's 13 to adult size 8, with half sizes in all width fittings. If a dancer has one foot larger than the other, Mark will make pairs in two different sizes by special order, if required.

The *Solo* is the name for the basic model shoe that comes in three main insole types. The first has a standard insole with a standard box. The second has a hard insole with a three-quarter cut (or full cut) and a standard box, and the third has a light insole and a lighter box. Mark's *Solo*

Light, designed to help young dancers, is made in a more flexible style, so that students can reach the on-pointe position more easily. All other shoes are specials.

This stock shoe can also be customized to an individual dancer's needs. Some of the adjustments available include any combination of vamp, side, and heel measurements; cotton or elastic drawstrings; varying box strengths; a wider or more narrow platform; a higher or lower platform; and a platform angle adjustable to the dancer's best foot placement (to help "pull back" or to enable the dancer to go "farther over"). There are many combinations of special insoles, including *arch break,* to enable the dancer to go farther over when on pointe, and *arch supports,* to give extra strength and support when needed; and an extended or reduced heel, which lengthens or reduces a shoe by a quarter size.

Other International Makers

Australia

Bloch

Bloch Australasia	Bloch Concept Store, United
P.O. Box 301 Roseberry 1445	Kingdom
Unit 1, Century Estate	35 Drury Lane, Covent Garden
476-492 Gardeners Road	London WC2B 5RH, UK
Alexandria 2015, Australia	Telephone: 0207 836 4777
Telephone: 61 2 9669 3777	Fax: 0207 836 6555
Fax: 61 2 9693 2960	E-Mail: info@bloch-uk.com
Bloch USA	Bloch Canada
1170 Trademark Dr., Suite 112	Voce Enterprises Ltd.
Reno, Nevada 89511	1456 E. Pender St., Vancouver
Telephone: 775-824-2550	Canada BC V5 L IVS
Fax: 775-824-2551	Telephone: (604) 320-0848
	Fax: (604) 320-0859
New York Retail Store	
304 Columbus Avenue (between	
74th and 75th St)	
New York, NY 10023	
Telephone: (212) 579-1960	

Jacob Simon Bloch founded Bloch in 1932. Russian-born, Jacob arrived in Australia in 1931 at the height of the Great Depression, and began making shoes by hand in the workshop where he lived. Loving ballet, he visited many dance studios. After noticing a young dancer having trouble staying on pointe, he promised he would make a better pair of pointe shoes. In the late 1930s he made shoes for Spessivtseva, Baronova, Riabouchinska, Toumanova, David Lichine, and others who toured Australia with de Basil's Ballet Russes de Monte-Carlo. Today, David Wilkenfeld, Jacob's grandson, is managing director of Bloch International.

Two different paste types and two different construction techniques are used in making Bloch pointe shoes. The shoes that fall into Category A require a little extra time to break in because they are made with a harder paste. Once broken in correctly, they have a long lifespan. The shoes that fall into Category B are made from a paste that is designed to soften when moisture is applied. These shoes take more care when being broken in.

CATEGORY A HARDER PASTE SHOES	CATEGORY B SHOES
1. *Aspiration*	1. *Alpha*
2. *Serenade*	2. *Professional BPS*
3. *Serenade Strong*	3. *Signature Performance*
4. *Sonata*	4. *Signature Rehearsal*
5. *Suprima*	5. *Signature Rehearsal Strong*
6. *Suprima Strong*	6. *Synergy* ¾ Shank
7. *Serenade II*	7. *Synergy* Full Shank

Break-in Instructions

Break-in Technique A

Since these shoes are made with a harder paste than in Technique B, they are susceptible to snapping, if treated roughly at first. Doing barre is the best way to break in this type of pointe shoe, but the shoe needs to be prepared for barre by gently softening the shank and box by hand. Concentrate on the *demi-pointe* area of the shank, being careful not to crush the box. Then work up to the heel, gently massaging the shank until it is at the point where *tendu* and *relevé* on *demi-pointe* are comfortable. Softening the box is not always necessary; it is up to the individual to decide. If softening is needed, concentrate on gently softening the sides of the box. Although many dancers stand on top of the box in order to soften and widen it, this is not recommended because it can damage the shoe permanently. Once the shoes are ready for barre, one to two hours of barre will be sufficient time to shape them to the foot. At this point the shoes will be evenly softened with no weak points.

Break-in Technique B

Follow break-in technique A. After one to two hours barre, the shoe will become moist and shape itself to the dancer's foot. Once the shoe dries, it will be set in this shape. At this point, it is possible to apply shellac to the inside of the block and shank. This will not only harden the shoe in its current shape, but will also stop any more moisture from entering the shoe.

Along with a variety of dance shoes and dancewear, Bloch carries thirteen models of pointe shoes.

The *Alpha-S0104* features the new three-quarter outsole design that has a half-inch skive cut to minimize underfoot bulk. The shoe is aimed at the advanced student, preprofessional, and professional market. The purpose of this new design is to offer a shoe that allows maximum bend at the arch without compromising support. Fully developed foot and ankle strength is advised for this shoe. Its box has room for the metatarsal joints and a generous platform. The *Alpha* utilizes "low-noise" paste, a fully cut insole that has been designed to work with the outsole, and comes in X, X, XX, XXX widths; European Peach.

The *Aspiration-S0105L* is a beginner shoe built for the student. It has a similar shape to the *Synergy* (below), but uses the same paste and pasting method as the *Serenade, Sonata,* and *Suprima* (below). The shank is a new construction, which encourages the shoe to bend at three-quarter level, while still providing full shank support. The *Aspiration* comes in European Pink color, in sizes 1 through 9, and is available in A, B, C, D, and E widths.

BPS Professional-S0111L is the stock shoe by Bloch; it is the basic model of the custom professional pointe shoe. The box is constructed with a similar pasting method to the *Synergy* shoe (below), using paste that is designed to shape itself to the dancer's foot when moist. The full red board shank contains no tack or glue on the heel. This shoe can be ordered by maker. The three makers available are *Spade, Triangle en Pointe,* and *M* maker. Each has his own individual style. *Spade* is a tapered, streamline design popular among Euorpean dancers. *M* is much squarer, featuring a bigger/wider platform, and is most popular in the United States. *Triangle en Pointe* is found in most countries around the world. This shoe is somewhere between *Spade* and *M*, featuring a slim line without compromising on balance. The widths for the *BPS* are Medium, X, XX, and XXX, and the color is European peach.

Serenade-S0131L is a similar shape to the *Suprima* and *Sonata* (below), and has a narrow heel. The platform is wide, which makes it well suited to a dancer with square-shaped toes. To help dancers with flexible feet or hyperextended legs, the *Serenade* has a long vamp and strong shank. It comes in B, C, D, and E widths, and the color is European pink.

Serenade Strong-S0131S is for the dancer who needs a little more support in the shank than the standard *Serenade*. All other features of the *Serenade* apply to the *Serenade Strong*.

Serenade II-S0141L is a stock *Serenade* with a few significant design changes. It features a sponge cushion in the pleats that helps reduce noise, and has an insole redesigned to assist with *demi-pointe*, while maintaining the support found in the original model. This series of pointe shoes has a similar shape to the *Suprima* and the *Sonata* in the sense that the heel is narrow, and fits snugly. The platform is wider, so it is better suited to a dancer with square-shaped toes. The shank is made with a six-iron body and a leatherboard centerpiece. The available width fittings for the *Serenade II* are B, C, D, and E, and the sizes range from 1-9. The color is European pink.

Serenade II with *Ultra V Vamp Shape-S0141LV* is a Bloch first, with the introduction of an ultra "V"-shaped vamp. The *Ultra V* gives an alternative look for dancers who like a longer, more slender line.

Signature Performance-S0162L is designed, like the other *Signature* shoes, as a professional shoe with a longer life span. These shoes are constructed with the paste that is designed to shape itself to the dancer's foot when moist. The composition of the paste is also responsible for a large reduction of noise on the floor. The platform is as high as it is wide, which provides for both forward and lateral balance. The difference between the *Signature* shoes is the shank. The *Performance* has a green board body with a leatherboard center piece. This is equivalent to a 1.8mm shank. The available widths are B, C, D, and E, and the color is European pink.

Signature Rehearsal-S0168L has a red board body with a leatherboard centerpiece. This is the equivalent of a 2.5mm shank. It is available in

B, C, D, and E and comes in European pink. The difference between the *Signature Performance* and the *Signature Rehearsal* is the shank.

Signature Rehearsal Strong-S0168S offers more support for the dancer in the shank than the standard *Signature Rehearsal*. It has a 2.5mm red board body, a 1.6 mm insole red board (second centerpiece), and a leatherboard (third centerpiece). All other features of the *Signature Rehearsal* apply to the *Signature Rehearsal Strong*.

Sonata-S0130L has a tapered heel for a snug fit. The platform is as wide as the *Serenade*, but taller, which makes it a good balancing shoe. The slightly shorter box allows for an easy *demi-pointe*, and it contains a cushion within the pleats to cut down on noise. A sponge inside the toe at the platform provides extra comfort and protection. The leatherboard shank is malleable and is less likely to snap when broken. It contains no tack or glue on the heel; this allows the shank to bend more easily at three-quarter level. The available widths are A, B, C, D, and E, and the color is European pink.

Suprima-S0132L has a streamlined shape, and is suited to a dancer with a narrow foot. The last itself is narrow and tapered, which also allows for a snug fit on the heel. The *Suprima* has the smallest platform and the most tapered box of all the Bloch pointe shoes. The available width fittings are B, C, D, and E, and it comes in European pink.

Suprima Strong-S0132S is for the dancer who requires more support in the shank than the standard *Suprima*. The shank is made with a five-iron board body and a red board centerpiece. All other features of the *Suprima* apply to the *Suprima Strong*.

Synergy ³⁄₄ Shank-S0101L is constructed on the Y-last, which has been developed for the more advanced dancer. The Y-last is wider around the metatarsals and their joints to accommodate bunions. The box is constructed with the paste that is designed to shape itself to the dancer's foot when moist, and it also has a very solid toe for support and longevity. The shank has a three-quarter red board body with leatherboard. This shoe is available in Y, YY, and YYY, and comes in European peach.

Synergy Full Shank-S0100L has the same qualities as the *Synergy ³⁄₄ Shank*, other than the shank. This full red board shank contains no tack or glue on the heel, which allows it to bend more easily at three-quarter level. The available width fittings are Y, YY, and YYY, and it comes in European peach.

In addition, Bloch has three other models, which are only available in Australia: *Concerta, Triomphe,* and *Sylphide.* The *Concerta* features an arched last, an inner rubber toe cushion, and a deep, sloped platform; it comes with a medium to short vamp. The *Triomphe* has a *Suprima* shape, a slightly wider platform, a suede toe cap, and an inner rubber toe cushion. The *Sylphide* has a rounder last, wider fittings, and greater depth in the toe box.

Salvio's Dancing Shoes PTY LTD.

34 St. Paul's Street	St. Paul's NSW 2031
Randwick NSW 2031	Australia
Australia	Telephone: (02) 9398-3502
Mail Orders: P.O. Box 126	Fax: (02) 9399-8647

Salvio's Dancing Shoes PTY Ltd. has been manufacturing dance shoes by hand since the early 1880s. The company makes all styles of shoes ranging from ballet to ballroom, Russian boots to can-can boots, acrobatic shoes to Scottish and Irish shoes.

In 1976 Salvio's changed their method of making pointe shoes by designing a molded box that will not break down or change shape with wear. The leather-reinforced shanks are handmade, which gives the makers the ability to change the area and amount of strength to suit individual requirements. Standard strengths are light, medium, and strong, but a light medium is also available.

The uppers are made of cotton-backed satin, which is extremely long-wearing. The vamp length, as well as the back height, may be adjusted upon request. The outsoles are chrome-split, as are the socks inside the shoes, and the size range is from 3 to 7.5, with the width fittings from A to BBB. Salvio's pointe shoes can be made in ballet pink, white, and black.

Austria

Schachtner

c/o Mary Price Boday	Telephone: (309) 672-2123;
The Dance Works	(800) 762-0789
719 W. Moss Avenue	E-mail: pavlova2@aol.com
Peoria, IL 61606	www.members.aol.com/
	dancearea/

Schachtner shoes, made in Vienna, Austria, can be purchased in the United States through The Dance Works in Peoria, Illinois, which has an active mail-order department. Mary Price Boday, who runs the shop, discovered Schachtner shoes when she was dancing with the Zurich Ballet. At the time, she was going through four pairs of pointe shoes a day. Then she discovered that she could wear one pair of Schachtner shoes for eight hours a day for seven days. When she returned to the United States and discovered that the shoes were not readily available, she began to import them.

Schachtner is currently run by Gerda Schachtner, whose father-in-law invented the shoes used by the dancers of the Vienna Opera Ballet. When her husband, who had taken over direction of the shoemaking process, died suddenly at the age of twenty-eight, Gerda Schachtner decided to carry on.

There are no "stock" Schachtner shoes; instead, shoes are made according to customer specifications from a broad set of choices. For instance, a dancer can order one width for the front of her shoes, and a separate width for the back as a standard option. Schachtner shoes are also available in a short, long, extra long, or regular vamp; a soft sole; and a regular, very soft, hard, or steel shank. Any of these shanks can be ordered three-quarters long. The shoes can also be ordered with a suede tip.

The width at the ball of the foot can be D (very narrow), E (narrow), A (middle), G (medium wide,) or F (very wide). The width at the heel of the shoe can be N (narrow), B (regular), or BB (wide). Any combination of ball and heel widths is possible. As a result, Schachtner offers more variety in width than can be found in most pointe shoe lines.

In length, the shoes go up by half-centimeters, while American shoes go up in half inches or full inches, resulting in a much bigger jump between sizes. The dancer has the option of a three-quarter size, in addition to conventional half and whole sizes. Pointe shoes can be made in canvas, leather, or satin, in red, white, black, or pink.

To mail order Schachtners, a dancer simply outlines her feet on a piece of paper and provides written information about the kind of shoe she currently wears, what qualities and features she is looking for in a pointe shoe, the wear patterns of current pointe shoes (what breaks first, what kind of arch, and so on), and how much support she wants.

Brazil

So' Dança

North America/Asia	Europe
320 N. Military Dr.	Telephone: 00 351 21 445 4123
Deerfield Beach, FL 33442	Fax: 00 351 21 445 4124
Telephone: (800) 269-5033	E-mail: sodanca.trinys@sapo.pt
Fax: (954) 428-2665	Latin America
E-mail: sodanca.com	Telephone: 55 18 561 9900
www.sodanca.com	Fax: 55 18 561 9904
	E-mail: sodanca@trinys.com.br

This Brazilian company has eight styles of pointe shoes, three of which are the special Cecilia Kerche *Roll On* line. All So' Dança shoes are created by a team of experienced makers, led by Pedro Krastchuk. Pedro's background as a dancer gives him unique insight into the needs of other dancers. It also enables him to be at the forefront of innovative design, such as the use of biodegradable glue to improve elasticity and lessen the effects of dampness on the shoe. All new designs are subject to thorough testing by professional dancers, students, and teachers before being released on the worldwide market.

The *Special Line* (EF 13) gives a choice of three-quarter or full shank; normal (N), reinforced (R), soft (S), or extra reinforced (X) shanks; widths in X, XX, or XXX; and colors pink, black, or white. The sizes range from adult 1 through 7.5.

The *Advance* (EF 25) has the same qualities as the *Special Line*. The widths are A, B, C, and D, and the adult sizes range from 1 through 9.

The *Equilibre* (EF 20) varies from the above two styles by having only A and B widths. The adult sizes range from 1 through 7.

The *Performance* (EF 26) also has the same four strength shanks, colors, and widths A, B, C, and D. In adult sizes 1 through 8, the widths are available in A, B, and C, and in adult sizes 1 through 7, D width is offered.

The *Danseuse* (EF 21) has only three shanks, as opposed to the four offered in the other styles (N, R, and S). It comes in two widths (A and B), and in adult sizes 1 through 7.

The *Cinderella* and the *Marie* are both designed as no-nonsense, economic shoes for beginners only. They have full shanks with a suede sole and come in Soft, Normal, or Reinforced shanks. Widths are A, B and C; sizing starts at 1 adult. The difference in the two shoes is in the box structure: *Marie* is wider through the metatarsals with a slightly flatter profile.

Named after a popular South American ballerina, the Cecilia Kerche line offers three styles. This pre-arched line needs almost no breaking-in, and is perfect for advanced and professional dancers. It is available in three box styles and a choice of shank strength and length. The design is based on the concept of rolling up and down from pointe effortlessly. All the Cecilia Kerche shoes include ribbon, elastic, leather toe tip. and shock-absorbing foam toe tip.

The *Grand Pas* (CK 01) has a half, three-quarter, or full shank available in (normal (N), reinforced (R), soft (S), and extra reinforced (X). It comes in four colors (pink, black, and white), and five widths (A, B, C, D, and E). Adult sizes 1 to 8.5 come in widths A, B, and C; adult sizes 2 to 8.5 also offer widths D and E. This shoe is designed for a dancer with a second toe longer than the big toe (referred to as a "Greek Foot.")

The *Nikiya* (CK 02) has the same characteristics as the *Grand Pas*. This shoe is designed for a dancer with toes that slant diagonally down (referred to as an "Egyptian Foot").

The *Pas d'Action* (CK 03) has the same characteristics as the other Cecilia Kerche shoes. It is designed for a square foot with squared-off toes.

Included in the catalog and brochure for all So' Dança shoes are descriptions of all their shoes, extensive information about pointe shoes in general, fitting instructions, and other interesting information.

Canada

Angelo Luzio

9185 Place Picasso	Customer Service:
Montréal, Quebec	andria@angeloluzio.com
Canada H1P 3J8	E-mail: info@angeloluzio.net
Telephone: (514) 322-8350	www.angeloluzio.com
Fax: (514) 324-1660	

In postwar Italy, Angelo Luzio, a shoemaker, traveled from his native village in the south far to the north in search of work. Many friends had moved to northern Europe for the same reason, but Angelo dreamed instead of America. After much debate with his wife, Celia, a seamstress, he booked passage on a boat to Canada.

Angelo was a fine shoemaker, but it took six months before he found work in his chosen trade. One day he met a man who ran a ballet shoe factory, and he was hired immediately. Angelo seized this opportunity, and had his wife hired as a seamstress. After eight years, they decided to return to Italy, but found that their country had changed greatly. They then realized that the New World was their only option, and returned to Montreal where they invested their savings and the rest of their lives making dance shoes of distinction.

Angelo Luzio now makes footwear for the Cirque du Soleil, Les Grands Ballets Canadiens, the Royal Academy of Dance, Le Théâtre Cheval, and other prominent companies. Today, Angelo's son and grandson run the company.

In the beginning, the company had different forms of pointe shoes: a round, tapered toe; a flat, wide toe; a round, wide toe; and a flat, tapered toe. In the 1990s, they found that dancers wanted a flatter outside, with more oval (not conical) shape inside.

From this arose the anatomical line, the *N* Series. A new last was designed along the natural anatomical lines of the foot. At present, Luzio is working on arch support, and researching cardboards, polymers, and fibers for the shank. Other studies are being carried out for safety, to find less slippery materials, without adding excess drag. In this line, one shoe is a little bigger than the other, since one foot is always larger. The shoes are designed to need less break-in time, the smooth interior means there are no creases against the foot, and the suede-brushed sole requires much less rosin. This *N* series has a flattened pleat area to help balance on *demi-pointe*. Its construction is no longer stitched, but glued.

The *O3Z* has a satin upper, leather sole, cotton lining, and a round tapered toe. It comes in black, beige, white, and pink.

The *O5Z* also has a satin upper, leather sole, cotton lining, and a suede toe. It also comes in the same four colors.

The *71Z* is the same as the two above, but it has a flat, wide toe.

The *83Z* has a round, wide toe, and comes in red as well as black, beige, white, and pink.

The *TS* has a flat, tapered toe and comes in black, beige, white, and pink.

Diamond Pointe

Principal Dance Supplies	Telephone: (416) 920-0639
26 Rowanwood, Avenue	Fax: (416) 920-6918
Toronto, ON	E-mail:
Canada M4W 1Y7	principalcanada@aol.com
	www.chanhongoh.com

Owned by Principal Dance Supplies, Diamond Pointe is a separate company that came onto the market in the fall of 2003. This new shoe was designed and developed with feedback from teachers, students, and professionals. Chan Hon Goh, the designer, wanted to come out with a combination of the Principal *D, F* and *J* shoes. She wanted a shoe like the one she wears (the *J*), but longer lasting. It is therefore made with a different type of glue to give it a stronger box. The platform is slightly wider than the *D*, to give support and help with balance in turns, and it has a graduating three-quarter shank. The color is American rosy-pink, while the *D, F and J* shoes are European peachy-pink.

Principal Dance Supplies

26 Rowanwood Avenue	Fax: (416) 920-6918
Toronto, Ontario	E-mail:
Canada M4W 1Y7	principalcanada@aol.com
Telephone: (416) 920-0639	www.chanhongoh.com

This new company is run by a principal dancer with The National Ballet of Canada, Chan Hon Goh, and her husband, a former professional dancer and now a ballet teacher in a college. He started designing dance shoes for them. They tried out several designs and passed them around the dance community. They were surprised when they got calls from distant places asking where they could buy the shoes. Now the shoes are available across Canada and some places in the United States.

The Principal pointe shoes style *J* (*Jewel*) was designed with the importance of a performance shoe in mind. It is lightweight with a squared, flat ninety-degree formed toe box to allow for easy balance and secure contact with the stage. The *J* shoe has a slight wing block, a graduating three-quarter shank, and a grip canvas lining on the heel. Although it is considered a professional shoe, it is also recommended for beginners because it is so lightweight, which helps them to get up onto pointe with ease.

The characteristics of the *D* style are a strong supportive wing block and a high, slightly V-shaped vamp. It has a medium-hard shank that includes an inner leather piece which is placed proportionally to the size of the shoe to offer added support in the metatarsal. The toe box is tapered, its drawstrings are elastic, and it has a grip canvas lined heel. It comes in three standard widths: X, XX, and XXX, with A (more narrow than an X) and XXXX widths also available.

The *F* style features a deep, wide box for the abundant foot. The shank is medium weight and has an inner leather piece that supports the foot to the three-quarter mark. The shoe has an average vamp height, and comes in three standard widths: X, XX, and XXX. Extra narrow or wide sizes can be specially ordered.

Custom-made shoes may also be ordered. Shoes can be made for people who have feet of different sizes, adjustments made for bunions, and even for feet with an outward sickle. The company makes shoes fit within the last, rather than by filling the shoe with sponges and liners.

France

Repetto

22, rue de la Paix	Repetto USA
Paris, France	65 Broadway, Suite 1802
Telephone: 33 1 44 71 83 27	New York, NY 10009
E-mail: mlebreton@repetto.fr	Telephone: (800) 858-5855
	Fax: (212) 635-0156
	E-mail: usa@novalys.com
	www.gambadance.com

Repetto, the largest manufacturer of pointe shoes in France, was founded in 1947 by Rose Repetto at the request of her son, dancer and choreographer Roland Pettit. Since then, the company has supplied shoes and dance apparel to the world of dance, from professionals in the largest French and foreign companies to local dancing schools. Interestingly, Rose created, in 1948, the shoes that Brigitte Bardot wore in the movie "And God Created Woman." In addition, the designers Givenchy, Balenciaga, Thimister, and Chanel regularly consult Repetto for their basic shoes and custom designs.

In 1990 the company diversified to include street footwear, fitness wear, and swimwear, and in 1992 bought Gamba, a major manufacturer of ballet, pointe, and theatrical shoes.

La Bayadère (207) is a new shoe with a fiber-carbon shank that is available in medium and hard strengths. This shoe features a tapered, flexible box that is shaped with a glue composed of natural ingredients. It absorbs the humidity of the foot and molds the box to the shape of the foot. Its flexibility does not block the foot at the toes, yet still gives the toes necessary support. The outside of the box is square, and has a platform that is very stable. The vamp is medium short, and has a low profile. It comes in narrow, medium, and large widths, and French sizes 6-26 or European 32-42 street shoe size. The color is pink.

Swanhilda combines traditional styling with an elastic top line instead of a drawstring. This shoe, which has a minimum break-in period, has a low profile, a broad platform, and long side wings. It is available in narrow, medium, and large widths, and in a choice of soft, medium, or hard shanks. It comes in pink (538) or salmon (531); white (050), and black (410) can be specially ordered.

Sansha Inc.

1717 Broadway, 2nd Floor	Melbourne: australia@sansha.com
New York, NY 10019	Madrid: madrid@sansha.com
Telephone: (212) 246-6212	Moscow: moscow@sansha.com
Fax: (212) 956-7052	Budapest: budapest@sansha.com
E-mail: marie@sansha.com	Barcelona: barcelona@sansha.com
www.sansha.com	Le Havre: lehavre@sansha.com
Paris: paris @sansha.com	

Sansha dancing shoes are designed by Frenchman Franc Raoul Duvall, originally from a French merchant family in Normandy. Mr. Duvall was nicknamed "Sansha" by his friends when he lived in Russia.

Following the success of his soft ballet shoes, he turned his attention to pointe shoes. He came up with a revolutionary idea for a replaceable shank that allows the shoes to be worn even after the original shank is broken, thus offering a longer-lasting shoe to professionals and students alike. He also developed the first "silent" pointe shoe in an effort to bring back the lightness and grace of the first pointe shoes as they appeared a century ago.

The shoes come in four widths, one vamp height, and canvas or satin uppers. Customized orders are possible from the New Jersey factory.

Sansha has five student pointe shoes and four professional styles. Beginning with the student shoes, the *Soprano* (101) has a wing block, a medium platform, and a narrow box for a long, fine look. The upper can be ordered in canvas (101C) or satin (101S), and the shoe comes in peach pink or UK pink.

The *Recital* (202), like the *Soprano*, comes in canvas or satin uppers and in addition to peach and pink, it comes in black canvas. All Sansha pointe shoes come in sizes 3-13, except for this model which goes up to a 16. These features are to accommodate the few men (Trockaderos and others who wear them to strengthen their feet in class) with the courage to wear pointe shoes. This model has a medium-strength box and a wide platform, which makes it ideal for wearing toe pads. This shoe is suitable for a "Grecian" or square foot.

The *Lyrica* (404) has a platform for medium feet, the same last as a *Premiere* (below), a V vamp, higher sides, and a stronger shank. It comes in peach pink and UK pink.

The *Partenaire* or *Partner* (300) has a reinforced, hard shank, a wide platform for medium and wide feet, and is made on the same last as the *Recital*. It comes in pink and peach pink. The fifth student shoe, the *DP 801*, is a *demi-pointe* shoe with a soft box and sole. It comes in peach pink and UK pink.

The professional models are the *Première* (808), the *Legende* (909), the *Ovation* (606), and the *Futura* (111), which as its name suggests, is quite unusual.

The *Première* has an extra-flat anatomical platform, a streamlined box, a medium-strength shank, and a wing block for more lateral support and comfort. It comes in peach pink and UK pink. The *Legende* has a pear-shaped three-quarter external sole for experienced dancers only. A medium hard (MH) or medium soft (MS) shank is available. It comes in peach pink only.

Another professional shoe is the *Ovation*. Its leather sole is hand-stitched, it has an easy *demi-pointe* passage and is also available with a ¾ shank (603). The colors are peach pink and UK pink.

The fourth professional Sansha shoe is the *Futura*. This unusual shoe has a lace-up vamp, for extra front support and a snug fit, and comes with elastics attached. It comes in black, red, dark blue, and peach pink.

Germany

Eva

Monika Fritsche	E-mail: 320036218816-
(address is unavailable)	0001@t-online.de

Eva shoes, manufactured in Germany by Karl Heinz Martin, are no longer available in the United States. The only distributor went out of business in 2002, and now the only way to order them is directly, by e-mail, from the factory in Germany.

Eva shoes are lightweight yet durable, aiming to combine optimal support and flexibility. A flat platform gives excellent balance and is designed to make the dancer feel lifted from the floor when on pointe. The shoe is available in various vamp lengths and four different-strength insoles, including three-quarter and half shanks. A unique toe box and wing configuration are designed to ensure stability and to allow the shoe to mold quickly to the foot. A hygienically safe paste formula was introduced to reduce the incidence of foot problems. Special orders are available for both advanced students and professionals.

Italy

E. Porselli Ltd.

Ufficio Comm: 20159 Milano	Telephone: 39 02 608 1439
Viale Stolvio 41, Italy	Fax: 39 02 608 0646

Porselli pointe shoes are manufactured in Italy, where they dominate the market. Eugenio Porselli founded the company in Milan in 1919, and the company is still owned and directed by the Porselli family.

The Porselli shop, run by Gine Chant-Grostern in London, no longer carries Porselli shoes, but they are still distributed in the United Kingdom by Alan Schofield. There is no distribution through retail shops in the United States

The shoes available are Style *A* (narrow), Style *B* (for beginners), Style *D* (narrow, with a suede toe), Style *E* (very wide), Style *F* (lightweight, with a flexi-back), Style *Gala* (a strong shoe with a double back/shank and a wing), Style *L* (a *demi-pointe* shoe), and Style *W* (wide).

Japan

Chacott Ltd.

E-mail: chacott@estate.ocn.ne.jp	Also distributed through
www.chacott-jp.com	Evolution Pirouette Inc.
Distributed through	6340 Green Valley Circle #318
Freed of London	Culver City, CA 90230
21-01 43rd Ave	Telephone: (310) 701-3730
London Island City	Fax: (310) 642-0529
New York, NY 11101	E-mail: Epdancing@aol.com
Telephone: 866-MY-FREED	
Fax: (718) 729-8086	

In 1951, a Japanese ballerina asked Makoto Tsuchiya, a shoe salesman, to create a pair of pointe shoes for her. At that time, not long after World War II, there was a shortage of good pointe shoes in Japan. After analyzing the ballerina's European shoes, Tsuchiya decided to start his own pointe shoe company. Now the largest dancewear manufacturer in the world, Chacott has introduced machinery that accomplishes several major pointe shoe construction steps traditionally performed by hand.

In October 2002, Chacott Iberica named Evolution Pirouette Inc. its distributor for the United States. Chacott Japan owns Chacott Iberica, Freed of London, and Gallardo Dance S. L. (The latter is a famous brand of flamenco shoes and garments.) Evolution Pirouette is the result of more than thirty years of experience in the dancing business.

The Chacott *Veronese II* pointe shoe is distributed in the United States through Freed of London. It is a very light and elegant shoe, suitable for beginner through professional level dancers. It has a low profile for a snug fit, especially for dancers with thin feet. The sizes are in centimeters (including half sizes), and the widths range from C through E. It has a split outer sole, but the insole is full. There is a choice of medium or hard insoles, and the color is European pink satin.

Chacott Iberica manufactures pointe shoes in Spain under the brand names of *Coppelia II, Sylphide,* and *Elvira.*

The Coppelia II was designed for beginning through advanced students. This shoe has a plastic reinforced tip, making it quite durable, and is designed on a regular mold. It has a standard vamp, wings, a hard box (made with water glue), and a regular platform, and it comes in U.S. sizes 3.5 through 9.5. The widths offered are B, C, D, E, and EE. The shank is standard, and the color is rose pink (salmon). Ribbons are included.

The *Sylphide* is designed on a narrow mold, has a narrow platform, a soft box (made with water glue), a standard vamp, and comes in U.S. sizes 3.5 through 9.5. Its soft block or box enables beginner dancers to strengthen their feet. It comes in widths C, D, and E, and the color is light pink. Ribbons are included

The *Elvira* is a pointe shoe for advanced students, or for dancers with wide feet. It is made on a wide mold, has a wider platform, and comes in widths C, D, and E. The box (made with natural glues) is hard, with a shock absorber; the vamp is standard, and wings are optional. The *Elvira* comes in U.S. sizes 3.5 through 9.5, and the color is European pink. Ribbons are included.

Evolution Pirouette has a detailed fitting service on the Internet. They say that this fitting system works not only for Chacott but for all brands. It is called EPFIT-InterFax Fitting Table, and is meant to be ninety-nine percent accurate. It is designed to save time and to help the dancer double-check the pointe shoes she is already wearing. The answers to the dancer's requests are processed and returned within twenty-four hours. Even though the system is extremely accurate, Evolution Pirouette says that it does not substitute for the fitting process done personally by a professional fitter.

Sylvia Co. Ltd.

2-23-10 Kouenji-Minami Suginami-Ku Tokyo, Japan 166-0003 Telephone: 03-3315-3100	Fax: 03-3314-3769 E-mail: info@sylvia.co.jp www.sylvia.co.jp

Shinobu Uchino, a member of the staff, says that Sylvia pointe shoes are designed for the dancer who does not have a strong foot. All of the shoes make it easy to get over on pointe. They have also tried to make the shoes lightweight to give the feeling of dancing in bare feet.

The newest style is the *Florina* (SSY/17020), with a shank made of nylon rosin, which makes it very durable. For dancers with a broad, square forefoot, its nearly square box provides stability on pointe. It is suited for intermediate, advanced, and professional dancers, and comes in European pink.

The *Satin Toe* (SSY/11010) is a basic pointe shoe for beginners to advanced students. It comes in pink satin.

The *Cherry Toe* (SSY/13010), designed to mold to the foot easily, but to remain durable, has a medium strength leatherboard shank. It comes in pink satin.

The *Session Toe* (SSY/15020) is a more stable shoe with a wider toe area. This European pink shoe is made of a special material that creates a beautiful line.

The other styles are the *Neo Cherry Toe* (SSY/14010), the *Leather Top Toe* (SSY/12010), and the *Session Toe Magic* (SSY/15020T).

The medium shank is stock, but soft or hard can be ordered at extra cost. Narrow width (S) and wide (E) must also be ordered, but at no extra charge. There is an extra charge for EE and EEE, however.

The website is in Japanese, but requests can be made in English using the e-mail address or fax number. When ordering, list the items desired and the address to which they are to be sent. You will receive an invoice by e-mail or fax to confirm your order. Reconfirm the details of the invoice, sign it, and return by fax. If you would like to pay with a credit card, fill in the required information; you may pay by credit card or wire transfer in Japanese yen. You may choose your preferred method of shipment. (The cost is added to the total cost of the order.)

Mexico

Miguelito

Canela No. 124	Wholesale And Retail Sales
Col. Granjas Mexico	7315 San Pedro
Mexico D. F., 08400	San Antonio, TX 78216
Telephone: 52 650-3755	Telephone: (210) 349-2573
E-mail:	Fax: (210) 349-9610
miguelito@miguelito.com.mx	E-mail: migueldancing@cs.com
www.miguelito.com.mx	

Calzado Teatral Miguelito was founded in 1940 by De Luz Serrano and Miguel Alvarez in Mexico City. Initially they produced only traditional ballet shoes, but over the years Miguelito's went on to develop another line of footwear to satisfy an increasing demand for new products in different areas such as Mexican folklore, flamenco, and other cultural traditions in the dance community of Mexico City. Now they have added shoes for jazz, highland dance, modern dance, ballroom dance, and tap, all of which are approved by the Academy of Dance in London.

In 1986, owing to demand, a store was opened in San Antonio, Texas. The sales in the first month amounted to $659.57. Now they have more than thirty-five distributors in the United States, Canada, and Puerto Rico, and manufacture more than four hundred products a day with the same quality and service as in 1940.

Miguelito's newest pointe shoe, the *Criselle,* is for dancers with a square forefoot and medium-length toes. The strong, durable box is angled for full stability on pointe. It also features a three-quarter red board shank, a tapered box, an absence of pleats, and a moderate crown. They can be ordered on-line.

Russia

Russian Pointe

P.O. Box 2596	Fax: (734) 996-2044
Ann Arbor, MI 48106-2596	E-mail: info@russianpointe.com
Telephone: (734) 996-2040	www.russianpointe.com

In May 1998, Aleksandra Efimova came in contact with the supplier factory in Moscow, and Russian Pointe Inc. was formed. As president, she is the exclusive representative of the company in the United States and Canada.

The company highly recommends that dancers be fitted professionally for pointe shoes by visiting one of their official Russian Pointe dealers. If that is not possible, the shoes may be custom-ordered. They suggest these five simple steps: 1. choose from six handcrafted models; 2. specify shoe size; 3. specify width; 4. choose your vamp; 5. choose your shank.

There are four widths from which to choose: W1 (narrow); W2 (Medium); W3 (wide); and W4 (extra wide). Vamps come in V1 (short), V2 (medium), V3 (long). V1 and V3 are special order at no extra charge.

Shanks come in two categories: standard and flexible. The standard shank, designed in the tradition of the Russian technique of "springing" onto pointe, is offered in HL (Super Hard), H (Hard), MH (Medium Hard), M (Medium), MS (Medium Soft), and S (Soft). The flexible shank, meanwhile, accommodates the technique of "rolling-through" *demi-pointe*, and comes in HLF (Super Hard Flexible), HF (Hard Flexible), MHF (Medium Hard Flexible), and MF (Medium Flexible). Shoes may be specially ordered in red, black, and white. Linen may be chosen as a lining, but changes in color or materials are billed ten percent extra, with no exchanges. The average time for back-ordered shoes is two to six weeks. Based on the traditions of the Russian classical ballet, and working closely with leading dancers around the world, Russian Pointe cobblers offer six models of pointe shoes to insure a proper fit for every dancer's foot.

The *Anima* is a narrow toe platform shoe with a high crown, ideal for dancers with naturally tapered feet.

The *Clarino* is especially designed for dancers with slim feet. This model features a narrow toe platform and low crown.

The *Brio* is a medium toe platform shoe with a high crown and generous box.

The *Dolce* is a wide toe platform shoe.

The *Entrada* is ideal for dancers with high arches. Its pre-arched shape and sole are designed for longevity, while minimizing break-in time.

The *Polette* is different from all the other shoes in the line in terms of lower heel height and elastic drawstrings. (The others have a high heel and no drawstrings.) It features a broad, stable toe platform with extra room for comfort pads inside. The new aerodynamic design of the low heel ensures a smooth fit without taking extra pleats. This shoe is available in all sizes and in five widths. The vamp is medium and it comes with a three-quarter shank.

Vozrozhdenie

Victoria Antonova
Import/Export Department
Vozrohdenie Ltd.
Chekova st. 2
Rus-191104 St. Petersburg
Russia
Telephone: 7-812-325-8487
Fax: 7-812-325-8486
E-mail: victoria@theater-
    decor.com
www.theater-decor.com
	Exclusive representation in the
	    U.S.:
	Theatre Link, Inc.
	4957 Shadow Rock Circle
	Carmel, IN 46033
	Telephone: (317) 571-0949
	Fax: (317) 580-1207
	E-mail: ealiev@indy.rr.com
	
	ZQI, Inc.
	1775 Mentor Avenue, Suite 402
	Cincinnati, OH 45212
	Telephone: (513) 396-6006
	Fax: (513) 396-6067
	E-mail: jzurick@zqi-inc.com
	http:://www.zqi-inc.com

Vozrozhdenie appeared on the Russian market in 1992, and since then has been working with most theaters in Russia. Among its main customers are the Maryinsky and Mikhailovsky Theaters (the largest in Saint Petersburg) and the Bolshoi Theater in Moscow. Vozrozhdenie has also been working with theaters in the United States, Japan, Italy, and Germany.

The company produces one type of pointe shoe that differs in terms of the type of last or boot tree. The three styles are *Jisell, Odetta,* and *Aurora,* all handmade. The *Jisell,* which is not very closed, is recommended for dancers with a normal instep; the *Odetta,* which is very closed, is for dancers with a big instep; the *Aurora,* with its flat toe part, is not very closed, and is for dancers with a normal instep.

There are two different types of insoles available in all three models (medium and high rigidity). Two more types of insoles can be produced by special request (soft for the beginners and super hard for a very big instep). The color options are white, flesh, or pink, but Vozrozhdenie is also willing to dye the shoes. The vamp can be of any form. The shoes come in sizes 5 to 9 and widths 1 to 4.

South Africa

Teplov Ballet Shoes

P.O. Box 3037	Telephone: 27 21 851 7313
Somerset West 7129	Fax: 27 21 851 5263
Republic of South Africa	

Teplov, located forty kilometers outside Cape Town, has been manufacturing all types of ballet shoes since 1980. Diana Teplitsky-Kessler, owner of the company, and formerly a principal dancer with Arts Cape in Cape Town and at the National Theatre in Munich, started the pointes line in 1993. Teplov is the only manufacturer of pointe shoes in South Africa.

The shoes come in satin and canvas, with sizes ranging from 1 through 8, including half sizes. The widths available are C (extra narrow), D (narrow), E (average), F (wide), and G (extra wide). Vamps come in low, medium, high, and extra high. The back, or shank, can be a soft back, medium back, or hard back.

NOTES

1. Rogers Corporation Poron® has the American Podiatric Medical Association Seal of Acceptance.

2. "Maker requests are not allowed" means that with the Freed stock shoe, which has been recently called the Classic Deep Vamp, dancers may not request specific makers. In other words, many different cobblers actually handmake these shoes and each one varies slightly because of the specific style of cobbling. It is the same as many cooks making the same cookie recipe—it is the same recipe, but the cookies will taste a little different from cook to cook. Dancers who want the *Wing Block* shoe have to take whatever maker they get; they cannot ask for a shoe by a specific maker.

Pointe Shoe Characteristics

This list has been compiled in collaboration with the manufacturers. The category headings are the result of the authors' numerous conversations with dancers and dance teachers, who were unsure of how to find the right shoe for their particular idiosyncrasies, sizes, or needs. In addition, because of recent technological developments, it was felt that some of the qualities of the shoes needed explanation.

Please note that, since some brands are primarily custom-made, they fit into many categories.

The Bloch models *Sylphide, Triomphe,* and *Concerta* are made and distributed in Australia only.

Narrow Shoes (A or N Widths)

Angelo Luzio *N31z* – A
Angelo Luzio *N51z* – A
Angelo Luzio *N83z* – A
Angelo Luzio *S66m* – A
Bloch *SO111 BPS* – no X available by special order
Bloch *Aspiration* – A
Bloch *SO104 Alpha* – no X available by special order
Bloch *SO130 Sonata* – A
Bloch *SO133 Sylphide* – A
Bloch *SO162 Signature Performance* – A available by special order
Bloch *SO168 Signature Rehearsal* – A available by special order
Bloch *Synergy* Series – no Y available by special order
Capezio *Nicolini (N 156)* – moderate strength, feathered box, #2 leatherboard shank, dual nail construction
Capezio *Pavlowa*
Dance Workshop Ltd. – all custom-made shoes
Diamond Pointe – can be ordered in A or AA

Fuzi – full shank

Fuzi – ¾ shank

Fuzi – split sole

Gamba *G97*

Gamba *G93*

Gamba *GPP* – NN and N; this shoe is special order only.

Gaynor Minden – narrow with the #2 box; the toe is narrow and tapered and is available in most lengths.

Grishko *2007* – X

Grishko *Elite* – no X

Grishko *Ulanova II* – X

Grishko *Vaganova* – X

Mark Suffolk *Solo* – nine widths from N to extra W; shoes may be made as narrow as a customer needs. The toe box is fitted until it is correct by using a smaller length N (which is narrower without the heel of the shoe on). Then the width is made, and the length is extended by the required amount. Mark Suffolk does not do this often, but the process works well for the very narrow foot.

Petrushka

Prima Soft *Royale* – fits N, M, and W; also good for shallow feet; V-vamp.

Principal D – can be ordered in A or AA. Of all the Principal shoes, this is the narrowest.

Principal F – can be ordered in A

Principal J – can by ordered in A

Russian Pointe *Anima* – narrow toe platform

(All Russian Pointe models are available in narrow width [W1], from the metatarsal to the heel.)

Russian Pointe *Clarino* – narrow toe platform

Sansha *Legend* (909) – ⅔ hard shank, reinforced poron heel, whisper toe

Sansha *Lyrica* (404)

Sansha *Partenaire* (303)

Sansha *Premiere* (808)

Sansha *Recital* (202)

Schachtner – no stock shoes are made, but shoes come in narrow (D) and (E) at the ball of the foot. There are different widths also for the heel.

So' Dança *Advance*

So' Dança, Cecilia Kerche *Grand Pas*
So' Dança, Cecilia Kerche *Nikiya*
So' Dança, Cecilia Kerche *Pas d'Action*
So' Dança *Danseuse*
So' Dança *Equilibre*
So' Dança *Performance*
So' Dança – *Advance, Performance, Equilibre, Special Line, Danseuse*
Teplov – comes in extra narrow (C) and narrow (D)

Shallow Shoes

Angelo Luzio *N03z*
Angelo Luzio *N31z*
Angelo Luzio *S66m*
Bloch *SO131 Serenade*
Bloch *SO132 Suprima*
Capezio *Aerial*
Capezio *Nicolini (N 156)*
Chacott *Veronese II*
Chacott *Veronese II* – C through E; medium and hard insoles; very
   light, low profile
Gaynor Minden – the #2 and #3 boxes are low-profile boxes,
   available in most lengths and widths
Grishko *Elite*
Mark Suffolk – can be made in low profile by request
Prima Soft *Royale* (709) – fits narrow, medium, or wide feet well;
   one graduated shank strength; extra wide is available.
Russian Pointe *Clarino* – low crown box
Russian Pointe *Entrada* – low crown box
Russian Pointe *Polette* – low crown box

Extra Wide Shoes

Angelo Luzio *N31z* – E
Angelo Luzio *N51z* – E
Angelo Luzio *N71z* – E
Angelo Luzio *N83z* – E
Angelo Luzio *NO3z* – EE
Angelo Luzio *NO5z* – EE
Angelo Luzio *S66m*
Bloch *SO130 Sonata* – E

Bloch *SO168 Signature Rehearsal* – E
Bloch *SO104 Alpha* – XXX
Bloch *SO105 Aspiration* – E
Bloch *SO111 BPS* – XXX
Bloch *SO131 Serenade* – E
Bloch *SO132 Suprima* – E
Bloch *SO133 Sylphide* – E
Bloch *SO139 Triomphe* – E
Bloch *SO141 Serenade* V – E
Bloch *SO162 Signature Performance* – E
Bloch *Synergy* Series – YYY (YYYY available by special order)
Chacott *Coppelia II* – EE
Chacott *Elvira* – E
Chacott *Sylphide* – E
Chacott *Veronese II* – E
Fuzi – A through E
Gaynor Minden – any shoe with the #4 box; available in most
    lengths
Grishko 2007 – stock XXXX and XXXXX. The latter is equivalent
    to an F width.
Grishko *Elite* – stock XXXX and XXXXX.
Grishko *Ulanova* – stock XXXX and XXXXX
Leo's *Inspiration*
Leo's ³/₄ *Inspiration* – E
Mark Suffolk – up to XXXX
Prima Soft *Prima Russe* – XXXX
Prima Soft *Royale (#709)* – can come in XXXX and even XXXXX
Principal D – XXXX and XXXXX can be ordered
Principal F – XXXX and XXXXX, can be ordered in A
Principal J – XXXX and XXXXX, can be ordered in A
Russian Pointe *Dolce* – wide toe platform
Russian Pointe *Polette* – wide toe platform; the only model avail-
    able in narrow through X-extra wide
Sansha *Lyrica (404)*
Sansha *Ovation (603)*
Sansha *Partenaire (303)*
Sansha *Premiere (808)*
Sansha *Recital (202)*
So' Dança – E width is special order in sizes 2 through 8.5 only
Teplov – comes in G (extra wide)

Student Shoes (longer-lasting)

Angelo Luzio *N05z*

Bloch *Aspiration*

Bloch *SO105 Aspiration*

Bloch *SO130 Sonata*

Bloch *SO131 Serenade*

Bloch *SO132 Suprima*

Bloch *SO133 Sylphide*

Bloch *SO141 Serenade V*

Capezio *Pavlowa* – reinforced, feathered box, #3 leatherboard shank, longer vamp, lower heel

Capezio *Plié I* – moderate shank, moderate toe box

Capezio *Plié II* – moderate shank, broad toe box

Chacott *Coppelia II* – made in Spain; for beginner through advanced students; durable plastic reinforced tip; medium and hard insoles

Chacott *Elvira*

Diamond Pointe

Freed *Studio I* – strong platform, wing block; also suitable for advanced students and professionals

Freed *Studio II* – wider and flatter than *Studio I*; strong platform; medium or hard insole; also suitable for advanced students and professionals

Gaynor Minden – all shoes have unbreakable elastomeric shanks and boxes, and generous platforms with a wide choice of stiffnesses

Grishko *2007* – the favorite student shoe of Grishko has a super soft shank; also used by advanced and professional dancers, and available in a medium and hard shank as stock

Grishko – all Grishko shoes are made to be long-lasting

Leo's *Pas de Deux Pointe 1* – the square, suede toe helps beginners stay on pointe

Mark Suffolk *Solo* – a strong insole shoe, popular with students, that lasts longer

Prima Soft *Gala* – requires no break-in. The natural shank is very light but supportive, owing to the graduated shank support.

Principal *D*

Principal *F*

Russian Pointe *Polette* – the only Russian Pointe shoes with a drawstring. All Russian Pointe models available in Super Soft, Soft, Medium Soft, and Medium shanks.

Sansha *Lyrica*
Sansha *Partenaire* or *Partner*
Sansha *Recital*
Sansha *Soprano*
So' Dança – *Advance, Performance, Equilibre, Special Line, Danseuse, Cinderella, Marie*

Lightweight, Professional Shoes (break in easily)

Angelo Luzio *N51z*
Bloch *Signature Rehearsal* – regular and hard shanks
Bloch *SO100 Synergy*
Bloch *SO101 Synergy* – ¾ 2.5mm shank
Bloch *SO102 Synergy* – ¾ 1.8mm shank
Bloch *SO104 Alpha*
Bloch *SO111 BPS*
Bloch *SO162 Signature Performance*
Bloch *SO168 Signature Rehearsal*
Chacott *Veronese II* – medium or hard shank; made in Japan
Freed *Classic Deep Vamp (SBTDV)*
Freed *Classic Wing Block (SBTWB)*
Gaynor Minden *FeatherFlex* – has an extremely pliable shank and box, available in all lengths, widths, and toe box styles. Note: Gaynor Minden shoes do not break in; they start soft and stay soft.
Gaynor Minden *Pianissimo* – even more pliable than *FeatherFlex*, comparable to an almost dead-paste (very lightweight and comfortable) shoe; available in all lengths, widths, and toe box styles.
Grishko *2007* – Grishko's most lightweight shoe; ¾ shank; available in supersoft, medium, or hard shank as stock
Grishko *Fouetté* – medium-height vamp; this facilitates springing onto pointe rather than rolling, which makes it good for fouettés; made on the same last as the *Ulanova I*.
Grishko *Maya* – For even-length toes which are slightly tapered; ¾ shank is available in soft, medium, or hard
Grishko *Ulanova I* – medium-height vamp; good for long toes; facilitates rolling through *demi-pointe*
Leo's *Split-Sole Pointe* – for an easier break-in
Mark Suffolk *Solo Light* – designed for young dancers, but can also be worn by more experienced dancers as a performance-ready shoe; low profile. The *Pro Flex* insole is very popular with professionals.

Principal *J* – squared, flat toe box; slight wing block; graduating
¾ shank; can be custom-made to dancer's specifications

Russian Pointe models – all available in super soft, soft, and medium soft

Sansha *Legende* (*909*) – ⅔ hard shank, whisper toe, cushioned poron
heel

Sansha *Ovation* (*603* and *606*) – *603* has a ¾ shank.

So' Dança, Cecilia Kerche – *Nikiya, Pas d'Action, Grand Pas*

Light Shanks

Angelo Luzio *N03z*

Angelo Luzio *N05z*

Angelo Luzio *N31z*

Angelo Luzio *N51z*

Angelo Luzio *N71z*

Angelo Luzio *N83z*

Angelo Luzio *S66m*

Bloch *SO102 Synergy* – ¾ 1.8mm shank

Bloch *SO104 Alpha*

Bloch *SO105 Aspiration*

Bloch *SO111 BPS*

Bloch *SO162 Signature Performance*

Capezio *Infinita* – #1

Capezio *Tendu II* – #1

Chacott *Veronese II*

Freed *Classic Deep Vamp*

Gaynor Minden *FeatherFlex* – available in all lengths, widths, and
toe box styles

Gaynor Mindon *Pianissimo* – superpliable

Grishko *2007* – supersoft shank, as well as soft, medium, and hard

Grishko *Elite, Maya, Ulanova I,* and *Ulanova II* – soft, medium,
or hard

Mark Suffolk *Solo Light* – with a lighter box; also standard with standard box

Miguelito *Criselle* – flexible, break-in support; good for roll-through;
durable and tapered box; for dancers with a square forefoot

Prima Soft *Prima Russe* – flex graduated shank; also regular graduated shank; shorter box

Repetto *Swanhilda* – comes in soft, medium, or hard

Russian Pointe (Flexible) – medium flexible, medium hard flexible (MHF)

Russian Pointe *Polette* – ¾ shank in super soft, soft, and medium soft

Russian Pointe (Soft) – super soft (SS), soft (S), medium soft (MS)

Sansha *Soprano* (*101*)

Schachtner – these special order shoes only come in very soft, regular, hard, or steel; can also be in ¾

So' Dança, Cecilia Kerche – *Nikiya, Pas d'Action, Grand Pas* – soft and reinforced by special order only; medium is stock; ¾ shank and pre-arched also

So' Dança – *Advance, Performance, Equilibre, Special Line, Danseuse* – soft and reinforced by special order only; medium is stock; ¾ shank and pre-arched also

Teplov – soft

Medium Shanks

Angelo Luzio – all models come in light, medium and hard shanks

Bloch *SO100 Synergy*

Bloch *SO101 Synergy* ¾ 2.5mm shank

Bloch *SO111 BPS*

Bloch *SO130 Sonata*

Bloch *SO131 Serenade*

Bloch *SO132 Suprima*

Bloch *SO133 Sylphide*

Bloch *SO141 Serenade V*

Bloch *SO168 Signature Rehearsal*

Capezio *Aerial*

Capezio *Contempora*

Capezio *Infinita*

Capezio *Nicolini*

Capezio *Tendu I* and *Tendu II*

Chacott *Coppelia II* – medium and hard

Chacott *Elvira*

Chacott *Sylphide*

Chacott *Veronese II* – medium and hard

Gaynor Minden *SuppleFlex* – is available in all lengths, widths, and toe box styles

Grishko *2007*

Grishko *Fouetté*

Grishko *Maya*

Grishko *Ulanova I* and *II*

Leo's *Split-Sole Pointe* – medium red board full-strength shank

Leo's *Inspiration*

Mark Suffolk *Solo* – standard insole with standard box; also hard with standard box

Prima Soft *Gala (701)* – also hard, graduated shank (good for "banana feet"); elastic drawstring

Prima Soft *Prima Russe* – regular graduated shank; also in Flex graduated; shorter box

Prima Soft *Royale* – fits narrow, medium, and wide feet; good for shallow feet; V vamp

Prima Soft *Silhouette* – this is a substantial shank, reinforced under the metatarsal; good for the long-toed, flexible-arched dancer; one graduated shank

Principal *D* – medium/hard shank

Principal *F* – deep, wide box with an inner leather piece that comes to the ¾ mark on the foot; for the abundant foot

Repetto *La Bayadère* – medium and hard

Repetto *Swanhilda* – soft, medium, or hard

Russian Pointe – all models available in medium (M) and medium flexible (MF) shanks

Sansha *Futura (S111)* – lace-up front

Sansha *Premiere (808)* – (professional shoe) extra-flat platform; wing block

Sansha *Recital (202)* – whisper toe, wide platform

Schachtner – these special order shoes come in very soft, regular, hard, and steel; can also be in ¾

So' Dança, Cecilia Kerche – stock in all three styles; soft, reinforced, and extra reinforced are special orders

So' Dança, Cecilia Kerche – soft, medium, reinforced

So' Dança – stock shoe is normal; soft or reinforced is special order

Sylvia *Cherry Toe*

Sylvia *Florina*

Teplov

Medium Hard And Medium Soft Shanks

Chacott *Coppelia II* – lighter than most hard shanks

Chacott *Veronese II* – much lighter than most hard shanks

Freed *Classic Wing Block* – stronger insole than the Freed *Classic Deep Vamp*

Gaynor Minden *ExtraFlex* – available in all lengths, widths, and toe box styles

Principal *D* – medium hard shank

Principal *F* – medium

Russian Pointe – all models available in medium hard (MH), medium hard flexible (MHF), and medium soft (MS) shanks

Sansha *Legende* – (professional shoe) pear-shaped ¾ external sole

Sansha *Ovation (603)* – ¾ shank professional shoe

Sansha *Ovation (606)* – full shank, hand-stitched professional shoe

Hard Shanks

Angelo Luzio – all models come in light, medium, and hard shanks

Bloch *SO131S Serenade* – strong

Bloch *SO132S Suprima* – strong

Bloch *SO168S Signature Rehearsal* – strong

All other Bloch models are available in strong and double strong by special order.

Capezio *Glissé (102/102A)* – broad toe

Capezio *Pavlowa* – #3 leatherboard

Capezio *Plié I* and *Plié II*

Chacott *Coppelia II* – SS, S, M, H, and HH

Chacott *Elvira* – SS, S, M, H, and HH

Chacott *Sylphide* – SS, S, M, H, and HH

Diamond Pointe – unique placement of the supportive inner shank offers maximum support when on pointe, and allows the toes to point with articulation when foot is stretched

Gamba *97*

Gaynor Minden – hard shank is available in all lengths, widths, and toe box styles; it is very hard and never softens. Hard shank with extra reinforcement is even stiffer; it is available in all lengths, widths, and toe box styles by special order.

Grishko – all Grishko shoes are available in hard shanks, and can be specially ordered in super hard. Note: Grishko shanks are considered harder than most other manufacturers'. Grishko medium is like most other companies' hard shanks; their stock hard is equivalent to a double hard; super hard would be equivalent to a triple shank strength.

Leo's *Pas de Deux Pointe 1* – fiber shank for durability

Mark Suffolk *Solo* – hard insole with ¾ shank and standard box; also hard insole full shank and hard insole full shank with arch supports

Prima Soft *Gala* – hard graduated shank; also natural graduated shank; elastic drawstring

Prima Soft *Silhouette* – comes in one strength, but can be ordered in extra hard

Prima Soft *Volé* – actually comes in medium, but harder shanks may be specially ordered in quantities of six (pairs)

Principal *D* – medium/hard shank

Repetto *La Bayadère* – medium, and hard

Repetto *Swanhilda* – soft, medium, and hard

Russian Pointe – all models available in hard (H), hard flexible (HF), super hard (HL), and super hard flexible (HLF) shanks

Sansha *Lyrica (404)* – V-vamp with high sides

Sansha *Legende (909)* – ⅔ hard shank; split outer sole; reinforced poron heel; whisper toe. The shoe runs narrow; Sansha suggests going up one width from normal.

Sansha *Partenaire* or *Partner (303)* – (student shoe) reinforced shank

Schachtner – these special order shoes come in very soft, regular, hard, and steel shanks; can also be in ¾

So' Dança, Cecilia Kerche – all three styles in soft, medium, and reinforced

So' Dança – all five styles

Teplov

Other Shank Qualities

Memory Shank
Each time the dancer goes from pointe to flat, the shank comes back to its former shape.

Gaynor Minden – all shoes

Leo's *Split-Sole Pointe* – red board has memory shank
Prima Soft *Volé* – graduated memory shank; one strength, but hard can be ordered
Principal *J*
So' Dança, Cecilia Kerche

Graduated Shank

This is a shank that is thicker under the forefoot, and is shaved or skived down to be thinner as it approaches the heel.

Bloch models (all)
Diamond Pointe
Leo's *Inspiration* – graduated shank
Prima Soft *Gala* (*701*) – natural or hard
Prima Soft *Prima Russe* (*702*) – flex or regular
Prima Soft *Royale* (*709*)
Prima Soft *Silhouette*
Prima Soft *Volé* – graduated, memory shank
Principal *J* – graduating ¾ shank; lightweight; flat, squared toe box

Roll Through Shank

Bloch *Alpha*
Bloch *Aspiration*
Bloch *Serenade*
Bloch *Serenade V*
Bloch *Signature Performance*
Bloch *Signature Rehearsal*
Bloch *Sonata*
Bloch *Suprima*
Bloch *Sylphide*
Bloch *Synergy*
Bloch *Synergy* – ¾ 2.5mm shank
Bloch *Synergy* – ¾ 1.8mm shank
Bloch *Synergy* – strong
Gaynor Minden – *SuppleFlex, FeatherFlex,* and *Pianissimo* have an easy roll through and a high *demi-pointe*
Grishko *2007*
Grishko *Maya*
Grishko *Ulanova I* and *II*
Russian Pointe – flexible in the ball of the foot of gradual *demi-pointe*; medium flexible (MF), medium hard flexible (MHF), hard flexible (HF), super hard flexible (HLF)

Sansha *Legend* (*909*) – ⅔ inner and outer sole with cushioned heel
Sansha *Ovation* (*603*) – ¾ shank with easy roll through *demi-pointe*
Sansha *Ovation* (*606*) – full shank

Three-Quarter Shanks/Insoles (or something similar)

Angelo Luzio *N03z*
Angelo Luzio *N05z*
Angelo Luzio *N31z*
Angelo Luzio *N51z*
Angelo Luzio *N71z*
Angelo Luzio *N83z*
Angelo Luzio *S66m*
Bloch *SO101 Synergy* – ¾ 2.5mm shank
Bloch *SO102 Synergy* – ¾ 1.8mm shank
Capezio *Infinita* (*183*) – ¾ skived, allowing heel to be flexible while the rest remains supportive
Capezio *Prelude*
Diamond Pointe
Fuzi – handmade fiberglass shank; one of three models
Gamba *97* – fiber, carbon shank is hard at bottom but flexible at instep; a hard shank is available for heavy dancers
Gaynor Minden – available by special order in longer sizes
Grishko *2007* – blunt cut, ¾ shank shoe with a drawstring; flexible, lightweight, and very quiet. Soft, medium, and hard shanks; sizes 3 to 8; X to XXXXX.
A new anatomical form and nonconstrictive vamp make this shoe extremely supportive while still allowing the dancer to roll through pointe easily.
Grishko *Maya* – ¾ shank available in soft, medium, or hard; flexible, lightweight, and quiet; for medium length toes that are tapered
Leo's *Inspiration* – graduated ¾ shank
Mark Suffolk *Solo* – the hard insole has ¾ shank with a standard box
Miguelito *Criselle*
Principal *J* – graduating strength ¾ shank
Repetto *Swanhilda* – also available in full shank
Russian Pointe *Polette*
Sansha *Lyrica* (*404*) – (student shoe) slightly more than ¾

Sansha *Ovation* (603) – (professional shoe) ¾ shank
Schachtner – these special order shanks can be ordered in ¾
So' Dança, Cecilia Kerche – all three styles in soft, normal, and reinforced; also come in full shank
So' Dança *Special Line, Advance, Equilibre, Performance,* and *Danseuse* – also come in full shanks

Split Outer Soles

Angelo Luzio *S66m*
Bloch *Alpha* – ¾ outer sole
Chacott *Veronese II*
Fuzi – full shank
Leo's – patent pending
Sansha *Legende* (909) – ⅔ insole (shank)

Split Inner and Outer Soles

Angelo Luzio *N66*

Broad or Wide Box

Angelo Luzio *N71z* – flat, wide toe
Angelo Luzio *N83z* – round, wide toe
Angelo Luzio *S66m*
Bloch *Alpha*
Bloch *Aspiration*
Bloch *BOS*
Bloch *Serenade*
Bloch *Serenade V*
Bloch *Sonata*
Bloch *Sylphide*
Bloch *Synergy*
Bloch *Synergy* – ¾ 1.8mm shank
Bloch *Synergy* – ¾ 2.5mmshank
Capezio *Glissé* (102-102A) – higher platform, graduated flat crown box. Top quarter of the hard shank is skived, u-shaped vamp, tapered satin around the heel, elastic drawstrings
Capezio *Plié II* (197) – moderate shank
Capezio *Tendu II* – (199) – light shank

Gamba *97* – wide platform; ¾ fiber carbon shank; offers hard shank for high arch

Gaynor Mindon – #4 box is available in most lengths

Grishko *Elite* – also flat box and platform; good for wide instep, wide spread toes and short toes, toes of even length, and feet that are shallow in depth. It is not pre-arched. Medium and hard shanks.

Grishko *Fouetté* – wide platform; medium-cut vamp

Leo's *Inspiration*

Leo's *Inspiration* ³/₄ – E

Leo's *Split Sole* – full length red board shank

Principal *D* – deep and wide box; medium shank

Prima Soft *Prima Russe* – regular and flex shanks

Russian Pointe *Brio* – high crown and medium toe platform; generous box

Russian Pointe *Dolce*

Russian Pointe *Polette*

Sansha *Recital* (202) – square block

So' Dança, Cecilia Kerche – *Pas d'Action*

So' Dança – *Advance*

Sylvia *Florina*

Sylvia *Session Toe*

Light Boxes

Angelo Luzio *N03z*

Angelo Luzio *N05z*

Angelo Luzio *N31z*

Angelo Luzio *N51z*

Angelo Luzio *N71z*

Angelo Luzio *N83z*

Angelo Luzio *S66m*

Capezio *Nicolini*

Chacott *Sylphide*

Freed *Classic Deep Vamp*

Gaynor Minden – all *FeatherFlex* and *Pianissimo* styles

Leo's *Split-Sole Pointe* – durable lightweight box, with sides for comfortable support

Mark Suffolk *Solo Light*

Principal *J*

Medium-Strength Boxes

Angelo Luzio – all models have regular box strength
Bloch *Alpha*
Bloch *Aspiration*
Bloch *BPS*
Bloch *Serenade*
Bloch *Signature Performance*
Bloch *Signature Rehearsal*
Bloch *Sonata*
Bloch *Sonata*
Bloch *Suprima*
Bloch *Sylphide*
Bloch *Synergy*
Bloch *Synergy* – ¾ 1.8mm shank
Bloch *Synergy* – ¾ 2.5mm shank
Capezio *Aerial* (191) – moderate to light box with #2 leatherboard shank. Dual nail construction allows a flexible heel while the rest of the shank remains supportive. A new last provides extra width at the ball of the foot, narrowed heel and enhanced arch.
Capezio *Contempora* (176/176X) – feathered box with broad platform and #2 leatherboard shank. Dual nail construction, longer vamp, lower heel.
Capezio *Infinita* (183) – moderate to light box with #1 leatherboard; ¾ skived shank
Gaynor Minden – all SuppleFlex styles
Grishko – all models have medium strength boxes. Hard boxes with reinforced wings are available by special order.
Mark Suffolk *Solo* – with the standard insole and hard insole
Principal *D*
Principal *F*
Sansha *Futura* (*S111*) – lace-up front
Sansha *Première* (*808*)
Sansha *Recital* (*202*) – broad platform; designed for square feet

Hard Box

Angelo Luzio – all models offer light, medium, and hard boxes
Capezio *Pavlowa* – hard shank; tapered box; longer vamp; lower heel

Chacott *Coppelia II*
Chacott *Elvira*
Diamond Pointe
Gaynor Minden – all ExtraFlex and hard styles
Grishko *Elite*
Leo's *Pas de Deux Pointe 1* – tapered box
Miguelito *Criselle* – also angled box

Tapered Box

Angelo Luzio *N31z* – flat, tapered toe
Angelo Luzio *N51z* – flat, tapered toe
Angelo Luzio *NO3z* – round, tapered toe
Angelo Luzio *S66m*
Bloch *Suprima*
Capezio *Infinita* – not as tapered as the *Aerial*; good for dancers with a medium to narrow forefoot and tapered toes
Capezio *Nicolini* (N156) – moderate strength that is narrow and tapered; slight V throat
Capezio *Pavlowa* (P103)
Gaynor Minden – #2 and #3 boxes
Grishko II – V-vamp, no drawstring, tapered heel as well as tapered box; available in soft, medium, and hard shank
Grishko *Vaganova* – high vamp; good for dancer with a strong flexible arch; medium and hard shank
Leo's *Pas de Deux Pointe 1*
Mark Suffolk *Solo* – slightly tapered toe box
Miguelito *Criselle* – strong, durable box, angled box for stability
Principal *D* – strong wing block; medium hard shank
Repetto *La Bayadère*
Russian Pointe *Anima*
Russian Pointe *Clarino*
Sansha *Soprano* (101) – designed for a regular shaped foot with a slight taper in the toes

Flat Box or Block

Angelo Luzio *N51z* – flat, tapered toe
Angelo Luzio *N71z* – flat, wide toe

Capezio *Glissé* – graduated flat crown box for maximum support without extending to the top of the vamp. The top quarter of the hard shank is skived.

Chacott *Veronese II*

Freed *Studios II*

Gamba 93

Gamba 97

Grishko *Elite*

Principal *J* – squared box; ¾ graduated shank; lightweight

Principal *D*

Russian Pointe *Dolce*

Russian Pointe *Entrada*

Russian Pointe *Polette*

Sansha *Legende* (909)

Sansha *Lyrica* (404)

Sansha *Ovation* (603)

Sansha *Ovation* (606)

Sansha *Premiere* (808)

So' Dança – all five styles

Wing Blocks

Angelo Luzio – all models offer wing blocks

Bloch – by special order only

Chacott *Coppelia II*

Freed *Classic Wing Block* (*SBTWB*) – V-cut deep vamp to lend support to the metatarsals; M, X, XX, XXX, strong insole

Freed *Studios* – V-vamp; medium or hard shank; C, D, E, EE

Freed *Studios II* – same as *Studio I*, but wider platform and flatter profile

Gaynor Minden – by special order only

Mark Suffolk *Solo* – wing block on all styles except *Solo Light*

Principal *D* – supportive wing block; medium hard shank with an inner leather piece

Principal *J* – slight wing block; graduated ¾ shank

Repetto *Swanhilda*

Sansha *Première* (808) – professional shoe with extra-flat platform and a medium-strength box

So' Dança, Cecilia Kerche – all three styles

So' Dança – all five styles

Quiet Boxes

Angelo Luzio *N51z* – light box construction
Bloch *Alpha*
Bloch *BPS*
Bloch *Rehearsal* (SO168L)
Bloch *Serenade V*
Bloch *Signature Performance*
Bloch *Signature Rehearsal*
Bloch *Synergy*
Bloch *Synergy* (SO100L/SO101L) – special pasting method that reduces noise
Bloch *Synergy* – ¾ 1.8mm shank
Bloch *Synergy* – ¾ 2.5mm shank
Diamond Pointe
Freed *Classic Deep Vamp*
Freed *Classic Wing Block*
Gaynor Minden – all models have a patented noise-reducing cushion system using real Rogers Corporation Poron® cellular urethane foam
Grishko 2007
Leo's *Split-Sole Pointe* – quiet and stable for comfort and confidence
Miguelito *Criselle*
Prima Soft *Gala* (701) – natural or hard graduated shank
Principal *D*
Principal *F*
Principal *J*
Russian Pointe *Polette* and *Polette* – ¾ shank; revolutionary formula glue that minimizes noise
Sansha – all models feature the whisper toe construction
So' Dança, Cecilia Kerche – all three styles
So' Dança – all five styles

Box for Long Toes

Angelo Luzio – all models have boxes and a high vamp for long toes
Diamond Pointe
Gaynor Minden – all boxes in deep vamp styles
Grishko *Ulanova II* – high vamp; lightweight shoe; medium and hard shanks; good for over-extended arches and a narrow heel

Grishko *Vaganova* – same as the four above
Mark Suffolk *Solo* – extended toe shoes made to order
Prima Soft *Silhouette* (703) – graduated shank and V- vamp with
   no drawstring; for the longer-toed dancer with a flexible arch
Principal *D*
Russian Pointe – all models available in high vamp (V3)
Sansha *Soprano* – (student shoe) narrow box; for long and fine feet
So' Dança, Cecilia Kerche – *Nikiya*
So' Dança – *Special Line* and *Equilibre*

Box for Longer Second Toe

Grishko *Ulanova II* – supports the foot in such a way as to prevent
   curling of the extra long toe, thus preventing arthritis
So' Dança, Cecilia Kerche *Grand Pas*
Prima Soft *Royale*

Box for Short Toes

Angelo Luzio – all models offer boxes for short toes
Gaynor Minden – all boxes in regular vamp styles
Grishko *Elite*
Prima Soft *Prima Russe* (702) – for short toes and the squarer foot
Prima Soft *Volé*
Principal *F*
Russian Pointe – all models available in short vamp (V1)
Sansha *Partenaire* (303)
So' Dança, Cecilia Kerche – *Pas d'Action*
So' Dança – *Advance*

Perfect Placement Box

The *Perfect Placement Box* was originated by Grishko in Moscow. Each shoe is hand balanced by the cobbler before it leaves his work station. The goal is for the shoe to stand on its own with a weight in the toe; if you put a handful of quarters in the shoe, a Grishko shoe will not fall down. This design is supposed to achieve to perfect placement; the dancer does not have to use body alignment to compensate for a shoe that is not balanced or does not have a perfectly flat platform.

Prima Soft has changed the way its box is shaped in order to avoid "knuckling under;" in other words, to get the dancer on the floor and off the vamp. It is made with natural materials (no fiberglass, plastics, or rubber).

Grishko *2007*
Grishko *Elite*
Grishko *Fouetté*
Grishko *Maya*
Grishko *Ulanova I* and *II*
Prima Soft *Gala*
Prima Soft *Prima Russe* – shorter box
Prima Soft *Silhouette*
Prima Soft *Royale*
Prima Soft *Volé*

Natural Placement Box

This is made with natural materials (no fiberglass, plastics, or rubber).
Angelo Luzio – all models

Narrow Platform

Bloch *Suprima*
Chacott *Sylphide*
Grishko *Ulanova II*
Grishko *Vaganova*
Russian Pointe *Anima* – high crown
Russian Pointe *Clarino* – low crown; for dancers with slim feet
Sansha *Legende* (909)
Sansha *Ovation* (603 and 606)
Sansha *Première* (808)
Sansha *Soprano* (101)

Broad Platform

Bloch *Aspiration*
Bloch *Serenade*
Bloch *Serenade V*
Bloch *Sonata*

Bloch *Sonata* – high and wide platform
Bloch *Sylphide*
Bloch *Synergy* Series
Capezio *Contempora* – #2 shank
Chacott *Elvira*
Diamond Pointe
Gamba *G97*
Gaynor Minden – all #4 box styles
Grishko *Elite* – for wide instep
Grishko *Fouetté*
Leo's *Split-Sole Pointe*
Principal *F*
Repetto *Swanhilda*
Russian Pointe *Dolce*
Russian Pointe *Polette* – room for extra pads inside; low heel
assures a smooth fit without extra pleats; elastic drawstring.
This shoe is different from other Russian Pointe shoes, with the
drawstring and low heel.
Sansha *Lyrica* (404)
Sansha *Partenaire* or *Partner* (303) – student shoe
Sansha *Recital* (202) – student shoe
So' Dança, Cecilia Kerche, all three styles
So' Dança – all five styles

Medium or Regular Platform

Angelo Luzio – all models come in medium or regular platforms
Bloch *Alpha*
Bloch *BPS*
Bloch *Signature Performance*
Bloch *Signature Rehearsal*
Bloch *Sonata*
Chacott *Coppelia II*
Gaynor Minden – all #3 box styles
Grishko *2007*
Grishko *Fouetté*
Grishko *Maya*
Grishko *Ulanova I*
Principal *D*

Russian Pointe *Brio* – high crown, generous box
Russian Pointe *Entrada* – model E, for dancers with high arches
Sansha *Lyrica* – V-vamp, stronger shank
Sansha *Soprano* – (student shoe) with narrow box for long, fine feet; wing block

Extra Flat Platform

Capezio *Nicolini*
Capezio *Pavlowa*
Grishko – all shoes have extra flat platforms
LaRay/Eva
Mark Suffolk *Solo* – all have very flat platforms
Prima Soft *Royale* – all Prima Soft pointe shoes have a flat platform
Principal *J*

Tapered Platform

Angelo Luzio *N03z*
Angelo Luzio *S66m*
Bloch *Suprima* (SO132L)
Capezio *Nicolini* (N156)
Capezio *Aerial* (191)
Chacott *Veronese II* – tapered V shape; lightweight; minimal break-in time (Japan)
Freed *Studios* (STU)
Grishko *Ulanova I*
Grishko *Vaganova*
Miguelito *Criselle*
Principal *D* – tapered toe box
Russian Pointe *Anima* – narrow toe platform with high crown
Russian Pointe *Clarino* – low crown; for dancers with slim feet
Sansha *Legende* (909)
Sansha *Ovation* (603)
Sansha *Ovation* (606)
Sansha *Première* (808)
Sansha *Soprano* (101)

Square Platform

Bloch *Serenade*
Bloch *Serenade V*
Bloch *Synergy*
Freed *Studio II* – square at the toe
Gamba *G93*
Gaynor Minden – all #4 box styles
Principal *F*
Repetto *La Bayadère*
Sansha *Lyrica* (404)
Sansha *Partenaire* (303)
Sansha *Recital* (202)

Vamps

Angelo Luzio – all seven models have a ¼ inch higher vamp
Bloch *Alpha* – new higher vamp
Bloch *Serenade II* – new ultra V-shaped vamp; also long vamp; narrow heel
Bloch *Synergy* – higher vamp and sides
Capezio *Contempora* – longer vamp, lower heel; moderate-strength box; broad platform
Capezio *Glissé* – longer vamp; U-shaped; tapered satin around the heel
Capezio *Nicolini* – longer vamp; lower heel; moderate-strength box
Capezio *Pavlowa* – longer vamp; lower heel
Capezio *Plié I* and *II* – vamp extends beyond the toe box
Capezio *Prelude* – longer vamp than *Aerial*
Chacott *Coppelia II* – standard (60 mm)
Chacott *Elvira* – standard (60 mm)
Chacott *Sylphide* – standard (63 mm)
Diamond Pointe – high U-shaped vamp with elastic drawstrings
Freed *Classic Deep Vamp* – U-cut vamp; deep vamp
Freed *Classic Wing Block* – V-cut deep vamp
Freed *Studio* and *Studio II* – slight V-vamp
Gamba *G93* – high vamp
Gamba *G97* – high vamp; flat box, wide platform; two different blunt-cut ¾ shank strengths

Gaynor Minden – a deep vamp is medium high and U-shaped; a regular vamp is shorter and more open.

Grishko *2007* – new higher vamp designed to be supportive but not restrictive

Grishko *Elite* – cut slightly lower

Grishko *Fouetté* – medium height vamp

Grishko *Ulanova I* – medium height vamp

Grishko *Vaganova* and *Ulanova II* – high vamp design with a tapered box

Leo's *Pas de Deux Pointe 1* – medium vamp

Leo's *Split-Sole Pointe* – high vamp

Mark Suffolk *Solo* – round; sharp V can be ordered.

Prima Soft *Prima Russe* (702) – V-vamp with no drawstring; flex or regular graduated shank; shorter box for a square foot with shorter toes

Prima Soft *Royale* (709) – V-vamp shoe for the dancer who likes the feel of an American shoe, but also likes the style of Russian shoes.

Prima Soft *Silhouette* (703) – V-vamp with no draw string; for the long-toed dancer with flexible arch; Perfect Placement Box; one graduated shank strength; can be specially ordered

Principal *D* – a high, slightly V-shaped vamp; strong, supportive wing block; medium hard shank; tapered box

Principal *D* – high V shape

Principal *F* – regular height U vamp; elastic drawstring

Principal *J*

Repetto *La Bayadère* – medium-short length

Russian Pointe – all models available in short (V1), medium (V2), and long (V3) vamps

Sansha *Lyrica* (404) – (student shoe) V-vamp; higher sides; medium-to-hard shank is slightly longer than ¾

Sansha – all models, except #303, have a medium-high vamp

Schachtner – these special order shoes come with short, long, extra long, or regular vamp

So'Danca (Cecilia Kerche) – vamp length is tailored to particular box

Teplov – low, medium, high, and extra high

For Dancers With High Arches

Angelo Luzio – all models accommodate dancers with high arches

Capezio *Aerial* – longer-lasting; tapered box; medium shank, medium box

Capezio *Prelude* – like *Aerial* but with a longer vamp

Diamond Pointe

Freed *Classic Wing Block*

Freed *Studio II*

Freed *Studio*

Gamba *G97* – comes with a hard shank for very hard arches and high instep

Gaynor Minden – all deep vamp, extra flex, or hard styles

Grishko *2007, Ulanova I* and *II, Fouetté, Maya* – the only model not appropriate is the *Elite*

Prima Soft *Gala* (701) – hard, graduated shank; elastic drawstring; Perfect Placement Box

Prima Soft *Silhouette* (703) – for longer toes with a flexible arch; graduated shank; no drawstring; Perfect Placement Box

Principal *D*

Russian Pointe *Entrada* – pre-arched shape and sole to enhance longevity while minimizing break-in time

Sansha *Legende* (909)

Sansha *Lyrica* (404)

Sansha *Ovation* (603)

Sansha *Partenaire* (303)

So' Dança, Cecilia Kerche

So' Dança – *Special Line, Performance*

Prima Soft *Royale*, due to the way the vamp is "more closed"

Flat Outer Sole

Angelo Luzio – all models have flat outer soles

Chacott *Veronese II*

Diamond Pointe

Gamba *G97*

Gaynor Minden

Mark Suffolk *Solo*

Principal *D*

Principal *F*
Principal *J*
Sansha – all pointe shoe models have flat outer soles
Schachtner – these special order shoes come in a soft sole

Very Unusual Shoes

Angelo Luzio *N 66* – called a classical jazz shoe; a free arch jazz shoe
with a pointe box asymmetrical jazz form.

Angelo Luzio *S66m* – called a fusion shoe; it fuses jazz and ballet
for the classically trained dancer wishing to experiment. Featuring
a symmetrical pointe form, an arch supporting shank, and slip-
on elastic with response sides, it allows for more
lateral-free choreography. Angelo Luzio says it is a fun shoe for
the choreography of new moves, while respecting the classical
rules.

Sansha *Futura* (111) – lace-up front, medium box, high vamp, medium shank; available in white, red, black, dark blue, and pink.

No Pleats

Angelo Luzio *N03z*
Angelo Luzio *S66m*
Gaynor Minden
Miguelito *Criselle*

Triangular Shaped Feet

Angelo Luzio *N83z*
Bloch *Serenade* – for square toes
Capezio *Aerial* (191) – dual nail for flexible heel; #2 leatherboard
shank; B, C, D, E
Gaynor Minden *Sleekfit*
Grishko II
Grishko *Vaganova*
Russian Pointe in general
So' Dança, Cecilia Kerche *Pas d'Action*
So' Dança *Advance*

Square Shaped Feet

Angelo Luzio *N71z*
Gaynor Minden – #4 box styles
Grishko *Elite*
Leo's *Split-Sole Pointe* (0051)
Miguelito *Criselle* – for square forefoot and medium length toes; flexible red board shank; tapered box; strong and durable box
Prima Soft *Prima Russe* (702)
Principal *F*
Sansha *Recital* (student) – medium strength box; comes up to size 16; also available in black

Narrow Heels

Angelo Luzio *N31z*
Bloch *Serenade*
Bloch *Serenade V*
Bloch *Signature Performance*
Bloch *Signature Rehearsal*
Bloch *Sonata*
Bloch *Suprima*
Gaynor Minden – *Sleekfit*
Grishko II
Grishko *Vaganova*
Prima Soft – all are made with a tapering of the heel
Principal *J*
Russian Pointe – all models in narrow width (W1)
Schachtner – makes no stock shoes, but a narrow heel can be ordered with any number of width at the ball of the foot

Other Heel Qualities

Principal D – all of the Principle shoes (D, J, and F) have the grip canvas lining on the heel to ensure that the foot and shoe move as one.
Principal *J*
Principal *F*

Pre-Arched Shoes

Capezio *Contempora* (176) – medium #2 shank; medium box, longer vamp, lower heel height
Capezio *Nicolini* (N156)
Capezio *Pavlowa* (P103)
Gaynor Minden – ExtraFlex and hard styles
Grishko *2007*
Grishko *Fouetté*
Grishko I and II
Grishko *Maya*
Leo's *Pas de Deux Pointe 1* – this shoe has Leo's Rainbow Arch to insure that the shank and the soles form to the bottom of the foot
Russian Pointe *Entrada*
So' Dança, Cecilia Kerche

Longer-lasting Shoes

Angelo Luzio – all seven models offer a double box
Capezio *Aerial*
Capezio *Infinita*
Chacott *Coppelia II*
Chacott *Elvira*
Diamond Pointe
Freed *Studio* – extra durable platforms
Freed *Studio II* – wider platform and lower profile
Gaynor Minden – all models
Russian Pointe *Entrada* – significantly increases the life of shoes for dancers with strong, high arches
Sansha – all models are long-lasting

Colors

Angelo Luzio – peach, pink; all colors and materials are available with a minimum order of twelve pairs
Bloch *SO100, SO101, SO102, SO104, SO111* – European peach
Bloch *SO105, SO130, SO131, SO132, SO133, SO141, SO162, SO168* – European pink
Chacott *Veronese II* – can be specially ordered in black and white satin

Freed *Classic Deep Vamp* and *Wing Bloch* – can be specially ordered in black, white, and red satin

Gaynor Minden – pink and white

Grishko – European pink, white, black, red, green, purple, yellow, and blue

Principal – can be ordered in any color

Russian Pointe – red, black, and white

Sansha *Futura* – black, red, dark blue, peach, and white

Sansha *Recital* – black canvas, as well as peach-pink canvas or satin; up to size 16 for men (black is available in canvas only)

Schachtner – red, white, black, or pink

So' Dança – pink in stock; white, black, red, and green are special order shoes

Unusual Fabrics

Angelo Luzio – stretch canvas

Freed *Classic Deep Vamp* and *Wing Block* – can be specially ordered in canvas or leather

Gaynor Minden – optional peach suede platform

Grishko – can be specially ordered with reverse satin and canvas

Sansha – canvas or satin

Schachtner – canvas, leather, or satin

Drawstrings

Angelo Luzio – cotton or elastic drawstrings available

Bloch styles – all available with cord drawstring; elastic by special order

Diamond Pointe – elastic drawstring; can be made with cord, if specified

Gaynor Minden – elastic drawstring that opens at the side

Leo's *Split-Sole Pointe* – elastic drawstring

Prima Soft *Gala* and *Volé* have elastic drawstrings

Principal – all shoes have elastic drawstring; can be made with cord, if specified

Russian Pointe – no drawstrings except *Polette* and *Polette* ¾ shank

Sansha – all Sansha pointe shoes offer elastic drawstrings

So' Dança, Cecilia Kerche – elastic drawstrings

So' Dança – elastic drawstrings

Primarily Handmade Shoes

Bloch *SO104 Alpha*
Bloch *SO105 Aspiration*
Bloch *SO111* BPS
Bloch *SO130 Sonata*
Bloch *SO131 Serenade*
Bloch *SO132 Suprima*
Bloch *SO133 Sylphide*
Bloch *SO139 Triomphe*
Bloch *SO141 Serenade V*
Bloch *SO162 Signature Performance*
Bloch *SO168 Signature Rehearsal*
Bloch *Synergy* Series
Capezio
Dance Workshop – all bespoke shoes made for individual dancers; they must be fitted correctly so that the dancer suffers no discomfort
Diamond Pointe Shoes
Freed *Classic Deep Vamp*
Gamba
Grishko
Leo's
Mark Suffolk
Prima Soft
Principal
Salvio's Dancing Shoes
Sansha #603 *Ovation* ¾ shank
Sansha #606 *Ovation* full shank
Sansha #909 *Legende*
Schachtner
Sylvia

Primarily Machine-made or Manufactured Shoes

Sansha #101 *Soprano*
Sansha #202 *Recital*
Sansha #303 *Partenaire*
Sansha #404 *Lyrica*
Sansha #801 *Soft Toe*
Sansha #808 *Première*

Combination of Handmade and Machine-made Shoes

Angelo Luzio

Chacott Iberica – the box is premolded and produced in a press. Then the entire shoe is handmade around the box. The sewing is done on a sewing machine.

Freed *Studios* and *Studios II*

Fuzi

Gaynor Minden

NOTE

Dancers should be sure to inquire about the length of time between ordering and receiving special order or custom-ordered shoes; in many cases, it can take several months.

10 Basics of Teaching Pointe

The Basic Issue: When is a Dancer Ready to Go On Pointe?

The most pressing question facing a teacher of pointe is how best to determine a student's readiness to begin pointe training. During our interviews with medical specialists and master teachers, we concluded that there is no simple answer to this question. There is agreement that the teacher must consider a combination of factors, including the age, anatomy, bone development, strength, length of training, weight, and attitude of a student before making this judgment. Discovering consensus on a set of guidelines to use in evaluating these factors is quite another matter.

In his book *Dance Technique and Injury Prevention,* Dr. Justin Howse, former orthopedist for the Royal Ballet School, says that, for many years, twelve was considered the age to begin pointe work. He himself feels that there is no particular age at which pointe work should begin. Dr. Howse states, "The only factor which matters is the state of the development of the child, and to be dogmatic about an age does not make any reference to the child's maturity or immaturity."[1]

Howse adds that there is no shame or disadvantage in beginning pointe work at a later age, while an early start before physical and technical readiness are present can be potentially harmful. A dancer who waits to go on pointe until the correct time for her particular body and skill development level will have less risk of injury, be able to achieve the correct technique with greater ease, and progress more speedily. He notes that a number of well-known dancers were not strong enough to start pointe work until they were teenagers, but found this no handicap to their careers.

In training situations where the only route to a professional career is through company schools, as in the Russian system, there would be no questions of a student going on pointe who was not anatomically equipped to do so. The screening process for admission weeds out applicants with such limitations, or they are dropped from the school. However, a pointe teacher in the United States may very well be confronted with such cases, since the only requirement for studying ballet may be a desire to dance.

This more democratic approach puts a great deal of additional responsibility on the teacher to decide when and if a student should go on pointe. The decision is one that can only be made on the basis of skill and knowledge, and should not be subject to student or parental pressure. Dancing on pointe is serious business, and teachers must protect their students from the risk of doing permanent damage to the bone and muscle structure of their bodies and feet. Such risks far outweigh the temporary disappointment a student may experience when told she is not ready or physically designed for pointe work.

It is entirely possible that some students may never "be ready" to go on pointe. If a teacher takes the course of least resistance, and allows such a student to go on pointe, using the excuse that she will only find another teacher who will put her "up," that teacher is overlooking his or her responsibility for the student's current and future physical health. For this reason, it is important for teachers to develop a strong rapport with parents. Once parents have confidence in a teacher's judgment, they are more likely to understand a thoroughly explained and scientifically supported discussion of why their child should not be placed on pointe.

It is also important that going on pointe not be made a key to studying ballet. If students who should not go on pointe, or may not want to do so, are made to feel a significant part of a studio program, they will be far more likely to remain on the roster.

Avoiding the concept of putting whole classes on pointe and thinking of readiness as an individual matter seems to be a good strategy. This is helpful both because children mature at different rates and because it takes some of the peer pressure off a child who is asked to wait or defer beginning pointe work. If a student appears in class who has been incorrectly placed on pointe at another school, and shows evidence of such problems as bent knees and incorrect placement, she should be taken off pointe until her problems are resolved.

Too often the issue of when students will get pointe shoes overshadows the importance of adequate prepointe training. Great care needs to be taken to design a curriculum preceding pointe work that stresses the development of the necessary strength and muscle tone. Particular emphasis must be placed on developing strength and suppleness in the feet and the strength of the postural muscles.

For this reason, students at the Royal Ballet School at White Lodge wear socks instead of tights during their prepointe training to enable teachers to watch the manner in which they are working their feet and legs. They wear elastic on their ballet shoes instead of ribbons, to make the shoes easier to slip on and off. Teachers are concerned with checking the students' bare feet to be sure they are not clenching and gripping with their toes in *tendu* or forming other patterns that will have a negative impact on pointe work.

Christine Beckley, former ballet teacher at the Royal Ballet School, stresses the importance of touching children as a teaching method, rather that standing at a distance and demonstrating. The tactile element makes them aware of what they should be feeling. It is unlikely a child can fully comprehend the muscular actions related to pointe by merely imitating what she sees on someone else's body.

Students need to understand that "taking pointe" is not undertaking the study of a new technique. They are working on their pointe technique each time they do an exercise at the barre, since these exercises are preparing them to be able to execute movements on their toes. The principles of classical ballet movement are the principles of pointe work as well.

Once a dancer has excellent placement, she can approach pointe work as a series of adjustments in weight distribution, areas of stress, and of timing—not as a new form of dance. Pointe work is an additional skill to be practiced and mastered.

Many teachers have convinced themselves that the only way to have a successful studio is to allow every female student to go on pointe as soon as possible. Part of this practice is rooted in a lack of understanding of the anatomical and technical foundation of pointe work, and part of it is based on poor logic. Putting every female student on pointe probably does as much to drive students away as to retain them. Many students who have gained reasonable proficiency in soft shoes find the reality of being on pointe so frustrating that they are discouraged from continuing their dance studies.

Some teachers take the position that children taking dance for enjoyment, as opposed to preprofessional training, should not go on pointe at all.

They feel that a child should only begin pointe if she remains interested in dance at age thirteen or fourteen, and has a sound technical foundation with strong feet, legs, and back.

In *Anatomy and Ballet* Celia Sparger questions putting a student on pointe unless she is in a systematic, concentrated, professional training situation. Sparger explains that a once-a-week class can never be a suitable preparation for pointe work, and carries with it the risk of lifelong disability. Teachers rarely see the results of poor pointe training, which may appear later in life in the form of foot, knee, or back trouble.

Clearly stated policies on pointe dancing, that are explained upon entrance to a school program, can go a long way to reducing the tension surrounding this issue. One possibility is to offer a pointe preparation option, requiring that children preparing for pointe take several classes a week for at least two years. Parents not choosing this option will be aware from the start that pointe is not a probability for their child.

Another strategy is to begin analyzing a child's anatomical problems from the time of admission, to prepare her and her parents to accept any possible unsuitability for pointe work. Capezio distributes copies of a free handout called "Why Can't I Go on My Toes?" through its retail stores; it is well written and ideal for distribution to parents.

Knowledge is the best weapon in successfully dealing with the issue of readiness. Teachers must know how to evaluate a child for pointe readiness and be able to interpret the process clearly for parents. Helpful guidance can be obtained by talking to podiatrists and orthopedists who work with dancers, attending seminars at conventions, and conferring with fitting specialists at dance shops. Many colleges offer courses in anatomy, and some are designed especially for dance majors. Taking such a course on a not-for-credit basis could provide a valuable base of knowledge. Outside support for a cautious approach to placing students on pointe can be gained by requiring that students have the consent of their physicians, indicating when they are at an appropriate stage in their growth and physical development to begin pointe.

Edith Royal, who, with her husband, Bill, ran a successful dance school and company for more than thirty years, developed a method of teaching pointe that sought to maintain professional standards in a private studio setting. Her approach is a vivid demonstration that this is possible. Royal based her method on her own training at the Royal Ballet

School in London, the Paris Opéra Ballet School, and with Robert Joffrey.

Royal gave a pointe test to students at her school when they reached age eleven to determine their readiness. Before taking the test, a student had to take classes for two years. The test examined pull-up in the legs, articulation of the feet, and back strength. Students who did not pass the test stayed in the same class as those who got their pointe shoes, but they did the pointe exercises on *demi-pointe*. In other words, pointe was a possibility and not an inevitability.

In surveying teachers around the country, we asked them their reasons for telling their students not to begin pointe work. Answers include improper placement, students are too young, they are not pulled up in the body and feet, their feet not arched enough, they are overweight, they have a lack of strength in the torso, their knees or ankles are too weak, their basic stance on *demi-pointe* is not strong and correct, they are taking too few classes per week.

In determining a system for evaluating readiness for pointe, a teacher should consider the following areas.

Length and Intensity of Study

Time and preparation are needed for students to develop adequate strength and technique to begin pointe. It is essential that the student's musculature be strong enough to support her entire body. Much of the lift in pointe work depends on the two calf muscles, which meet in the Achilles tendon. Most of the teachers we interviewed require at least two or three years of serious ballet training, and insist that a student be taking two or three classes a week. Many require four years of training.

In *Anatomy and Ballet*, Celia Sparger states, "The ability to do pointe work is the end result of a slow and gradual training of the whole body, back, hips, thighs, legs, feet, general coordination of movement, and the placing of the body, so that weight is lifted upwards off the feet, with straight knees, perfect balance, a perfect *demi-pointe*, and no tendency of the feet to sickle in or out, or the toes to curl and clutch."[2]

Dr. William Hamilton, official doctor of the New York City Ballet, espouses George Balanchine's theory that a student should have studied ballet for four years before beginning pointe. It should be noted that

Hamilton is not convinced by available research data that putting a child on pointe before a particular age is necessarily damaging. However, he does feel that a child with four years of training will have the strength and technique required to begin pointe. He adds that learning technique on *demi-pointe* puts less strain on the foot than wearing pointe shoes, since the weight is still bearing on the metatarsals.

Some teachers place the greatest emphasis on the training factor. For instance, Nathalie Krassovska, former ballerina with Ballet Russe de Monte Carlo and the Grand Ballet du Marquis de Cuevas, feels that training level and body development are more important than age. She believes that if a student takes class every day, she can develop strength very quickly and occasionally can go on pointe as early as eight, after several years of intensive study. However, she would keep less serious dancers, who take fewer classes, off pointe until as late as age fourteen or fifteen. Krassovska insists that students come at least three times a week to be able to take pointe class.

Strength

Dr. James Garrick has stated that, contrary to finding that going on pointe "too early" produces significant musculoskeletal problems, the Dance Medicine Division of his Center for Sports Medicine at St. Francis Hospital in San Francisco observes students who physically struggle with pointe because they lack the strength and technique necessary for "this demanding endeavor." He believes a student should be able to do a solid *passé* on *demi-pointe* with a straight, pulled-up knee. This requires that she put all her weight on one leg, with full knee extension and full *relevé*. He adds that if a dancer can go from a *grand plié* in center to standing with her knees straight, no wobbling, and without altering foot positions, it may be time for pointe.

Dr. Richard Braver, former medical consultant to Capezio, states that a student should be able to stand on *demi-pointe* for forty-five seconds on each foot, without faltering or wobbling.

Dr. Justin Howse says that strength must have been achieved in the feet and around the ankles, with full control of all relevant joints. Students should be able to hold turnout at the hips and be stable in the hip area when standing on both legs or one leg alone. There also needs to be strength and stability in the trunk. Inadequate control of the muscles of the trunk, hip, and thigh can make a student unstable and unsafe on pointe. If the feet and body are in any way soft, mobile, or floppy, pointe work must be delayed.

Many children come to ballet with loose ligaments, says Dr. Louis Galli, New York City podiatrist, who works with dancers in Broadway shows as well as the leading ballet companies. They usually discover ballet because they are able to do things other children cannot, and because of their loose ligaments (which simply means that they are loose-jointed), they have better extension and better lines.

Dr. Galli's concern regards the fact that ligaments support the joints: if the ligaments are loose, what will support them? The answer is the muscles and tendons; but that is not their primary function. Their primary function is to move the body. Therefore, these children have a false sense of flexibility. They are loose-jointed, but their muscles and tendons are tight. They are asking their muscles and tendons to do the job that their ligaments would normally do.

Dr. Galli feels that these students never get strong enough, and he suggests exercise such as Pilates or swimming to strengthen them. He stresses the importance of this; otherwise, these students are likely to get injured because their muscles work too hard.

Age/Bone Development

Bones have different rates of ossification. The *epiphyses* are layers of cartilage or solid, resilient cellular tissue present in bone that has not yet completed its growth. Some of these layers of cartilage do not totally ossify until humans reach their twenties. Bones harden gradually from the center outward. In the long bones, such as those of the leg, forefoot, and toes, that bear the weight of the body when the dancer is on pointe, the shaft ossifies first. The epiphyses remain connected to the shaft by cartilage only, until the early teens. There is great variation among children as to when the cartilage becomes bony; ossification may not begin until the age of fourteen. To compensate for this fact, the muscles must be particularly well developed, to protect joint alignment. Otherwise, the pressure of body weight on feet and toes, which are still soft and growing, can cause malformation of the bones and joints. With correct training, the weight of the body should be held and distributed in such a way that minimum weight falls on the toes.

In light of these developmental considerations, few of the teachers we interviewed think children should go on pointe before the age of ten. Many wait until students are eleven or twelve, regardless of how young they have begun their training. Joanna Kneeland, a noted dance teacher who did extensive research in the field of dance movement, suggested sending children to a doctor and having the feet X-rayed to determine if the tips of the toes have changed from cartilage to bone. She suspected that the body may reach this stage of maturity faster in warm climates.

Even after determining that students are ready to go on pointe, some teachers carefully chart their growth spurts by keeping height charts at the studio. If a beginning pointe student experiences a growth spurt, she is taken off pointe for three or four months until her growth stabilizes. During growth spurts, weight distribution changes, the center of gravity changes, and the proportions of body parts change. Rapidly growing dancers run a greater risk of injury than others. Since muscles may not keep up with bone growth and may grow tightly, the resulting strain on the body can have a long-lasting impact. Students are kept in the same class structure, but work in flat shoes until the growth spurt ends. They might be given additional exercises to stretch the quadriceps, hamstrings, and calf muscles, to keep them strong, stretched, and flexible.

Anatomy of the Foot and Ankle

A teacher must evaluate the structure of the student's foot and ankle. Although "ideal" feet are rarely found, extreme problems that may cause difficulties should be identified. The ideal foot for pointe is thought to be wide, with two or three toes of the same length and a strong ankle. This kind of foot provides a broad base for weight distribution. A student with a long big toe can do pointe work, but those with extremely long second toes find it more difficult. A narrow pointed foot with a high arch also signals potential problems.

The flexibility of the ankle and the amount of natural arch in the instep should be examined. With limited flexibility and arch, a student may have problems aligning her ankle between knee and toes on pointe. A student with inflexible feet may experience Achilles tendon problems from pointe work because of the pressure created when the heel bone goes into the tendon.

A weak ankle and an instep with too much arch can also be limiting.

When this kind of foot is placed on pointe, the toes usually curl under, forcing the front of the foot and instep down and forward from the ankle. The thigh and knee muscles are strained, and weight is not centered over the bones of the legs. The shoulders, neck, and whole upper torso can be adversely affected. Students with this problem need to do additional strengthening work before they begin pointe work.

A student with pronated feet or fallen arches that roll toward the inside, with more weight placed over the big toe and arch, should not go on pointe until the muscles around the ankle can be retrained to hold the ankle in the correct position. Pronation can cause bunions and longitudinal arch problems.

While the muscles of the ankle joint can adjust to changing positions, on pointe they are held in a fixed position and cannot move. Consequently, they must be strong enough to keep the foot from *sickling* out and causing the weight of the body to be shifted to the inside of the foot. When this happens, ligaments and muscles can be overly stretched and the additional weight that presses on the side of the big toe can cause it to become displaced. Sickling can make the ankle prone to sprains. A student with supinated or sickled feet that roll toward the outside, with the majority of weight placed over the fourth and fifth toes, should not go on pointe until the muscles of the ankle can be retrained.

A student with a weak instep who goes on pointe without correct preparation can suffer lasting damage to the foot and ankle. The muscles of the foot and ankle need to be strengthened so that the foot is well controlled and able to be held in the correct position, rather than the over-pointed position.

Weight

Overweight students should be encouraged to lose weight before going on pointe. Otherwise they risk damaging themselves by placing extra pressure on their toes.

Attitude

An enjoyment of dance is a definite prerequisite for pointe study. A negative attitude toward dance class before pointe training will only worsen, once pointe shoes are introduced.

Preparing a Student for Her First Pointe Class

At first students are often upset by how different pointe shoes feel from ballet slippers or street shoes. The teacher should spend time discussing the parts of the shoe and their function.

She or he should remember that first-time pointe students need careful directions on such matters as sewing and tying ribbons, toe protection, and shoe care.

The Length and Form of Pointe Class

There is general consensus that pointe training must be slow and careful to give the bones and muscles a chance to develop properly. Individual attention is vital, since no small errors or sloppy movements can be overlooked. The student should not wear legwarmers during this early phase of pointe work, to allow the teacher to carefully observe the knee, calf, and ankle.

Pointe training is scheduled in widely varying formats. Beginning students may wear their pointe shoes for ten to thirty minutes at the end of every ballet class, after they are fully warmed up, from one to five times a week. Or, at first, they may wear their shoes once a week, then twice a week, gradually building up to wearing their shoes for forty-five minutes. In some studios beginners take a separate one-hour pointe class. Many teachers mentioned preferring to teach beginning pointe at the end of barre rather than the end of class, before students become too tired.

More advanced pointe students may take pointe classes for half an hour twice a week, or they may take half an hour of each hour-and-a-half class on pointe. At some schools, students are slowly introduced to a full hour-and-fifteen-minute class on pointe, based on the theory that they will eventually dance almost entirely in pointe shoes and need to develop the endurance to do so early in their training. A more detailed description of how pointe education is integrated into the curricula of major training schools and private studios can be found in this chapter and chapter 11.

Some Tips on Teaching Pointe

Dame Ninette de Valois once said, "When you are on your toes, keep off them." Failure to lift weight away from the hips results in toes being clenched and curled under, instead of elongated and narrowed. Weight should be lifted out of the shoes and distributed throughout the body. Sinking down into the shoes causes stress and pain to foot joints, and creates excessive wear on the pointe shoes. (See chapter 12, Sample Pointe Classes, for full notes on exercises for the first and second day on pointe, and classes ranging from beginner to advanced levels.)

The teacher must guide the student to stand correctly on pointe, with the entire tip of the platform flatly touching the floor and the toes perpendicular to the floor. The foot should not be pushed back or pushed forward. The instep must be fully stretched to accomplish this. Leslie Browne, star of the movie *The Turning Point* and former principal dancer with American Ballet Theatre, says she stresses this position of the foot on pointe, as well as the shape of the foot, to her students. The teacher should be able to draw a straight line through the center of the hip, knee, ankle, and big toe joints when watching a student stand on pointe from a side view. From the front, the teacher should see a straight line from the hip, knee, and ankle joints through the box of the shoe, between the second and third toes. Nathalie Krassovska encourages beginning pointe students to look up and focus at eye level.

The teacher should stress working on both sides to avoid having students develop one foot more than another. This can be a particular problem with turns, where students tend to favor a "good" side. Remember that the way a student comes down from pointe is as important as the position she assumes on pointe.

A teacher should use correct language, based on knowledge of the muscles, tendons, ligaments, and bones and how they operate. Do not try to teach pointe by using vague verbal images. Carefully educate the student about the mechanics of what they are learning. Encourage them to ask questions.

A teacher should look at each pointe student as an individual, and not try to impose the same movement principles on everyone. If one student's foot structure is different from another's, she may need to carry her weight differently. Positions should not be forced; not all bodies can take it.

In *The Teaching of Classical Ballet,* Joan Lawson[3] advocates teaching the student to find her own center of balance through the use of the spring. She explains that this center of balance falls between the first and second, and sometimes third, phalanges of the metatarsal arch.

After rising through quarter, half, and three-quarter pointe, the dancer makes a slight spring to reach the tips of her toes. If a dancer has long toes, this spring is taken sooner. It is a slightly backward motion with toes going under the heel to cause the ankle and toes to stretch downward and out- ward, so that the heel is not pulled backward into the Achilles tendon.

In discussing the spring, Delores Lipinski of the Ruth Page Foundation School faculty points out that the English method of springing onto pointe by pulling the feet under is "nice and light," but does not work for students who have "banana feet" that lack strength. She feels that while springing tends to stretch out the foot and make it looser, rolling builds strength.

Advocates of rolling, have students rise slowly to full pointe and roll back from the ball down through the heel, using the whole foot. The instep is developed as it raises and lowers the heel. Nathalie Krassovska stresses the roll; she starts her students facing the barre and has them practice rolling up onto pointe. She does not teach beginners to spring. Joanna Kneeland also advocates the roll; she says the rise to pointe should require minimal adjustment. It should be a smooth rather than jerky feeling. It is not a matter of springing and replacing the heel with the toes, but of develop- ing the strength needed to lower softly through the metatarsals. She says, "It is not the toes' job to jump under the body. The foot is the foundation and cannot be disturbed."

Christine Spizzo, former soloist with American Ballet Theatre and now on the faculty of the North Carolina School of the Arts, dislikes shoes that do not allow a student to roll through the foot. Some of them are made so that only a springing *relevé* is possible, and Spizzo feels that this does not allow the student to develop the muscles of the feet properly.

Another prominent ballet teacher, Nancy Bielski, has taught children's classes, professional open classes at Steps, New York, and also has been on the faculty of American Ballet Theatre. Bielski emphasizes the proper use of the foot with slow rises and *demi-pointe* work. She wants her beginning students to be able to get up and down without jumping or dropping.

Pliés and *relevés* are avoided because beginners tend to jump while trying these movements on pointe.

Posture is also stressed in Bielski's classes because young students tend to stick their stomachs out and bend their knees while looking at the floor.

It is a good idea to videotape pointe classes so that students can observe their mistakes and also their progress. This allows students to see their feet in close-up. It also allows a teacher to see a mistake made by one student that might have been missed while attention was momentarily focused on another. Professionally-made pre–recorded tapes, or those made with more advanced students at the studio, can also be used to show students examples of a step being done correctly.

David Howard's Philosophy of Pointe Training

Master teacher David Howard's insights on pointe training are both provocative and informative.[4] The roots of Howard's movement philosophy are found in his study of kinesiology and many years spent observing dancers in the studio and in performance. He has his own syllabus gleaned from various systems, incorporating the best features of all of them.

David Howard is particularly concerned with patterns of energy. He notes that while most people stand with two feet on the floor and pull the body up, he works from "up" first and thinks in terms of going through to a "down," then stretching away from the floor using the calf as a depressor rather than a pulling agent. He says the calf should push on the way up, and push against the floor on the way down. It never changes its function as a muscle. According to Howard, if the calf is used as a pulling muscle, the knees lock and the natural coordination in the joint areas is gone. The calf must be thought of as a pushing muscle. When a person walks, he or she does not pull the calf but pushes through it every time.

The same dynamic must be applied to pointe. When it is, the dancer can achieve the quality of having pointe work appear to be an extension of the toe, rather than a function of the box of the shoe. Most dancers resort to artistic camouflage to roll up and down on pointe. They roll up and down by pulling away from the floor instead of using the calf as a depressor to get them onto pointe. When the calf is used as a depressor on the way down, it offers great control since the muscles of the leg are being used as they were designed.

Howard believes that pointe work is an extension of natural movement. He feels that many teachers teach one thing at the barre and then expect their students to do something else in the center. They lock students into a different state at the barre, and then scream at them when they do not move freely in the center. If bad patterns of energy are started at the barre, these patterns are inevitably going to be repeated in the center. But if the energy pattern is right, then the student will lift under the ankle, have a strong arch, and not "knuckle."

The nature of pointe work is that it makes the body stiff. Howard finds that boys often progress in dance training more quickly than girls at the age when girls go on pointe. He thinks this is because traditional pointe training conspires to give a female dancer two straight stiff legs under a spastic body, while boys are experiencing a greater range of motion. Although boys start later, they end up more coordinated.

Girls are always told their legs should be straight and pulled up, which they translate as stiff. Then when they move stiffly, they are screamed at to move. The emphasis should be on strong, stretched, and elongated rather than straight legs.

Howard observes that divers always have good feet because they stretch their feet instead of pointing them. They think of lengthening through the ankle and instep as much as possible, and a point is the result. Howard feels that "point your foot" is the right expression in terms of imagery but wrong in terms of teaching feelings. He explains:

> You don't point your feet. You lengthen them to the end of the extremity. You get energy to the end of the extremity and then feel the stretch happen. Rather than pull and point, you push down to the end of your toes. Stretch and lengthen. It is not static. You need the energy flow. It is a circular action. It is straight in look but not in feeling. *Demi-plié* is down under and out, and under up and through. It is a circular pattern in the knees and ankle joints. These areas have to sustain weight. They must go up to go down, to stretch against the floor.

He cautions that a dancer should never go lower down than her calf can push in a *demi-plié*. She should feel as if she could thrust away from the floor without doing anything. The idea that the farther a dancer goes down, the farther she can go up is not valid, according to his theory.

Howard stresses that he has not invented these concepts but is simply incorporating the way the body functions into ballet technique. He thinks ballet is trapped by its reliance on two-hundred-year-old ideas and is not taking advantage of contemporary knowledge about the body. He feels ballet has gone as far as it can, chained to these outdated practices. To reach another level, dancers and teachers have to be retrained with a different kind of understanding about body mechanics and special stress on the pattern of energy that goes through the muscles. Without the proper pattern of energy, the dancer will struggle. Dancers have to turn away from learning by imitating, and must deal with what they *feel* to gain strength and accomplish beautiful movement.

Howard sees gravity as the one obstacle to human movement, the "kiss of death" to a dancer. He says:

> If we use gravity as an aid rather than a harmful agent, we can use it to help us. If we push our energy down toward gravity and only stretch in the opposite direction, we are using gravity to help us. And if we are thrusting in a downward thrust to send the body away from the floor like a trampoline, then we are using gravity to help us. But if we are pulling the body away from the floor, we can never win. We can get certain height, but we cannot reach our fullest potential.

In other words, Howard suggests that we use rules and physics and nature to help us end up with much stronger, more elongated bodies and to accomplish things in the air. Otherwise we are relying on miracles, and as he observes, "Sooner or later time runs out." Unless a dancer is working in harmony with nature, sooner or later something goes wrong.

He feels that Gelsey Kirkland, Jennifer Gelfand, Tamara Rojo, Alexandra Ansanelli, and other dancers who have worked with him look different when they dance because their center of gravity is high. While their bone structure is up, their muscles are pushing down in opposition, resulting in a two-way energy pattern. Dancers using his method have the ability to release each area—the shoulders, diaphragm, and stomach. They have flexibility in their hips and knees. Each of these factors contributes to taking the dancer onto pointe. The *relevé* comes from the torso to the foot, whereas pulling up in *relevé* produces hyperextension.

Howard notes that dancers are so determined and strong that they will find a way to stand on pointe, even if their mothers glue their feet to the floor. A few students survive in spite of teachers by finding a way around what they are being taught in order to make things work.

To Howard, "pull up" is a look, not a feel. In keeping with his philosophy of starting up and going down instead of starting down and going up, he begins pointe work with *piqués* at the barre rather than *relevés*. For the first two years he uses *piqué plié* rather than *relevé plié*.

Howard is not in favor of doing all class work in pointe shoes because he thinks there is a lot of speed and flexibility to be gained from working on *demi-pointe*. He stresses that pointe work is only another level of ballet, not an individual discipline unto itself. Pointe work is a level the body can work from, and not a matter of someone standing up on her toes.

Throughout his training process Howard creates exercises and combinations to build energy patterns, always stressing that energy must come from the torso through the bone structure to the ends of the extremities. He sees the body as an expressive instrument that has to act. Dance steps are not a series of frenzied movements but represent a need to communicate; they are a means of expression.

Howard feels that Katherine Healy is the purest realization of his training theory. Although Gelsey Kirkland, whom he describes as the greatest exponent of classical dance he has ever seen, was highly receptive to his concepts, Healy was much younger when she began working with him. She reached an incredible level of technical and artistic achievement under his tutelage at a very early age. Howard believes that to train a dancer on pointe is to take something inherently artificial and transform it into genuine art.

Peff's Thoughts on Pointe

Peff Modelski, New York City–based ballet teacher and Feldenkrais Method instructor, thinks that many dance injuries are unnecessary and could be avoided. She says that when students are put into pointe shoes too soon and spend too much time in them in early training, they are setting themselves up for arthritis later in life. "Teachers don't do enough preparatory work," she says. "When dancers are not ready to do pointe work, the weight of the body can't travel through the toes. It travels into the toes which starts a problem all the way up the system. The toes are very small. The bones are very small. The dancer starts to grab her calves, then the knees, hip sockets, and back. She'll do anything not to fall down and disappoint the teacher or herself."

Peff says that it is very easy to teach beginner pointe students if the right amount of time is spent in class and if there is enough time in between lessons. This way, a dancer can build a strong, comfortable, pliable foot because the bones that bear weight on the top of it are not inhibited, torqued, or twisted. She feels there is a problem with the thinking of schools that put all of their classes on pointe at a certain age, whether nine years old or fifteen. To make her point she continues, "Pointe shoes were invented for a principal dancer who already had strength, stamina, timing, and professional expertise. Marie Taglioni was not nine years old when she started on pointe even though she may have been the darling of her father [a dancer and choreographer]."

Peff also says that the language used to teach pointe work has to be different from that used to teach a technique class, although the two do need to be linked. She feels the biggest controversy in ballet is whether to "pull up" or to "push down." The language a teacher uses and the tone of voice can determine whether the student truly comprehends what she should be experiencing. Instructions must be patiently delineated over and over again.

Some of her students who were professional dancers have suffered from tendinitis of the ankles as well as problems with their thighs and hips because of extreme hyperextension of the leg. Explaining that they must not pull up anything except their pelvic floor and their eyelids, and that everything else must be lengthened in the direction of the floor, helped dancers understand how to work successfully with this problem. She asks dancers to visualize lifting from under the heart. Going further, she continues, "If you see the legs as a platform that the heart sits above, you can push the feet into the floor in specific lines that provide for balance without gripping. I think teachers have to be more knowledgeable about how the human body actually functions—how it takes a visualized message and how the message is translated."

Pointe Training for Adults

The upper age limit for putting adults on pointe depends on how many hours a week they study, their general physical condition, muscular strength, and dedication. Patricia Klekovic, who teaches an adult pointe class at the Ruth Page School in Chicago, describes her students as "very brave ladies who have either had the dream of wanting to dance on pointe all their lives, or have danced as children and wanted to experience the feeling again." She only allows them on pointe if they are taking a minimum of three classes a week and take a ballet class immediately before their pointe class. She never encourages adults to go on pointe and insists that it be completely their own decision. Klekovic notes that it is much easier for children to learn to work on pointe than it is for adults, because adults have so much more weight on their ankles. Children also have less fear when confronting a challenge such as a *pirouette* on pointe.

Most of the women in the adult pointe class are fairly young and few older women have made the request. Klekovic feels that many of her adult pointe students cannot injure themselves because they are not exerting enough energy. Rather than trying to perfect their pointe technique, she allows them to move at their own pace.

Edith Royal also taught adult pointe in her studio in Orlando, Florida, and applied the same standards as her beginning children's classes. Most of the students in these adult classes were in their early twenties or thirties and were women who had studied dance until they attended college. They wanted to resume their ballet training both for physical conditioning and the satisfaction it afforded them. Royal insisted that they have the basic strength for pointe and take the same number of classes required of younger pointe students. Since these students were fairly skilled at basic technique from their past training, often they were able to become quite proficient at pointe.

Pointe Training in Higher Education

Participants in college dance programs may range from serious majors undertaking the full dance curriculum as a preparation for performing or teaching careers, to students who wish to take several dance courses on an elective basis. They may arrive on campus with years of pointe training of varying quality, or with no prior experience on pointe. The question of how best to serve these divergent populations in terms of pointe training is not a simple one to answer. A look at how pointe training is approached at the University of South Florida at Tampa, under the direction of Professors Gretchen Ward Warren and Sandra Robinson Waldrop, offers some insight into how this issue may be handled.

Any student applicant at the university is admitted into the Fundamentals of Ballet course, meeting twice a week for one semester. Students must audition for subsequent levels, Ballet I, II, III, or IV, and are placed according to their ability, regardless of their undergraduate status. They may remain at any level for three semesters, but cannot advance until judged ready.

Students in the Performance Track B.A. Degree Program are not formally accepted as dance majors until they have been placed in a level III (or IV) technique class. Once admitted to the program, either a ballet or modern dance emphasis is selected. The ballet major includes more pointe and variation requirements.

Pointe work is usually begun in Ballet II, a two-hour class that meets four times a week. For the last ten minutes of each class, the students work on simple pointe exercises such as *pliés* and *relevés* facing the barre, *échappés*, *pas de bourrée*, and, in the center, *pas couru* across the floor. Male students and students whose feet are deemed unsuitable for pointe work are excused from this part of class.

In Ballet III, which meets four times a week, more pointe work is part of the curriculum. Female students do a pointe-barre twice a week, and wear their pointe shoes for the last part of class on the other two days. The pointe exercises in the center alternate with men's work for the male students. In addition, many of the students in Ballet III also take a full pointe class on the fifth day of the week. The most advanced class, Ballet IV, meets five times a week with pointe work integral to every class.

Warren and Robinson Waldrop created the program now being followed, and established a syllabus designed to achieve their objectives. Their approach was influenced by their experiences at the Royal Ballet, American Ballet Theatre, North Carolina School of the Arts, and the Pennsylvania Ballet. They use the Vaganova system as a basis for their syllabus, but have added elements from the Bournonville and Paris Opéra Ballet schools, and the School of American Ballet (Balanchine).

The University of South Florida approach offers a quick progression through the syllabus for the older dancer who is ready mentally as well as physically. A constant concern is balancing the students' physical readiness with their need to know the mechanics of the entire classical vocabulary.

When advising dance majors about their future potential, Warren and Robinson Waldrop try to point them in an honest direction. Depending on each individual's strength, they may suggest auditioning for a small company, teaching, or graduate school for those who show talent as choreographers or writers.

They have found that some students who begin ballet in college may not advance at all, owing to lack of physical facility rather than age. On the other hand, many students learn to do the most with what they have. For instance, Warren and Robinson Waldrop had a student who lacked the necessary hypermobility in her ankle joints to allow her to stand fully vertical on pointe. She was a trained dancer who moved well and had nicely developed legs. They were able to help her learn to work her feet to their maximum potential, but there was little they could do to change the inherent limitations caused by the structure of her feet.

The expense of pointe shoes is a real stumbling block for students in the program. Since many are working to pay for their education, the added burden of paying for pointe shoes is a great strain. Consequently, they often work in broken shoes or cannot afford to experiment widely enough to find the right fit.

Pointe Training for Men

Whether it is useful for male students to study pointe is an area in which there is wide disagreement. Men may be interested in experimenting with pointe because they wish to strengthen their feet. Or they may plan on teaching pointe at some time in the future and want to have first-hand knowledge of the process. Or they may be part of performing ensembles such as Les Ballets Trockadero de Monte Carlo or Les Ballets Grandiva, which require pointe work.

Associate Professor Richard Sias, at Florida State University at Tallahassee, feels that pointe training offers male students a level of stretch not possible on *demi-pointe* or in soft ballet shoes. Rodney Irwin, who teaches *pas de deux* at the Ruth Page School in Chicago, thinks that a male dancer who has experienced pointe finds it easier to understand the pointe problems of his female partner. He also believes that it helps a male choreographer understand the limits of pointe work.

Mikhail Messerer, ballet master for the Royal Swedish Ballet and the Munich Opera Ballet at the time of our research (and nephew of the famed Asaf Messerer), thinks pointe training for men is sensible if they can find pointe shoes that will not damage their feet. Messerer trained at the

Bolshoi School, where men took pointe classes for strength and better balance. Joanna Kneeland, however, doubts that pointe shoes build men's strength that cannot be gained through other exercises. Another concern of those opposed to men's pointe training is that men may bear more weight on their ankles and feet, possibly resulting in injury.

One of the major drawbacks for American men who wished to experiment with pointe was the problem of finding proper fitting shoes. Most stock shoes were not made above a woman's size 8 or 8.5, and were frequently not wide enough for men's feet. Even now it is a problem, but pointe shoe manufacturers have recently expanded their choices of sizes and widths, and Sansha's *Recital* (202) is now made up to size 16 in black, specifically with men in mind.

Dancer Anton Wilson began pointe work to strengthen his feet while a student at Towson State University. He initially wore stock Capezio *Pavlowas* in size 8.5 D, and to give his feet extra support, he elongated the vamp with pink denim. After finishing his education at the North Carolina School of the Arts, he joined Les Ballets Trockadero de Monte Carlo, the all-male ballet company that performs classical and original works, with men in female dress performing women's roles. The members of the Trockadero are classically trained dancers who perform on pointe and are also skilled comedians. Once in the company, Wilson had his shoes custom-made and began wearing 8.25 E *Contempora*. The squarer box gave his toes more room.

He suffered from a large number of blisters when he began pointe and also encountered a major problem with bruised toenails. Even the weight of a bed sheet became excruciating. His nails also hurt in flat shoes, and he dreaded the thought of performances because of this condition. On the positive side, Wilson's performing experience on pointe gave him new respect for female pointe dancers, and a more thorough understanding of partnering. He discovered new muscles in his calves and thighs when he danced on pointe, and also learned valuable lessons about pulling up "out of" his legs.

The director of Les Ballets Grandiva, Victor Trevino, has some interesting observations concerning men on pointe. The company was formed in 1996, after the original Trockaderos splintered a couple of years earlier. He points out that men's feet tend to be wider than women's, and that their heels are also bulkier. This means that, when on pointe, the line of a man's foot is not as attractive as that of a woman's. Trevino thinks that men need to wear toe pads for extra cushioning, since their toes are generally much bigger than women's, and their general size and weight put much more pressure on the shoe.

NOTES

1. Howse, Justin. *Dance Technique and Injury Prevention* (New York: Theatre Arts Books, 1988), p. 59.

2. Sparger, Celia. *Anatomy and Ballet* (New York: Theatre Arts Books, 1970), p. 121.

3. Lawson, Joan. *The Teaching of Classical Ballet.* (New York: Theatre Arts Books, 1983), p. 121.

4. Information attributed to David Howard in this chapter was gathered during an interview at his studio, May 19, 1989, and further interviews prior to the publication of the Second Edition.

Note: In addition to the teachers referred to throughout the chapter, material on the basics of teaching pointe was gathered in surveys from teachers across the country. Teachers surveyed were asked at what age they placed students on pointe, what determined pointe readiness, which shoes they suggested, how they integrated pointe into their curricula, how much time was spent on pointe per week, and what kinds of exercises they used in beginning pointe classes. Additional material was gathered on location at the schools profiled in chapter 11.

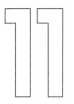

Profiles of Pointe Training Methods

Pointe Training in Company Schools

The Royal Ballet School

46 Floral Street, Covent Garden
London WC2 9DA, England
Telephone: 00 44 207 836 88 99
Fax: 00 44 207 845 70 80
E-mail: Rachelh@royalballetschool.co.uk

The Royal Ballet Lower School

White Lodge, Richmond Park
Richmond
Surrey TW10 5HR, England
Telephone: 00 44 208 876 5547
Fax: 00 44 208 392 8037

The Royal Ballet School, founded in 1931, consists of a Lower School for children between the ages of eleven and sixteen, housed in White Lodge in Richmond Park, Surrey, and an Upper School, for students aged sixteen and over, in central London, directly opposite the Royal Opera House. Both the Lower and Upper Schools are under the direction of Gailene Stock A.M.

The Royal Ballet School is not to be confused with the Royal Academy of Dance, which is a teacher-training institution with its own syllabus and system.

While the Royal Ballet School's graduates enter many ballet companies in Britain and Europe, the main purpose of the training program is to provide dancers for the Royal Ballet and the Birmingham Royal Ballet. Entrance to the Lower School is by preliminary auditions held throughout Britain, and a final London audition, which is highly competitive.

Students must be eleven years old to be admitted, and they come from all over the world. Potential talent and physical suitability are both considered. While foreign students have to pay for their schooling, British students can be assisted with grants. No one who is eligible to attend has ever been turned away because of financial difficulties.

There are 125 male and female students at the Lower School, most of whom board at the school. While students entering at age eleven dance for approximately three-and-a-half hours per day, by the time they leave the school, they will be taking approximately twenty-eight hours of dance classes a week. In addition to the dance syllabus, children also pursue their academic studies. The school year runs from September to July.

Students go on pointe about halfway through their first term at the Lower School. Initially the girls wear their pointe shoes only once or twice a week. Younger students often look to older students for advice about pointe work.

The ballet teachers oversee the entire shoe-fitting process for every student in the Lower School. They are deeply involved in helping each student select the proper shoe for his or her foot, and in determining what changes are needed in shoes as the student progresses. Lower School students wear Freed pointe shoes and soft ballet shoes. The students are taught to darn their shoes and attach their ribbons. Lower School students wear uniforms for both their dance and academic classes. They are not allowed to wear make-up, jewelry, plastic pants, flashy colored leotards or leg warmers.

The Upper School students often work with The Royal Ballet, which provides great inspiration to them. Graduates of the Lower School, and students from other British and foreign schools, complete their final training in a nonresidential setting. The curriculum includes classical ballet, character dance, *pas de deux*, contemporary dance, stage make-up, variations from repertory, music appreciation, art appreciation, and dance composition. In the final year of the training they are involved in many performances and usually one international tour, presenting a variety of works and styles of dance. International tours have included visits to Kobe, Japan; Stuttgart, Germany; and Salt Lake City and New York in the United States.

The Royal Ballet School has its own system of training, which evolves over the eight years of schooling. Students are appraised each year by a panel of school staff and professional dancers and teachers.

When students transfer to the Upper School, they can wear any shoes they wish and are not limited to Freed shoes; instead, they are encouraged to experiment. Students in the advanced classes at White Lodge and at the Upper School wear deshanked pointe shoes for ballet classes.

City Ballet School of San Diego

941 Garnet Avenue (alley entrance)
San Diego, CA 92109
Telephone: (858) 274-6058
Fax: (858) 272-8375
E-mail: info@cityballet.org
www.cityballet.org

Before starting the City Ballet Company and School of San Diego in 1993, Steven and Elizabeth Rowe-Wistrich danced with the Boston and Stuttgart Ballet Companies. Steven is the artistic director of both the company and school.

The school offers classes in technique, pointe, variations, *pas de deux*, jazz, and Pilates. There is also an extensive adult program with both technique and pointe classes.

There are six levels of ballet in the student program starting at the age of six. Twice a year the students' progress is evaluated. Advanced students may be asked to work as trainees or apprentices for the company.

Pointe work begins at the second level. (There are two levels below this, Ballet I and IB.) Usually the students are required to be in Ballet II for two years before going on pointe, and will have prepointe classes once a week with Elizabeth Wistrich. The students in this level take four classes per week, and the age range is eight to ten. All pointe exercises are done facing the barre, and the children work on pointe for fifteen to twenty minutes, one day a week. These young students must leave their pointe shoes at the studio, where they are placed in boxes with individual name tags.

At level III the children must take six classes a week, three of them pointe classes after an hour-and-a-half technique class. The students do a pointe-barre following the same format as a regular ballet class, and then come to the center.

By level IV they are taking eight classes a week. Pointe class has a shorter barre, including roll-up and spring *relevés, échappés,* and *piqués.* Center work follows the same format as a ballet technique class.

The advanced level, V, takes ten to twelve classes per week. The students are on pointe every day, except on the day they have jazz class. They put on their pointe shoes after barre in several of the ballet technique classes.

As well as a very extensive summer camp program for the younger students, the advanced students are fortunate to participate in a three-week intensive in August. Dancers from all over the United States and abroad come to study with world-renowned artists such as Gelsey Kirkland, Fernando Bujones, David Howard, and Susan Jaffe.

Houston Ballet Ben Stevenson Academy

1921 West Bell
Houston, TX 77019
Telephone: (713) 523-6300
E-mail: info@houstonballet.org
www.houstonballet.org

The Houston Ballet Ben Stevenson Academy is housed in a large, two-story building, which it shares with the Houston Ballet. Stanton Welch serves as artistic director of both the Houston Ballet and the Ben Stevenson Academy. Mr. Welch succeeds Ben Stevenson, who currently serves as artistic director emeritus of Houston Ballet. Clara Cravey, principal of the academy, is currently supervising the eight-level program designed for the academy. Students who reach levels seven and eight are judged by the school's staff to have potential to function at a professional level, either as dancers or choreographers. The school at this time typically provides fifty-five percent of Houston Ballet's company members.

Young students begin training in the Pre-School Division, which includes Creative Dance and Pre-Ballet. The Creative Dance program is designed for students four and five years old. At age six, students are moved into a Pre-Ballet program for one full year. Students begin the Main School Division, which houses levels one through seven, at age seven. The lowest levels, Ballet 1 and 2, meet once a week. Ballet 3 meets three times a week, Ballet 4 and 5 meet four times a week, and Ballet 6 meets five times a week. The students at the seventh level take class daily. The Professional Division, Ballet 8, is designed to prepare students for a professional career in dance, and students are present daily, from 9 A.M. until 4 P.M., for classes and rehearsals. These students are also called into company rehearsals when needed.

Throughout the training process, students proceed through the program on an individual basis. They are not automatically moved from level to level, but are evaluated on the basis of physical and emotional readiness. Parents are invited and encouraged to watch class twice a year during an observation week, which helps them understand how their child is progressing through the year. Students with professional potential are advised to forgo a university education until they have established their professional careers. However, students are encouraged to continue their academic studies while attending the program with correspondence courses offered by various universities.

Students begin pointe classes in level four, with three pointe classes a week, two of which last forty-five minutes and the other thirty minutes. In Ballet 5 the students have three forty-five-minute pointe classes a week, and in Ballet 6 the students have two one-hour pointe classes a week. In Ballet 6 and Ballet 7 a *pas de deux* class is added to the schedule once a week, in which pointe shoes are also necessary. The *pas de deux* class is extremely critical in determining the student's stamina and endurance on pointe. Ballet 8 students have a daily technique class, two pointe classes a week, and two weekly *pas de deux* classes. They also have five additional rehearsals for which they must wear pointe shoes.

Pointe classes generally follow technique classes. The upper levels have a fifteen-minute break between classes, but the younger students do not. All students in levels five through eight are encouraged to take technique classes in old, broken-down pointe shoes, two to three times a week. This is encouraged in order to develop strength, and to prepare the students for jumping, running, and other technical movements in pointe shoes. Younger students are not allowed to do this because of the potential for injury. Forcing students is avoided throughout the program of study in favor of slow, careful progress toward an ultimate goal of using the body to its maximum capability.

Children beginning pointe are introduced to both the roll and spring action of the foot in *relevé*. The faculty feels that the roll (going up through the top of the foot, and then through the top of the pointe shoe, so that the instep is lifted and rolling through the foot) strengthens the foot and ankle, which allows the dancer to spring without wobble or give. Both are valuable tools for a female dancer.

Academy students are allowed to use elastic on their shoes in addition to ribbons, and must wear tights while wearing pointe shoes. Teachers at the academy use a combination of Cecchetti and RAD methods, but do not follow a set class syllabus. Teachers carefully fit shoes and properly assist in helping each and every student to find the correct shoe for his or her foot type.

National Ballet School

105 Maitland Street
Toronto, Ontario
Canada M4Y 1E4
Telephone: (416) 964-3780
E-mail: info@nbs-enb.on.ca
www.nbs-enb.on.ca

Canada's National Ballet School (NBS) was founded in 1959 by Celia Franca and Betty Oliphant to train professional dancers for the newly formed National Ballet of Canada. By the time it was incorporated four years later, NBS had expanded its mandate to include training dancers for companies across Canada and around the world.

NBS combines professional dance training, academic education, and residential care in an integrated, student-centered site. One hundred and fifty students, from age eleven to nineteen, are enrolled in the full-time Professional Ballet/Academic Program and Post-Secondary (Intensive Dance) Programs. Admission to the full-time training programs is by audition only, with students being assessed for physical suitability, coordination, flexibility, musicality, and expression. NBS also offers a full-time teacher training program (by audition) and part-time classes for children and adults. In total, close to seven hundred students enter the school's facilities and programs each week.

NBS is housed in a collection of buildings on two heritage blocks in downtown Toronto. Facilities include nine studios, each with a sprung floor, surfaced in either unfinished pine or linoleum, and custom-built to dance specifications; eight academic classrooms and various labs; two residences (one each for males and females); a 297-seat stage training facility, and The Shoe Room®, the school's pointe shoe and dancewear retail store.

The school is currently engaged in an $87.5 million (CDN) capital expansion and renovation project. Called Project Grand Jeté, it will triple the size of its physical plant, providing twelve double-height studios, a resource center and cross-training facility in a new Dance Training Center; new academic classrooms and labs in an Academic Center; new and renovated residences, and expanded space for The Shoe Room®.

Mavis Staines succeeded Betty Oliphant as the artistic director in 1989. Under Staines, NBS has developed an increasingly strong international reputation for achieving artistic excellence through a holistic approach to ballet training. The school has pioneered the use of health professionals to support its goal of developing healthy, critically thoughtful artists, who will expand the parameters of ballet as an art form. NBS graduates dance in close to forty companies throughout Canada and around the world, and make up eighty percent of the National Ballet of Canada, including the company's artistic director, James Kudelka.

Since the demands placed on professional ballet dancers are broader and more intense than ever before, NBS has developed a sophisticated training program that extends far beyond the ballet studio to include modern dance, exposure to non-Western dance forms, conditioning, music, history of art and ballet, anatomy and neuromuscular understanding, nutrition, emotional counseling, professional performance experience, career counseling, choreography, and more.

NBS has developed its own dance curriculum that is divided into seven levels. These are studied over an eight-year period (from grade six to post-secondary). The first four levels form the foundation of the students' technique. Since physical development varies greatly from student to student, it is not unusual for students to study one level for two academic years. Students have a full day, with four to five hours of academic classes interspersed with four or more hours of dance, dance-related activities, and conditioning. Students' schedules are often individualized, and can include tutorial sessions to address specific technical concerns.

Performance experience is gained through regular presentations from the school's theater, as well as participation in the productions of the National Ballet of Canada. In addition, NBS has an exchange program, where selected senior students are introduced to the larger dance community by spending part of their summer studying with other professional academies around the world.

Pointe work is introduced in the second half of level one, typically at age eleven. From this level on, pointe classes augment all girls' daily ballet class training. Each girl is accompanied by her ballet teacher for her first pointe shoe fitting. One of two full-time footwear specialists employed by NBS is also present at every fitting. It is the collaboration between the fitter and the teacher that ensures the best fit for each individual student.

The NBS philosophy is that students who are beginning pointe work should be fitted in a flexible shoe with a lighter insole and a softer wing block, in order to encourage them to increase their articulation and foot strength. For their first pair of pointe shoes, most NBS students are fitted with either a Freed *Studio Light* or a Suffolk *Solo Light*™, both of which were developed in collaboration with NBS to meet the school's specific needs. Since the insole is more flexible, students are better able, from the very beginning, to roll through their foot to establish correct placement on pointe. Also, the softer shoe forces the students to work on increasing their foot strength, since the shoe will not hold them up on pointe if the dancer's muscles are not fully engaged. This approach encourages young dancers to develop their own strength instead of "sitting" in the shoe and relying on the hardness of the shoe to hold them up—often in an incorrect position.

The Pointe Shoe Coordinator (who is also a full-time ballet teacher at NBS) is the liaison between the artistic staff, the footwear specialists, and the individual dance students. Any ballet staff member can request a consultation among all parties involved whenever the need arises. Consultation with the NBS physiotherapy department and the podiatrist is also encouraged so that the health of the dancer and her feet are always of primary concern. The open communication between the artistic staff and The Shoe Room® means that many problems with pointe shoes can be addressed before they become an issue.

More than twenty years ago, NBS created its own in-house shoe room similar to ones commonly found in professional ballet companies. This was because the school was not in close proximity to any of the pointe shoe manufacturers favored by professional dancers, nor were there any dance retail stores in Toronto supplying the required type of pointe shoes. NBS undertook to stock pointe shoes in all sizes and widths in order to fit their own students. A footwear specialist was also hired to oversee the ordering and fitting of the shoes.

Over the years, the stock of pointe shoes at NBS grew to reflect the more sophisticated requirements of today's classically trained dancers. Carol Beevers joined NBS as their footwear specialist in 1986, and split her time between the shoe rooms of both the National Ballet School and the National Ballet of Canada. Along the way, she gained a wealth of experience fitting all kinds of feet, from those of the very beginner to dancers well established in their careers. During the course of her dual career, Carol has worked with several different pointe shoe manufacturers to develop and then, together with students of the National Ballet School, test many of the pointe shoes on the market today. Currently a pointe shoe is being designed by Suffolk Pointe Company specifically for the National Ballet School.

In 1998, the National Ballet School opened a retail store called The Shoe Room® so that the expertise developed over the years could be shared with the larger dance community. The care taken with NBS students is now available to all other dancers. Many pointe shoes not available locally are now accessible through The Shoe Room® at Canada's National Ballet School.

Paris Opéra Ballet School

École de danse de l'Opéra National de Paris
20, allée de la Danse
92000 Nanterre
France
Telephone: 00 33 1 40 01 8000
Fax: 00 33 1 40 01 8050
E-mail: vhurteloup@opera-de-paris.fr
Website: www.operadeparis.fr

Claude Bessy was director of the Paris Opéra Ballet School from 1972 to 2004. Her successor, Elisabeth Platel, oversees a magnificent facility that includes twelve dance studios, academic classrooms, and dormitories. The school, in existence since the reign of Louis XIV, is funded by a foundation.

Students are accepted into the school at the age of nine. They may be beginners or students who have studied elsewhere before applying to the Paris Opéra. Great emphasis is placed upon accepting students with perfect bodies. The school prefers students to have a long Achilles tendon to allow a very deep *plié*, as well as a high instep with a flexible ankle. Successful candidates should also have natural turnout.

Once accepted at the school, students live there during the week and spend weekends at home with their parents. A typical school day finds them in academic classes in the morning and dance classes in the afternoon.

The majority of the students who enroll in the school complete six years of training there and then enter the Opéra Ballet. Exams are administered at the end of each year to determine which students are qualified to continue in the program. Those students who do not enter the Opéra Ballet may seek work in other countries or decide not to pursue professional careers.

Pointe is introduced into the curriculum in the second year, when the children are strong enough to work on *demi-pointe* and on one foot. At the beginning of the year, students have a full class off pointe, then put on pointe shoes and return to the barre. As students progress through the second year, they graduate to doing pointe exercises in the center.

No particular style or make of shoe is suggested, and each student is encouraged to find the shoe best suited to her foot. Shoes are fitted in dance shops and then brought to the school for final approval. Students use Kleenex and cotton in their shoes, but are not allowed to wear anything synthetic.

The school requests that students use pointe shoes with half insole for class rather than soft ballet slippers, which are called *demi-pointe* shoes. *Demi-pointe* shoes are only worn by very young students, for occasional rehearsals, or in the event of injury.

Royal Swedish Ballet School

Box 17516
SE-118 91 Stockholm
Telephone: 46 (0) 8 508 33 510
Fax: 46 (0) 8 508 33 520
E-mail: stockholm@svenskabalettskolan.com
www.svenskabalettskolan.com

The Opera Ballet School was inaugurated in Sweden by King Gustaf III in 1773, and until 1981 it offered classes after regular school hours. However, in 1981, the school's traditions and resources were transferred to the municipal school system of Stockholm, under the authority of the Board of Education, and the school was renamed the Royal Swedish Ballet School. While the Royal Swedish Ballet School maintains close contact with the Royal Opera Theatre, it now integrates traditional academic studies with dance education, a goal achieved after years of planning and discussion.

Royal Swedish Ballet School provides professional dance training to the Royal Ballet and other ballet companies in Sweden and around the world, as well as offering dance education to those interested in allied dance professions such as teaching and choreography.

The school, now directed by Kerstin Lidström (Gösta Svalberg at the time of our original research), offers a six-year comprehensive program and a two-year *gymnasium* (high school) program. It is located in an impressive facility, which contains nine studios, academic classrooms, and a 260-seat theater.

Auditions are held every March for entry into the school, which strives to have an equal number of girls and boys. Boys currently make up about forty-five percent of the enrollment of one hundred girls and eight-five boys. The Junior School is shared between four cities in Sweden: Stockholm, Gothenburg, Malmo, and Pitea. Continuation at the college level (after the age of sixteen) is only available in Stockholm, however. Students can enter the school at the beginning of any year, but are encouraged to start at age nine or ten for the best results. Students entering during the first six years usually come from the Stockholm area, but those who enter during the final two *gymnasium* years may come from other parts of Sweden or outside the country. Such students live in dormitory facilities, while most other students live at home throughout their schooling. Because of illness, a shift in interest, or a family move, students drop out of the program and are replaced by others each fall. As a consequence, class size can fall to eight or nine students.

Most entering classes of nine- and ten-year-olds have about thirty-two students. Boys and girls study dance in separate classes because of both technical and social considerations. The school is sensitive to the fact that boys may initially advance more slowly than girls, and does not want to subject boys to feeling "silly" in a co-educational class. Also, a concerted effort is made to provide boys with challenging, male-oriented dance training and repertory.

Academic classes are taken with children from the dance program, and from other programs as well, broadening the children's social contacts. By the time the students are fifteen, they are taking nineteen hours of dance classes a week, in addition to their academic load. However, their academic teachers are well aware of the nature of their special interest and are involved in the curriculum planning process. Issues like rehearsal and performance schedules are discussed by the entire faculty. The faculty finds that dance and academics seem to reinforce each other here, motivating students to care about their schooling.

Since the school is part of the Swedish public school system, tuition is free. Students wear standardized uniforms but must supply their own leotards and tights.

Shoes are provided free of charge. The school tries to find the right pointe shoes for each student, and makes a variety of brands available, including Freed, Gamba, Capezio, and K.H. Martins. A staff member handles all shoe purchasing and distribution for the student body, which is a more difficult job than in a traditional ballet company because of constantly growing and changing feet.

Girls go on pointe at age nine or ten after three months in the school, beginning very slowly at the barre with both hands. Their rate of progress is determined by their individual strength.

Students have one teacher for their first two years, then usually stay with another teacher for a one-year period, until their *gymnasium* years, when they again stay with one teacher for two years. For the first two years, students take ballet class for one-and-a-half hours, five times a week. They also take an improvisation class and a gymnastic-acrobatic class weekly. The acrobatic class is popular with the boys as well as the girls, since it allows them freedom at a time when precise, limited movement is stressed in their ballet classes.

Character classes are introduced in the second year and are continued until graduation. Modern and jazz training are introduced in the fourth year, and repertory classes start in the fifth year. Students are often taught repertory being performed by the Royal Swedish Ballet at the Opera House, so they can substitute for *corps* members. In the sixth year, they begin *pas de deux* work once a week and then add an additional *pas de deux* class the last two years.

The school has its own syllabus created by the staff, but students are exposed to a variety of styles as they progress to an advanced level. Most of the teachers have been professional dancers in Sweden, although teachers from other professional backgrounds have taught at the school as well.

At the time of our original research, Marianne Orlando, who was a prima ballerina with the Royal Swedish Ballet and also danced with American Ballet Theatre, taught the female students during their last two years at the school. Orlando trained at the Opera Ballet School from the age of eight, and studied in Russia and Hungary. Consequently, she is anchored by the Swedish tradition, but is also able to enrich her students' training with her diverse experiences.

Orlando's students were sixteen years old, and took class for an hour and a half, six times a week. At the beginning of the *gymnasium* year, she gave twenty to thirty minutes of pointe at the end of each class. As the year progressed, she built up to one full pointe class a week. She taught a combination of springing and rolling. Since Orlando believes that muscles should do the work for the beginning dancers, she felt that hard shoes were dangerous and encouraged students to work in lighter footwear.

Svalberg compared some classes at the school to fine wine from a particularly good vintage; others classes are not as good, she explained. However, because of the public school setting, the teachers' mission is to treat every student with the same concern, whether they appear destined for a professional career or not. The school believes that dance training is never wasted, and offers extensive benefits in later life.

San Francisco Ballet School

455 Franklin Street
San Francisco, CA 94102
Telephone: (415) 553-4641
Fax: (415) 861-2684
E-mail: school@sfballet.org
www.sfballet.org

Helgi Tomasson is the artistic director of the San Francisco Ballet, and director of the San Francisco Ballet School. Although Nancy Johnson Carter served as manager of the school at the time of our original research, today Gloria Govrin is the associate director. The school offers classes in technique, pointe, men's work, *pas de deux*, contemporary dance, music, and character dancing.

Students are accepted at age eight into a graduated curriculum with eight levels, and must attend at least two classes a week. Progress is evaluated twice a year. Advanced students may be invited to join the company as apprentices for one transitional year.

As a result of regional auditions, there are a large number of new students at the school each summer. San Francisco Ballet competes with the School of American Ballet and other major schools for these students, whom they consider "the cream of the crop."

There are eight graded levels of ballet. Pointe usually starts at the fourth level, depending on individual readiness. By this level, students take five technique classes a week, and pointe work is integrated into these classes. Each level has a "home-room" teacher who gives technique classes; other instructors teach special classes such as *pas de deux* and character. At levels six, seven, and eight, students wear their pointe shoes for all technique classes.

Faculty member Jocelyn Vollmar described an advanced pointe class that would follow a one-and-three-quarter-hour technique class. The pointe class begins with a short barre including a few *relevés, échappés, piqués,* rolling up and rolling through the foot, and springing up. She keeps the class in the center most of the time to discourage reliance on the barre.

School of American Ballet

70 Lincoln Center Plaza
New York, NY 10023-6592
Telephone: (212) 769-6600
Fax: (212) 769-4897
E-mail: info@sab.org
www.sab.org

Located at Lincoln Center Plaza, the School of American Ballet is the official school of the New York City Ballet and a constituent of Lincoln Center for the Performing Arts. Founded in 1934 by George Balanchine and Lincoln Kirstein, it is now financially supported by private and public sources. Nathalie Gleboff is executive director, and Peter Martins is chairman of the faculty. At the end of their schooling, many School of American Ballet students are taken into the New York City Ballet company, with which the school is affiliated. Ninety percent of the dancers in the company are trained at the School of American Ballet. The rest of the graduates are found in other major American and European companies.

Students are admitted to the school through auditions. General physical qualities sought are long legs, narrow knees, high insteps, long necks, small heads, and natural turnout.

The school has five children's divisions, and children are admitted between the ages of eight and nine. Students are placed on pointe in January of their first year of study. At that time they are given fifteen minutes of pointe at the end of their regular three weekly hour-and-a-half technique classes. By the fifth year, they are taking four hour-and-a-half ballet classes a week, and a one-hour pointe class a week.

There is a Parallel Division of ten- to twelve-year-old beginners who start pointe classes during their third year, with one hour a week. Stronger children in this division may start in their second year. In this program, students take three classes a week the first year, and six classes a week the following year, to allow them to catch up with the students in the Children's Division.

As the students enter the intermediate level, the Children's and Parallel Divisions merge. In the intermediate level, the students take six ballet classes and two pointe classes a week. By the time they move to the Advanced Division they are taking a total of ten classes a week. Students are evaluated at the end of each year, and after the age of fourteen may be encouraged to take as many as twelve classes a week, or eighteen hours of class work, plus rehearsals for a workshop performance in the spring.

The School of American Ballet also offers a summer program for gifted students from around the country; they must be twelve years of age and over, at intermediate and advanced levels. Regional auditions are held around the country for this summer course. A thorough knowledge of fundamental ballet positions and exercises is required. Applicants are expected to have well-proportioned, flexible, coordinated bodies, good turnout, and high insteps. They cannot be overweight and must be at a stage of technical advancement appropriate for their age. The summer course includes work in academic ballet, pointe, variations, *adagio,* and character.

Pointe Training in Private Studios

École Nationale de Ballet Contemporain

4816 Rue Rivard
Montréal, Quebec
Canada H2J 2N6
Telephone: (514) 849-4929
Fax: (514) 849-6017
www.enbc.org

The National School of Contemporary Ballet values the exploration of new ideas as well as the traditions of classical ballet. Classical technique is an integral part of their pedagogical method, acting as a base for future evolution with boundless possibilities.

The school's program was developed by two educators from the Opéra de Paris: Didier Chirpaz, executive director, and Françoise Vaussenat, director of studies. It relies on the elements of the French School. In tune with the realities of the international job market, the program encourages expression in all dance forms and styles. It also integrates character dance and contemporary dance. Studies take place over a period of ten years, from grade five through to the college level. Throughout the years of study, all students receive between three and five hours of dance courses daily.

To be admitted to the National School of Contemporary Ballet, the candidate must meet the age requirements for the level, satisfy the standards for dance, and be in good health. The selection process takes the form of an audition before a jury composed of the artistic director and pedagogical advisers from the school. The audition evaluates body type, coordination, flexibility, musicality, and expression, as well as the motivation a student has to pursue a career as a dancer.

All students registered in the program must also meet academic requirements at the beginning of the academic year, and provide a medical certificate attesting to the satisfactory health of the student. Before admitting a new student, the primary and secondary academic schools, École Saint-Joseph and Pensionnat St-Nom-de-Marie, evaluate the academic record of the candidate thoroughly. Admission to the college diploma program of the Cégep du Vieux Montréal requires that a candidate be a

Canadian citizen, have a high school leaving certificate or the equivalent, and have sufficient knowledge of French to complete the courses.

At the National School of Contemporary Ballet, pointe is introduced toward the end of the year for eleven-year-olds who are in the second or third year of daily classes. They have ten to fifteen minutes twice a week facing the barre, with very simple exercises, such as standing in sixth position on flat and pressing the arch of the other foot forward. This helps the student feel the shoe, and it develops the arch. In this beginning stage on pointe, they stand on both feet.

The following year the students do twenty minutes of pointe. They are still facing the barre, but as the year progresses, they will do the exercises with one hand on the barre. Basic work on two feet, such as *relevés* in first and second, and possibly *échappés*, are practiced in the center. Françoise Vaussenat points out that, of course, all of this depends on the dancers, since some classes advance earlier than others to more complicated steps.

As the dancers progress to higher levels, they will have hour-long pointe classes several times a week. The level is very high in the last two years since the school is for professional aspirants.

The teacher accompanies the students for their first shoe fittings and closely supervises not only the fittings, but also the sewing of the ribbons. The students do not darn their shoes, but the older ones with several years of experience, use shellac to prolong the life of the shoe.

Cumberland Dance Company

211 North Enola Drive
Enola, PA 17025
Telephone: (717) 732-2172
E-mail: scarlino@cumbelanddance.org
www.cumberlanddance.org

The Cumberland Dance Company, a preprofessional company and school is located just outside Harrisburg, Pennsylvania, and is directed by Sandra Carlino. When students decide they would like to pursue ballet on a higher level and have more performing opportunities, they audition for the company's Apprentice Level. While in the school, the students take ballet class two days a week. If they move to the Apprentice Company, they will stay there for one or two years and attend class three days a week. The next move is to Company Level I where they spend two years. When the students are nine years old, they are taken into Company Level II where they begin pointe training at the beginning of the year.

When it is time to choose first pointe shoes, Carlino recommends a shoe with a medium shank: not too soft, not too hard. When she has students who are especially muscular, she puts them into a shoe with a stronger shank. Most important for her is for them to have a shank that allows them all to "roll-through"; she dislikes the new shoes that are elastomeric, because it seems that the girls are either up or down—that there is no "in between." She has had good results with Capezio *Glissé* or *Plié*, Freed *Studio,* and Grishko shoes. She says that Grishkos are good roll-through shoes.

With Carlino supervising, the class goes as a group to the nearest dance shop. Helen, the owner, and a very knowledgeable fitter, patiently fits each new pointe student. They call in advance so that Helen can set aside the time she needs to find exactly the right shoe for each girl.

When they get back to the studio, they all sit down on the floor with their stitch kits. They are taught to cut their toenails, tape their toes, and sew on their ribbons. By allowing students to choose the best shoe (or about three properly fitted shoes), Carlino eliminates the annoying problem of students constantly adjusting their shoes in class, something she will simply not allow.

In Level II the dancers take class four days a week. They have a two-hour technique class and then an hour-long pointe class. Once a week they take a Variations Class. The girls leave their pointe shoes on, but the choreography is all two-footed work, including steps like *échappés.* The articulation of the feet is emphatically stressed. The girls are taught how to walk in the shoes on three-quarter, not half-pointe. They are encouraged to rise high up in the shoes so that their heels are not near the ground, and they are trained to take smaller steps. All this work aims, ultimately, to make the shoes feel more like slippers than blocks.

Level II introduces *sous-sus* traveling forward, walking in fifth position, simple *pas de bourrées,* and other steps on two feet at the barre. About ten minutes will be spent doing center work. When the girls reach Level III, they must come to class five days a week, when they will do a two-hour technique class and a one-and-a-half-hour pointe class.

When the students enter the highest level, level IV, and are taking class five or six days a week, all classes are taken on pointe. They are not necessarily pointe classes, but the dancers wear their pointe shoes at all times. Early in the company's existence, a principal dancer from the Pennsylvania Ballet set a ballet on the girls. He said then that they needed to wear their shoes every single day; that pointe shoes are not part of their costume.

Artistic Director Carlino says that the dancers are recognized throughout the area for their strong pointe work. She attributes that to her strong focus on consistent pointe training, and teaching students how to use their toes in the shoes. She feels that the hardest thing is for a teacher to have her students bend the shoes with the tips of their toes. She also is insistent that, for advanced dancers, pointe shoes be worn in all classes, so that they begin to feel like an extension of the body. Her advice to other teachers is to be stern with the students, and not to feel sorry for them. It sounds harsh, but in the end the dancers are always happy with themselves when they feel prepared for any professional experience they might encounter.

Unlike many professional schools, these students are encouraged to go to college or university after graduating from high school, even though several have gone directly into ballet or dance companies. Therefore, Carlino says she does not encounter problems with parents. It is quite common to have a struggle over whether to attend school or dance professionally. She looks for schools that have at least ten to fifteen hours of ballet a week, and says that she is partial to Mercyhurst, Butler, and Indiana University in Indiana; North Carolina School of the Arts; and SUNY-Purchase in New York. She has also had students with a preference for modern dance who attended Juilliard in New York City.

Ruth Page Foundation School

1016 North Dearborn Parkway
Chicago, IL 60610
Telephone: (312) 337-6543
Fax: (312) 337-6542
E-mail: info@ruthpage.org
www.ruthpage.org

The Ruth Page Foundation School, directed by Larry Long, has as its goal the production of dancers who can easily assimilate the style of various major companies. Long describes the school's curriculum as an American application of a Russian approach.

Students start pointe work at the intermediate (Ballet 4) level, when they are taking four classes a week. Children are evaluated for pointe based on individual readiness, and are not placed on pointe *en masse*, but when each is mentally and physically ready to accept the challenge. No student is placed on pointe before age ten. The school feels that once a child is strong enough, progress on pointe will be rapid.

During the first year on pointe, students take one pointe class a week, following a technique class. The staff finds an entire pointe class more useful to the student than relegating a portion of a technique class to pointe. During the second year, if they have not encountered any problems on pointe, students take one pointe class a week at a more advanced level. If they need to work on stretching their feet or gaining strength, they repeat beginning pointe and also take the second-year class. During the third year on pointe, students take a second-level and a third-level pointe class. When they enter the advanced class, they take an advanced pointe class and an intermediate pointe class. When the director feels they are strong enough, students take a *pas de deux* class. A special adult pointe class is also offered.

Beginning pointe students wear Capezios, with the staff favoring *Contempora* for those with wide feet, and *Nicolini* for narrower feet. Suede-tipped shoes are not allowed, but extremely soft shoes are also avoided for beginners. Parents are oriented to expect to buy at least three pairs of shoes from September to June if their child is taking one pointe class a week. They are told they may have to buy more than three pairs if their child has a problem finding the correct shoes.

Steps On Broadway

2121 Broadway at 74th Street
New York, NY 10023
Telephone: (212) 874-2410
Fax: (212) 579-1479
E-mail: theschool@stepsnyc.com
www.stepsnyc.com/school

Steps On Broadway, a private dance studio located at Broadway and 74th Street in New York, has been primarily known for its open classes, taught by some of the world's leading teachers, which attract top-notch professional dancers. A more recent addition to the school is the Children's Division, known as The School at Steps, which is directed by

Kate Thomas. This program, which is now ten years old, offers classes in ballet, jazz, modern dance, hip hop, theater dance, Isadora Duncan technique, pointe, and tap dance. Little Steps I and II is for ages two to four, Pre-Dance I and II for ages four to six, and Basic Technique for ages six to eight. At age eight, the graded levels and real curriculum begin. Prerequisites, in terms of the number of classes taken per week, begin at Level III.

The School at Steps is designed for students interested in exploring various dance styles, as well as those already focused on a career. Each child's level placement in class is carefully selected by the administration and faculty, and certain levels require an audition. Pointe work is carefully introduced, and is not offered until the student has developed enough strength and an understanding of placement to make a natural transition.

At Level IV at least three weekly classes are required in all disciplines. Ballet is required, in addition to all upper-level jazz classes. Faculty member Amanda Turner contrasts teaching in this type of environment to the vocational ballet boarding school she attended in England; her classes began at seven forty-five in the morning, and when she was rehearsing, she did not finish until ten or eleven o'clock at night. She said that she and the other students were "totally living" ballet. Here the children are doing many other things; they are at school all day, and many of them have other hobbies and interests. Director Kate Thomas tells the parents that when the students are twelve or thirteen, it is time to make some decisions: they cannot do everything. The parents and students become aware of the commitment needed to progress to the upper levels.

Turner says that certain sports can be counterproductive to dance training. She tells the story of a student who came in every week with various sports-related injuries to her legs and feet. Turner advised her, "When you see the ball coming, run away from it!"

Pointe begins when the children are eleven or twelve, and they have reached Level V. Amanda Turner starts her classes with a pointe-barre only because she feels they first have to build endurance before doing more pointe work. Pointe is done after a technique class so the students are already warm. Turner feels that the hardest thing for the dancers is making the transition from a flat, comfy canvas, slipper-type shoe to a pointe shoe. Suddenly they have this extra layer under their feet. Therefore, she puts great emphasis on shaping the foot. She has also found that beginner pointe students generally have a difficult time with second position because of a lack of inner thigh strength. She works the girls in a "baby" second position to guarantee that they will not end up in a split.

Faculty member Martha Chapman says that in her Pre-Pointe classes she uses a concept initiated by Peff Modelski, a well-known master teacher at Steps. She makes students familiar with the concept of "pushing down to go up," which is used in all ballet technique, but is particularly necessary for pointe. Exercises are done sitting and lying on the floor to strengthen abdominal and pelvic muscles, and to prepare these muscles for use when on pointe. To feel the energy through the lower leg, the students sit on their heels and push to an upright position, which engages the abdomen and pelvic area. In this exercise, the ankle is not lifted from the floor and the torso must be held.

Additional exercises have the students sit upright with their feet placed against a wall. They practice pushing away from the wall in parallel position. After this is accomplished, they do it turned out, and then with one foot. First it is executed barefoot, and then wearing shoes. It gives an accurate sense of how one must push through the entire leg in order to *relevé* properly.

Once they move to the barre, Chapman has them stand in parallel position. They step up to pointe, then press down through the right leg, and bring the left foot to pointe while rolling through the foot. They alternate, and may then do the exercise in fifth position. Chapman spends a lot of time in the first year articulating the foot and concentrating on being able to roll up and down through the shoe. She emphasizes going through three-quarter pointe on the way up and down, beginning with straight-legged *relevés* pushing down through the floor to go up. This is first done in parallel, often facing sideways to the mirror so the students can turn their heads and see what the foot must do. They then progress to a turned-out position in first and second positions.

Next the student progresses to starting a *relevé* from *plié*, maintaining the articulation of the foot on the way up and down. First-year students will do almost exclusively two-footed work which includes *relevés* in first and second positions, and also *sous-sus* and *échappé*. To understand the concept of sliding the shoe along the floor, as in *échappé*, Chapman uses an idea she learned from teacher Debra Jo Hughes. The students sit on a chair or bench, hold the barre, and slide the feet from position to position, without having weight on the legs.

By the end of the first year, depending on the student, *piqué* is added, which involves pushing from one foot to two, and then one foot to one, as in *coupé derrière* or *devant*. Next, they move on to the more difficult *pas marché*, which begins with a *piqué* and involves rolling through the foot, while the other leg does a *développé en avant*.

In the second year, the students take a half-hour pointe class after a full technique class. They start at the barre first, pushing from two feet onto one, as in *passé relevé*. Chapman spends a lot of time talking about the energy of the torso pulling away from the legs. When the students can *relevé* onto one foot with steady energy in the torso and a strong roll through in the feet, they then try it away from the barre. She also has the students do *piqués* starting away from the barre, and moving toward it. Later they raise the leg to *arabesque* or *attitude derrière*.

In the third and fourth years, the class progresses to multiple *relevés* and turns in all positions.

Leslie Browne, well-known star of the movie *The Turning Point* and other movies, danced with New York City Ballet and was a principal dancer with American Ballet Theatre. She now teaches the advanced level (Level VII) pointe classes at Steps. Leslie works at shaping the feet and developing the arch. "You're wearing pointe shoes. You've got to make them look good!" she tells her students. She stresses that while on pointe, students must place the weight directly in the middle of the shoe.

Leslie has worked with the advanced pointe class for several years. When the students first came to her, she very carefully introduced them to pointe. At first she found she had to work with them in two groups, because some girls have stronger ankles and good arches which makes it easier for them to progress. Her Ballet VII students are now learning classical variations from ballets such as *La Bayadère* and *Paquita*.

Until recently, most of the students in Leslie's Level VII class came from the School of American Ballet or other professional schools. The school is now achieving its goal of feeding its own students into this advanced level by building up the quality of the lower levels of the school.

Director Kate Thomas states that The School at Steps is committed to "developing a privately run dance program for New York City; for all levels, and with great teachers, a strong curriculum and high standards."

Sample Pointe Classes

While traveling across the United States and to Europe to gather information for this book, we had the opportunity to observe many wonderful pointe classes. Each of these classes had something unique and important to offer.

Because many of the teachers we surveyed indicated an interest in knowing how other instructors teach the various levels of pointe classes, we thought we would choose a representative sampling of exercises offered in some of the schools we visited. These exercises were notated by Janice Barringer.

The following abbreviations are used throughout this chapter:

    B+   Balanchine coined this phrase, meaning that the back foot is tendu derrière with both ankles touching.

    bk   back

    ft   foot

    frt   front

    L   left

    pt   pointe

    R   right

    xs   number of times, with 4xs meaning four times

References to the fixed points of the practice room and term definitions have been drawn from the third edition of Gail Grant's *Technical Manual and Dictionary of Classical Ballet* (New York: Dover Books, 1982).

BEGINNER CLASSES

First Day on Pointe, School of American Ballet

This segment is typical of a first pointe class; it takes place the last fifteen minutes of an hour-and-a-half ballet class.

BARRE

Exercise 1

Standing in parallel or natural position with both hands on the barre:
1 2 3 4   5 6 7 8
Roll slowly up through the metatarsal to full pointe, roll down. Repeat 4xs.

Exercise 2

Same as above except in 1st position.

Exercise 3

From 1st position: Roll up slowly to pointe (1 2 3 4), plié pushing out the instep (5 6 7 8), straighten legs (1 2 3 4), roll back down to 1st (5 6 7 8). Repeat 4xs.

Exercise 4

From 1st position: Press up to full pointe (1), hold, roll down to 1st (2 3 4). Repeat 8xs. Can be repeated in 2d position.

Exercise 5

From 1st position: Tendu R ft à la seconde (1), bring back to 1st in demi-plié (2), tendu L à la seconde (3), demi-plié in 1st (4), tendu R à la seconde (5), hold (6 7), bring back to 1st in demi-plié (8). Repeat 4xs.

Exercise 6

4th position, R ft frt: Rise to full pointe (1 2), press heel forward and release (3), press forward and release (4 5 6 7), roll down to 4th (8). Repeat and then same with L ft frt.

Exercise 7

5th position, R ft frt: Rise to full pointe (1), pull legs closely together (2), roll down (3 4). Repeat 4xs. Same with L.

Exercise 8

1st position, L hand on barre: Rise to pointe and walk down length of barre, turn to barre and return.

Second Day on Pointe, School of American Ballet

During this fifteen-minute segment, the instructor repeated continually that students must have an "excellent" position of the feet, meaning a nicely turned-out position. She would say, "Try to stretch the arch" as she took a foot in her hand and pressed the heel forward. Other instructions were, "Don't look down; stretch all your toes; chin up; push your foot more, and more, more, more!"

BARRE

Exercise 1

1st position facing barre: Tendu R à la seconde, demi-plié in 1st, tendu L à la seconde, demi-plié in 1st, tendu R à la seconde, hold, demi-plié in 1st and straighten. Same to L and repeat.

Exercise 2

1st position facing barre: Rise to full pointe, hold, hold, roll down off pointe. Execute 8xs.

Exercise 3

Same as exercise 2, but in 2d position.

Exercise 4

Same as exercise 2, but in 4th position. R ft frt first, then L ft frt.

The teacher took great care that the students pressed the heels forward.

Exercise 5

Same as exercise 2, but in 5th, and being sure to bring legs together into a tight 5th position in the rise. R ft frt first, then L ft frt.

CENTER

Exercise I

Changement 16 xs.
Révérence.

The teacher says, "Good-bye, girls," and they all reply, "Thank you."

Advanced Beginner Pointe Class, Ruth Page Foundation School

This class, inspired by Patricia Klekovic, is given at the end of the first year or beginning of the second and is done in ¾ time.

BARRE

Exercise 1

Facing barre, stand in parallel position: Step onto pointe in parallel position, R first, then L, holding barre with both hands. Roll off pointe slowly, demi-plié, and straighten knees. Step back slightly and repeat starting with L ft. (Teacher emphasizes aligning body as this is executed). Repeat. Music continues. Step away from barre; R ft tendu
$$\text{1-8} \quad \text{1-8}$$
devant, spring R L again, but this time into 5th en pointe, R ft frt.
$$\text{\& 1}$$
Bourrée down the barre to the R, passé L to place in frt, roll down into
$$\text{2 3 4} \qquad\qquad \text{5 6} \qquad\qquad \text{7}$$
demi-plié, step back onto R and tendu L devant. Repeat starting with
$$\text{8} \qquad\qquad \text{1-8}$$
L. Repeat last 16 counts.

Exercise 2

Facing barre, stand in parallel position, both hands on barre: Demi-plié,
$$\text{\&}$$
relevé, plié , relevé , plié, relevé , roll down. Repeat 7xs.
$$\text{1 \quad \& \quad 2 \quad \& \quad 3 \quad \& \quad 4}$$

Exercise 3

The stronger dancers place L hand on barre while the weaker ones use
both hands on barre. Feet in 1st position: Demi-plié, relevé en pointe,
$$\text{\& \quad 1}$$
plié, relevé, plié, relevé, roll down. Repeat 7xs.
$$\text{\& \quad 2 \quad \& \quad 3 \quad \& \quad 4}$$

Exercise 4

Facing barre, stand in parallel position, both hands on barre: Demi-plié,
$$\text{\&}$$
relevé en pointe, plié en pointe, straighten knees, roll down. Repeat 3xs.
$$\text{1 \quad hold 2 \quad 3 4 \qquad 5 6 \qquad 7 \quad 8}$$

The teacher tried to shape the feet correctly with her hands. She sat on the floor behind the dancer as she worked with the feet.

Exercise 5

Exercise 4 in 1st position.

Exercise 6

Facing barre, 1st position, both hands on barre. *One-half of class* begins.

    &   1   &

Demi-plié, échappé to 2d, return to 1st in plié. Continue for 2 counts

of 8. *The second half of* the class executes the exercise while the first half

    1–8   1–8

rests. Now the first group executes the exercise from 5th position fol-

    1–8   1–8

lowed by the second group.

Exercise 7

Facing the barre, 5th position, R ft frt, both hands on barre. *First half of*

    &   1   &   2

class: Demi-plié, sous-sus, plié, sous-sus. Continue through 8 counts.

Second half of class executes exercise. *First half* repeats 8 counts with L ft

frt. *Second half* repeats.

Exercise 8

The stronger dancers place L hand on barre while the weaker ones use

&

both hands while facing the barre. 5th position, R ft frt: Demi-plié,

  1   &   2   &   3   &   4

sous-sus, plié, sous-sus, plié, sous-sus, plié, relevé passé R leg from frt to

 &5&6&7&8   1–8

back. Same with L. Repeat. *Second group* executes the same 2 counts of

    &   1   &   2

8. *First group:* Demi-plié, relevé retiré devant, plié in 5th R ft frt, relevé

hold 3   4   5678   1–8 1–8

passé close 5th derrière. Same with L ft. Repeat.

Exercise 9

&

Facing barre, 5th position, R ft frt: *First group* starts: Demi-plié, relevé

1   &   2   &

retiré devant, plié in 5th R ft frt, relevé retiré devant, turn body slightly

3

to L (as a small windup to propel body in an en dehors turn), return

4   5 6 7 8

body, roll down to 5th, R ft bk. Repeat with L ft in frt. Repeat last 8

counts. *Second group:* Same.

Exercise 10

&

Facing barre, 5th position, R ft frt: *First group* starts: Demi-plié, relevé

1   2   3

passé en arrière to 4th position demi-plié, pirouette en pointe en dehors

4   5 6 7 8   1–8

closing 5th en arrière. Same with L ft in frt. Repeat. *Second group:* Same.

The teacher wants the students to hold the passé position for an extra

half count before closing in 5th en arrière.

Exercise 11

Repeat exercise 10 except the stronger students do it with one hand on the barre.

Exercise 12

Facing barre, 5th position, R ft frt. *First group* starts: Demi-plié, relevé
[&] ¹
on L with R in Russian sur le cou-de-pied pointed position, demi-plié
[&]
with R ft frt, relevé on R with L in Russian sur le cou-de-pied pointed,
²
demi-plié, continue alternating 3 & 4 & 5 & 6 & 7, demi-plié on L,
[&]
relevé on L (double relevé on & 7 & 8). Plié on both feet with R ft frt
and reverse last 8 counts. *Second group:* Repeat 1–16. *First group:* 1–16.
Second group: 1–16.

Exercise 13

L hand on barre, on the diagonal into the barre; standing on R ft, L in
croisé derrière. *First group* starts: Pas de bourrée en avant, pas de bourrée en arrière, pas de bourrée en avant, pas de bourrée en tournant en
dedans one-quarter turn (toward barre—ending facing into barre).
Now, with R hand on barre on diagonal, standing on R ft, L in croisé
devant: Pas de bourrée en arrière, pas de bourrée en avant, pas de bourrée
en arrière, pas de bourrée en tournant en dehors one-quarter turn (turning
toward barre—ending in original position). Repeat. *Second group:* 1–16.

Exercise 14

Facing barre, 5th position, R ft frt. *First group* starts: Demi-plié, relevé
onto L with R in Russian pointed sur le cou-de-pied devant, demi-plié
with R ft frt in 5th, relevé onto R with L in Russian pointed sur le
cou-de-pied derrière, demi-plié with R ft frt in 5th. Continue alternating
feet for the counts & 3 & 4 & 5 & 6 & 7. On the counts & 8 repeat the
relevé on L (double relevé). Demi-plié and begin by doing the relevé onto
the R with the L in sur de cou-de-pied derrière and continue for 8 counts.
Second group: Same. *First* and *Second groups* each repeat.

Exercise 15

Facing barre, both hands on barre. *First group* starts: Demi-plié, sous-sus, pas de bourrée suivi (Russian) or pas de bourrée couru en cinquième (French) commonly called bourrée-in place, slowly lifting only slightly off the ground. Lift [1]R to very low pointed sur le cou-de-pied position devant, [2]close to 5th, lift [3]L derrière, close to 5th, [4]lift [5]R, [6]close, lift [7]L, [8]close, lift [1]R, close, [2]lift [3]L, close, [4]lift [5]R, close, [6]lift [7]L, [8]close; faster-lift [1]R, step on R as L is lifted (simultaneously), [2]step on L as R is lifted, [3]lift [4]L, lift [5]R, [6]lift [7]L, [8]lift L; even faster, typical quick [1 2 3 4 5 6 7 8]bourrées in place. *Second group:* Same. *First* and *Second groups* each repeat starting with L ft frt in 5th.

Exercise 16

Facing into the barre (croisé), L hand on barre, R ft frt in 5th position. *First group starts:* Quick pas de bourrée suivi (commonly called bourrée) [& a]in place, [1]demi-plié on L and dégagé the R foot to 4th position devant en l'air à la demi-hauteur. Bring the R foot to 5th position [& a]devant, rising onto pointe and quickly bourrée in place. Immediately [2]plié on the R ft and dégagé the L derrière en l'air à la demi-hauteur. Continue [&a3]front , [&a4]back, [&a5]front, [&a6]back, [&a7]front, and [&a8]back. *Second group:* Same. *First* and *Second groups* each repeat starting with the L ft frt in 5th with R hand on the barre in croisé.

Exercise 17

Facing barre, both hands on barre, R ft in frt in 5th position. *First group* starts: [&]Plié, [1]sous-sus, plié in 5th, [&]relevé on L with R in retiré devant, [2]plié [&]on L, take R leg to attitude derrière, [3 en relevé]plié on L, [&]extend to arabesque and [4 en relevé]quickly close to 5th behind. [& in plié]Same with L leg. [5&6&7&8]Repeat. *Second group:* Same: [1–8]*First* and *Second groups* each repeat two more times.

Exercise 18

Facing barre. *First group* starts: Piqué en pointe stepping back onto L [1]with R in retiré devant, [2]coupé onto R, [3]piqué onto L as R does ballonné

à la seconde sur la pointe, roll into plié (as R goes to sur le cou-de-pied
derrière). Same in other direction starting on L. Same R except close
into 5th position plié on count 4, sous-sus, roll down releasing back ft
in cou-cle-pied derrière. Repeat those 2 counts of 8 starting in other
direction. *Second group:* Same.

Exercise 19

Repeat exercise 18 except the tempo is faster, which means the leg cannot go as high.

Exercise 20

Facing barre, standing farther back than typical, standing on L ft, R
behind in B+. *First group* starts: Fondu on supporting leg (L), R does a
piqué onto pointe in arabesque, balancé en arrière (L, R, L), repeat,
fondu on L, R does a piqué onto pointe in arabesque and hold, roll off
pointe, step back onto L, then R and point L tendu devant to prepare
to repeat the step starting on the L. Repeat starting on L ft. Repeat on
other side. *Second group:* Same.

Exercise 21

Similar to exercise 20, but with L hand on barre, R ft in 5th position frt.
First group starts: Fondu on supporting leg (L) as the R does a piqué
onto pointe in arabesque, balancé en arrière (L, R, L), repeat, fondu on
L, R does a piqué onto pointe in arabesque on R and holds—(now exercise changes)—turning toward barre (en dehors), bring L leg into retiré
devant as R hand takes barre, roll off pointe into plié as left leg développés devant, close 5th. Repeat by stepping onto L leg into arabesque.
Repeat entire sequence. *Second group:* Same.

Exercise 22

The class lines up single file at the end of the barre. The girls start one
at a time, L hand on barre, R ft frt in 5th position: Fondu on supporting leg (L), step into 5th position en pointe. Roll into demi-plié on left
as R goes to sur le cou-de-pied devant. Repeat last 2 counts. Hold and

3 4 5   6
balance with arms in 1st, roll into demi-plié (or fondu) with R in sur le cou-de-pied devant. As there is room, the next girl follows the first and so on until the barre is filled with dancers. When they have gone the length of the barre, they turn around and go the other way.

CENTER

Exercise 1

One at a time, moving across the floor; this movement is exactly like a typical piqué turn en dedans except without the turn.

The teacher emphasized moving the body in one piece as the dancer springs, onto pointe. It is done slowly with typical arms.

Exercise 2

Dancers make several lines with their bodies facing wall 6 (Cecchetti method) and R shoulder to the mirror. They must be very far upstage so they have room to do chaîné turns toward the mirror. Stand on L, with R leg tendu devant.

INTERMEDIATE CLASSES

Intermediate Pointe Class (Level V), Houston Ballet School

This class, inspired by Allyson Swenson, follows an hour-and-a-half ballet technique class.

BARRE

Exercise 1

Facing barre in parallel position: Roll through foot to ball, to pointe into arch, roll back to ball, put heel down. Same with L foot. Repeat. Both feet press to pointe, R rolls down, both feet to pointe, L rolls down. Repeat 2xs. Repeat last part except from straight legs, roll down into the plié for same amount of time. Turn out to 1st. R ft tendu à la seconde, flex, roll through foot to touch pointe on floor, press into arch bending R leg, straighten up, close to 1st. Same L. Tendu R, close in 1st with

189

demi-plié, tendu L, close in 1st with demi-plié. Tendu R à la seconde,
close 1st, press up in a rise with straight legs, lower heels into demi-plié.
Same L. Repeat R and L. Demi-plié, staying in plié, lift the heels, rolling
onto pointe, staying en pointe straighten legs, lower heels to 1st. Reverse
by pressing up to pointe, demi-plié en pointe pressing into arches, lower
heels to 1st while still in plié, straighten legs. Repeat.

Exercise 2

Facing barre in lst: R leg tendu à la seconde, close 1st, L tendu à la seconde, close 1st, demi-plié, spring onto pointe in 1st, lower to plié,
spring onto pointe, lower to plié. Straighten standing leg as the R leg
tendus to side to repeat. Repeat exercise except plié on counts 2 and 4.

At this point the teacher saw one girl knuckling. She said to press out
the elastic of the shoe—pull up in the upper part of the foot. The end
of the shoe must be on the floor. Don't pull back on the foot. Also think
of pressing the foot out where the ribbons cross. The teacher manually
shaped their feet and checked to see how much of the shoe was dirty,
which shows how much of the shoe is on the floor. The student should
pull the heel "out of your shoe."

Exercise 3

Facing barre, R ft frt in 5th: Sous-sus, plié, sous-sus, plié, échappé to 2d,
plié in 5th, échappé to 2d, plié in 5th. Sous-sus, plié, sous-sus, plié,
échappé to 2d, plié in 5th, sous-sus, plié. Same with L ft frt. Repeat
both sides.

Exercise 4

Facing barre, R ft frt in 5th: Échappé to 2d, plié in 5th, échappé to 2d,
plié in 5th, passé R ft, plié, sous-sus, plié, passé L ft, plié, sous-sus, plié
in 5th. Repeat. Same with L ft frt.

Exercise 5

Facing barre, R ft frt in 5th: Fondu on L, développé à la quatrième devant, demi-hauteur, piqué en avant $^{\&}$ to 5th sur la pointe. $^{3\ 4}$ Pas de bourrée suivi (commonly known as bourrée) ^{56} in place. Passé R leg closing ^{78} derrière while still en pointe (R arm comes off barre and moves to Russian 3rd or Cecchetti 5th on the passé; then as the leg closes behind, the arm goes to 2d and back onto the barre. The head turns to the L when the R leg and arm are moving and vice versa). $^{\&}$ Fondu on the R, and repeat using the other leg. Repeat both sides.

CENTER

Exercise 1

5th position, R ft frt. Preparation: arms move from preparation to 1st to 2d and back to preparation position as the R ft tendus à la seconde and closes to 1st position. $^{\&}$ Demi-plié, ^{1} spring to relevé in 1st, $^{\&}$ plié, ^{2} relevé, $^{\&}$ plié, ^{3} relevé, $^{\&}$ plié, ^{4} straighten legs, $^{\&}$ plié. Repeat 3xs.

Exercise 2

Repeat previous exercise except with different timing. This time plié on 1 and spring up on &.

Exercise 3

Repeat center exercise 2 except on the last & 5 & 6 & 7 & 8 the front row splits in the middle and runs upstage to form the back line as the 2d line runs forward to form the 1st line.

Exercise 4

Croisé, R ft frt in 5th. Same arm preparation as center exercise 1: ^{1} Sous-sus, ^{2} plié, ^{3} sous-sus, ^{4} plié, ^{5} sous-sus, ^{6} plié, ^{7} échappé changing direc- tions to finish in plié facing corner 1 with L ft frt in 5th, ^{8} plié. ^{1} Sous-sus, ^{2} plié, ^{3} sous-sus, ^{4} plié, ^{5} sous-sus, ^{6} plié, ^{7} échappé to croisé facing corner 2, ^{8} plié. ^{1} Sous-sus, ^{2} plié, ^{3} échappé (to corner 1), plié, sous-sus, plié, ^{7} échappé (corner 2), ^{8} plié, ^{1} sous-sus, ^{2} plié, ^{3} échappé (corner 1), ^{4} plié, ^{5} sous-sus, ^{6} plié, ^{7} and straighten legs plié. Repeat starting with L ft frt in 5th croisé facing corner 1. Repeat entire exercise, except on the last 8 counts the students change lines as in center exercise 3.

COMMENTS ON LEVEL V POINTE BY ALLYSON SWENSON

Students usually spend two years in level IV pointe, which is the first pointe level, before progressing to level V. In level IV they do not actually do much work on pointe. In the level V class described here, the students stay mainly on two feet. They are just starting to work on one foot. They may spend two years in level V, more or less.

Level V is just starting to do single turns from 5th position. The students are ages 11 through 13. One girl is 14, but 12 is the average age. Level IV students are aged 10 through 12. They do not start on pointe until they are 10 and then only if they're ready.

At level IV students are given one-half hour of pointe a week. The level Vs get a half hour twice a week. The level IVs stay on two feet the whole time. They work entirely in first and second positions. For example, they do the same warm-ups as the level V students—the same 1st, 2d, and 3rd exercises. When they do the 1st exercise, I tell them not to stretch the foot over, but to place the foot on pointe so it will be exactly the way it would be if it was up on pointe. They are not standing on it yet; they are just placing the foot.

What I'm looking for is exactly where they would be on pointe. I don't want them to fold the toes over or anything like that. I want them to be straight up on the end of the shoe so they feel the shape of the foot before putting any weight on it. After that they go up on pointe and do the changeover from one foot to the other.

With the older classes, starting with the Vs and VIs, I'll take them into plié on pointe. Now there is more pressure on the foot, but they are still supposed to keep the foot's shape and not push the arch out yet. The plié makes it a little harder.

Also with the IVs, Vs, and VIs I'll do the flex through the demi-pointe to try to get them to use the shoe. And then the tendu and plié with the stretch and rise is the first time they have really gone on pointe; they've done it with their feet parallel, but not in a rotated position. And then with the VIs I'll have them do rise, plié, rise, plié, which the IVs and Vs don't do. I'll usually have them take a balance at the end of that.

Sometimes toward the end of level IV I'll throw in a few sous-sus in fifth, but most of their time is spent doing exercises like tendu side, plié in 1st, tendu, plié in 1st, échappé and plié in 1st. They might try sous-sus, plié, and stretch (straighten their legs), plié, sous-sus, plié, and stretch, plié, sous-sus, plié and stretch, plié échappé, plié and stretch, plié. They repeat this on the other side. While level V can do continuous relevés from two feet to two feet, the IVs do better if they have a breather in between, whether it's a plié and straighten or a tendu.

I spend a lot of time correcting in level IV. I work with kids who can't make it all the way up and kids who are pushing over. They don't know how to work the feet on pointe yet. We also spend time learning to tie ribbons, how to cut them to the right length—they don't know to cut them on an angle, they don't know to turn the ribbon under when they sew it-they don't know how to put the shoes on.

I take new beginners to the center, and the first thing we do is turned in walking on pointe. Again, I always keep them on two feet. We might do the exercise described above in the center. After we get going along, we might do real simple bourrées. Sous-sus, bourrée in place, and change feet. I do that a lot with the level IVs to get them used to being on one foot. After they have been in class for a year, we'll do the bourrées and change feet in the center. Newer students change feet, but older ones change with a passé or retiré so they get used to coming into a position. Sometimes I'll take a separate group of the older kids and do a relevé on one foot at the barre, like jeté, relevé, hold, plié, and pas de bourrée under. Just that one little relevé for the older kids because they have been doing the pointe work for two years. This gets them ready to move to level V because that's when they do more work on one foot.

In level V, the students don't do piqué turns across the floor. They do piqués across the floor without a turn. Instead I'll start them with turns from 5th position. Because there's a lot they have to hold on to with a piqué turn. There's a lot of placement that you can lose. Whereas from 5th, it's cleaner. It's harder for them to lose the position and placement of the body. We might do, for instance, a tendu side, a plié, half turn, roll down, tendu, plié, half-turn, roll down; and then the same with a full turn. When the kids move up to level VI, they do pirouettes in the center so they've got to have had a little bit of that in V. Then their teacher at level VI will start giving them double turns from 5th position; she starts things across the floor like piqué turns. Usually they can make the transition all right because they've had time to get used to the feeling from the exercises in IV and V. A lot of the time I spend, particularly with the IVs, is just learning how to put the feet on pointe. You see every single foot is different and a teacher can't just say, "This is how you do it." I'll get them all to watch what I do with one person so they get an overall understanding, but each person is different. Some people I have to tell, if they have a low arch or instep, "You'll have to work to get the foot over more." If they have a high arch, then they have to keep the foot stretched in the shoe so they don't break over. I spend a lot of time in IV just working on that kind of thing. By V, they've pretty well got it, but there are still some problems. Especially the kids with high arches and insteps. They need more special care. They go up more easily, but need help with breaking over. Sometimes they sew elastic across the top or get a high vamp for extra support. And then some of them need to break the shoe in one place, while other girls need another place. By the time they get to level VI, they should know what they're doing.

Intermediate Pointe Class (Level VI), Houston Ballet School

Inspired by Swenson, this follows an hour-and-a-half technique class.

Exercise 1

Same as exercise 1 in level V.

Exercise 2

Same as exercise 2 in level V.

Exercise 3

L hand on barre; in 5th position, R ft in frt: Sous-sus,[1] demi-plié,[2] échappé[3] to 2d,[4] closing in 5th with L ft in frt. Sous-sus,[5] plié,[6] échappé to 2d[7] closing in 5th with R ft in frt.[8] Échappé to 4th with R ft in frt,[1] return to 5th in plié (arm goes from 2d to preparation position, 1st arabesque with palm facing floor, inclining head),[2] échappé changé to 2d taking[3] arm to 2d, plié in 5th, R ft bk.[4] Same with L ft in frt.[5 6 7 8] Repeat.[1-8] Quickly turn to other side and repeat entire exercise.

Exercise 4

Facing barre with R ft in frt in 5th: Fondu on L with R in sur le[&] cou-de-pied devant (pointed),[1] développé R ft devant and piqué onto[2] pointe to 5th with R ft frt.[3 4] Small bourrées in place.[5] Retiré R leg devant,

take to attitude derrière, take R arm to high 5th, extending to arabesque [6] [7]
as arm turns to allongé. Close R leg in 5th derrière, roll down to [8] [&]
demi-plié. Same starting with L ft. Repeat both sides.

Exercise 5

R ft frt in 5th, L hand on barre: Développé en fondu à la quatrième [&]
devant à demi-hauteur, piqué to 5th position sur la pointe R ft frt, roll [1] [2]
down off pointe to demi-plié. Repeat. R ft relevé passé en arrière, plié, [& 3 4] [5] [6]
relevé passé en avant, plié. Repeat counts & 12 & 3 4 5 6, but on count [7] [8]
6 remain en pointe. Turning away from the barre (demi-détourné), [7]
simply bring L foot to close en pointe in 5th devant. Now R hand is
on barre. Same starting with L ft. Repeat entire exercise. [1–8] [1–8]

CENTER

Exercise 1

Croisé, R ft frt in 5th: Sous-sus, plié, sous-sus, plié, sous-sus, plié, échap- [1] [2] [3] [4] [5] [6] [7]
pé changé, finishing in croisé with L ft frt in 5th (facing corner 1). [8]
Repeat with L ft frt in 5th. Sous-sus, plié, échappé changé (changing to [1–8] [1] [2] [3] [4]
face corner 1), sous-sus, plié, échappé changé (facing corner 2), sous-sus, [5] [6] [7] [8] [1]
plié, échappé changé (to corner 1), walk backward on the diagonal to [2] [3] [4]
corner 3, R, L, R, close L ft frt in 5th. Repeat entire exercise starting [5] [6] [7] [8] [1–8] [1–8] [1–8] [1–8]
with L ft frt in croisé.

The teacher wanted the students to rotate their legs by taking the seams
of their tights and bringing them forward.

Exercise 2

Croisé, R ft frt in 5th: Hands on hips, plié , sous-sus, plié, passé R to bk [&] [1] [2] [3]
(R arm opens from 1st to 2d and bk on hip on the plié), plié. Turn to [4]
face corner 1 on the passé. Same with L. En face passé R close bk plié [5678] [1] [2]
(R arm opens from 1st to 2d), passé L to bk plié (L arm opens from 1st [3] [4]
to 2d), passé R bk plié (R arm moves quickly through 1st to high 5th to [5] [6]

195

2d), passé L to bk plié (L arm moves quickly through 1st to high 5th to
$\overset{7}{}$ $\overset{8}{}$
$\underset{1-8}{}$ $\underset{1-8}{}$ $\underset{1-8}{}$ $\underset{1-8}{}$ $\underset{1-8}{}$ $\underset{1-8}{}$
2d). Repeat 3 more times. After executing 4xs, repeat with L ft frt.

The teacher's corrections were that when students do retiré or passé, they should lift from underneath their "rear." In the plié, they must lengthen out the body—not settle into the plié or sit into it. They must pull out of the hip flexor, not collapse it.

Exercise 3

Moving across the floor to the R: Piqué tour en dedans R 2xs, piqué on R with L sur le coup-de-pied derrière (making half turn to R), plié, piqué on L lifting R to sur le cou-de-pied devant (making half turn en dehors), plié, piqué en dedans R, plié on L. Continue across floor. Then to L across floor.

A Typical Vaganova
Intermediate-Advanced Pointe Class (Level VII)

BARRE

Exercise 1

1st position, facing barre: Demi-plié, relevé to pointe, hold, roll down to plié. Execute 8xs.

Exercise 2

2d position, facing barre: Demi-plié, relevé to pointe, plié, relevé, plié, relevé, press in plié over the pointes, straighten knees, roll down. Execute 4xs.

Exercise 3

5th position, R ft frt facing barre: Plié, sous-sus, demi-plié, sous-sus, plié, relevé on L with R in sur le cou-de-pied pointed devant, plié, relevé on L and low développé à la seconde with R, close bk in 5th. Same with L ft frt. Repeat 2xs.

Exercise 4

5th position, R ft frt, L hand on barre: Sous-sus, développé R ft devant, demi-rond de jambe en l'air en dehors to 2d, bring to retiré devant. Demi-plié on L as R ft is brought to pointed sur le cou-de-pied devant, relevé on L as R goes to attitude derrière while turning to face barre. Place R hand on barre making a quarter turn and stretch into 1st arabesque. Close to 5th and roll off pointe, demi-plié, and straighten. Same starting with L and repeat.

Exercise 5

5th position, R ft frt, facing barre: Coupé dessous onto pointe on L, coupé dessus to demi-plié on R, pas de bourrée dessous. Same other direction. Relevé onto L on pointe as R leg does double rond de jambe en l'air en dehors, close 5th derrière demi-plié; same relevé double rond de jambe en l'air but en dedans, and again en dehors, close 5th derrière demi-plié, sous-sus, demi-plié. Repeat entire exercise to L.

Exercise 6

Reverse exercise 5.

Exercise 7

5th position, R ft frt, facing barre: Pas de bourrée suivi en pointe moving R. Passé L ft from back to front closing in 5th remaining en pointe. Same moving to L. Repeat.

CENTER

Exercise 1

5th position, R ft frt in croisé: Développé à la quatrième devant à la demi-hauteur en fondu, turning en face, bourrée en avant (arms moving through first to 2d position), passé R ft to 4th position derrière. Pirouette en dehors, finish in croisé in 4th, tendu R ft, close to 5th derrière. Same starting with L ft frt.

197

Exercise 2

Poser on L with R ft behind in B+ in croisé: Moving en diagonale to Vaganova corner 2 ballonné devant sur la pointe en relevé in effacé, traveling forward. Relevé, roll down, relevé, roll down, relevé, roll down, relevé while sweeping R leg into attitude effacé derrière. Step on R ft and execute to, L.

Exercise 3

Croisé, 5th position, R ft frt: Développé écarté devant en relevé, close 5th in demi-plié. Relevé to 2d arabesque on R, close L in plié 5th derrière. Développé écarté devant en relevé with L, close in 5th devant sous-sus, plié. To R piqué tour en dehors on L 3xs, close R ft derrière in 5th, sous-sus, lower to demi-plié. Same to L. Repeat.

Exercise 4

Poser on L with R ft tendu in effacé devant: Moving toward corner 2 Vaganova en diagonale, soutenu en tournant en dedans, step into original poser position. Repeat continually across floor. When finished, travel across the floor to L.

Exercise 5

5th position, R ft frt, en face. Preparation, tendu R ft à la seconde, demi-rond de jambe to 4th position derrière, demi-plié: Single or double pirouette en dehors and then three fouettés rond de jambe en tournant en dehors (Russian school) finishing in 4th position derrière, tendu R on straight leg, return to 4th position preparation and continue with the fouettés. On the last set, tendu R and close in 5th derrière. Do the same combination to L.

Exercise 6

Croisé, R ft frt: Retiré devant en relevé, close 5th devant demi-plié, 3xs, relevé passé closing in 5th derrière as body turns to croisé with L ft frt. Same with L ft frt. Repeat.

ADVANCED CLASSES

Advanced Pointe Class (Level VIII), Houston Ballet School

This class was inspired by Clara Cravey.

BARRE

Exercise 1

Facing barre, feet in parallel position: Standing on L, cross R leg over L and place ft en pointe beside the heel of the L ft. Demi-plié on the L and push over the pt of the R ft. The L knee bends and pushes into the R
knee which is bent. Push into the pointe, release back, into the pt,
1 & 2
& 3 & 4 & 5 &
release back, into the pt, release, into the pt, release, into the pt, release,
6 7 & 8 1–8
into the pt, hold, release, step on R in parallel position. Same with L ft
1 2 3 4
crossed over. *Next*, with L ft in same place, put R ft heel directly in front of the L toe and knees are bent as the hips push in toward the barre to
1 2 3 4   1 2 3 4
stretch the calf muscles. Change feet and do same. *Next*, the R foot goes into same position, but with a space the length of a foot between the R
5 6 7 8
and L feet to get a bigger stretch of the calves. Same with L. *Next*, place
1 2 3 4
both legs together in parallel position with the legs straight, press the
5 6 7 8   1 2 3 4
hips to the barre, putting hips back on top of legs, lean forward on
5
straight legs until back is flat but head is up, arch back as head lowers
6 7   8
and roll up through the spine to a standing position. (The leaning forward and rolling up should stretch the arms and the upper back.)

Exercise 2

1   2
Facing barre in 1st position: R ft sur le cou-de-pied, extend devant about
3   4   5
two inches off floor, flex ft and bring it back to 1st position. Tendu R à
6   7
la seconde, bring to 5th devant with demi-plié, tendu R à la seconde,
8   &   1–8
and bring to 1st with demi-plié and straighten legs. Same en dedans. Execute entire exercise starting with L ft.

The teacher's corrections were that students must be sure that all five metatarsals are on the floor in plié. They should not be all "clinched up." Let the ligaments and tendons relax in the plié instead of holding or gripping.

Exercise 3

Facing barre, 5th position R ft frt: Tendu R à la seconde [1], roll down [2] through foot [3], point tendu again [4], close 5th derrière [5 6 7]. Repeat [8], finishing cou-de-pied devant [1 2 3]. Frappé à la seconde 3xs [4], hold, frappé à la seconde [5 6 7] 3xs [8 &1 & a 2 & a], hold [3 & a 4], battement frappé double à la seconde 4xs [5 6], tendu R ft à la seconde [7], demi-plié, straighten R and tendu L [8], close L in 5th devant [&]. Same starting to L. Repeat all.

Exercise 4

Facing barre, 1st position, both hands on barre: Take R hand off barre [1 2] and extend to seconde (looking into hand) as the body leans slightly in same direction. Bring arm to high 5th (same as Russian 3rd) as feet press [3] up to pointe [hold 4]. Leaving arm in 5th, lower through the metatarsals to the [5] balls of the feet [6], press back up to full pointe [7], lower down to demi-plié (as arm is placed back on the barre) [8], straighten legs [1–8]. Same with L arm. Repeat [1–8 1–8], this time taking both arms off barre for a quick balance on count 4 before lowering through the metatarsals. Repeat all 4 counts of 8.

Exercise 5

Facing barre, 1st position, both hands on barre: Demi-plié, spring into [&] relevé [1], down [2], up [3], down [4], up [5], down [6], up [&], down [7], up [&], down [8]; repeat two [1–8 1–8] more times. Pick up L foot sur le cou-de-pied derrière [&], pas de bourrée [1 2] dessous ending in 5th [3]. Pick up R foot to sur le cou-de-pied derrière [4], pas de bourrée [5 6] dessous ending in 5th en pointe (pas de bourrées are done [7] picking up feet), extend L foot with small développé à la seconde and [8] roll down gently to 1st position and plié [&]. Repeat exercise, but start the [1–8 1–8 1–8] pas de bourrée with R foot [8 counts of 8]. Repeat entire exercise.

The teacher's corrections were to "lift" the body up as the dancer springs down so the body will not be heavy going down.

Exercise 6

Facing barre, L ft in frt in 5th. Échappé to 2d^1, plié in 1st$^&$, échappé to^2 2d$^&$, plié in 5th R ft frt^3, échappé to 2d$^&$, plié in 1st^4, échappé to 2d$^&$, plié in 5th L ft frt$^{5\,\&\,6}$. Pas de bourrée dessous 2xs$^{7\,\&\,8}$ lifting feet as in Exercise 5, but closing in 5th in demi-plié at the end. Repeat the échappés$^{1\,\&\,2\,\&\,3\,\&\,4\,\&}$, relevé on R with L in retiré devant, hold the balance and passé the leg to close in 5th^7 derrière^8, demi-plié. Repeat, but this time with the L leg closing 5th the first time.

The teacher's correction was that when students go up into the retiré for the balance, they make the adjustment to position themselves for the balance after they have arrived—that their body weight is too far to the center. On the spring they should pull the foot directly underneath themselves so they will be immediately on balance; no shifting of the weight should be necessary. Also, the teacher wants a beautiful cou-de-pied position—shape the foot beautifully, don't just let it hang.

Exercise 7

5th position, R ft frt, L hand on barre: Pas de cheval 3xs$^{\&\,1\,\&\,2\,\&\,3}$, fondu on L (R^4 is in tendu devant), piqué onto pointe on R with L sur le cou-de-pied^5 derrière^6, plié^7, relevé^8, plié, relevé^1, turn into barre (put both hands on barre) and développé L leg à la demi-hauteur à la seconde^2, petit batte-ment alternating closing back and front starting devant-frt, bk^3, frt$^&$, bk^4, frt$^&$, frt, bk^5, frt$^&$, bk^6, frt$^&$, make a quarter turn placing R hand on barre closing^7 L ft frt in 5th^8. Same starting with L. Repeat exercise.$^{1-8\ 1-8\ 1-8\ 1-8}$

Teacher calls sur le cou-de-pied the "kissing heel" position.

Exercise 8

Repeat exercise 7 with ballonné simple.

Exercise 9

R ft frt in 5th position, L hand on barre: Chassé en avant$^&$, relevé into^1

attitude derrière, extend ^{2}into ^{3}arabesque, close ^{4}5th, roll down into $^{\&}$demi-plié, repeat the chassé ^{567}relevé and extend. Then bring L leg into ^{8}retiré devant as body turns to face barre with R hand holding barre and L arm 5th en haut. Extend L leg into ^{12}arabesque (passer la jambe) as L hand does allongé. Make another quarter turn en dehors bringing L leg into ^{3}retiré and closing in ^{4}5th devant with R hand now on barre. $^{\&}$Demi-plié, ^{5}relevé to retiré devant, close ^{6}5th L ft devant, $^{\&}$demi-plié, ^{7}pirouette en dehors, close ^{8}L ft 5th devant. $^{1-8}$Same $^{1-8}$starting to L. $^{1-8}$Repeat $^{1-8}$entire $^{1-8}$exercise. $^{1-8}$

The teacher explained that the heel, hip, and head all move together on the chassé to attitude relevé.

CENTER

Exercise 1

Croisé, R ft frt: ^{1}Échappé sur les pointes to 2d, closing 5th in croisé ^{2}L ft frt. ^{3}Échappé again ending croisé R ^{4}ft frt. Sous-sus en face ^{5}R ft frt (arms in 5th en haut), lift R ^{6}ft sur le cou-de-pied pointed devant, place $^{\&}$back into 5th en pointe, lift L ^{7}ft to sur le cou-cle-pied pointed derrière, place $^{\&}$back into 5th en pointe, ^{8}demi-plié returning to croisé R ft frt (arms open to 2d on counts 6 7 and arrive in preparation position on 8). $^{1-8}$Repeat $^{1-8}$2 more times. Repeat counts 1 2 3 4 and execute one more ^{5}échappé ^{6}ending facing corner 1 (Cecchetti) or croisé L ft frt in 5th, ^{7}sous-sus, ^{8}plié. $^{1-8}$Same $^{1-8}$starting $^{1-8}$with $^{1-8}$L ft frt. Repeat entire exercise.

Exercise 2

Moving across the floor to the R. Preparation, standing on L, R ft tendu ^{123}croisé devant: Attitude turn R, ^{1}step onto L in fondu as R ft does tendu croisé devant to corner 2 and R arm extends back and L arm moves from ^{2}1st position moving parallel with the leg as it stretches into allongé (typ- ^{3}ical révérence). ^{123}Bourrée ^{123}to corner 1 with arms extended in 2d allongé,

123   123   123
piqué on R (to corner 2) croisé en avant 2xs, attitude croisé derrière on
        123   123
R, step back on L into original preparation. Repeat the attitude turn
            123   123   123   123   123
into the reverence posé and the bourrée R. Pas de bourrée dessous 2xs
                                                         123
with lifted feet (LRL, RLR), ending with R ft 5th in frt. Pirouette en
                              1 2 3
dehors ending in 4th R ft behind, temps lié en arrière ending with L ft
tendu devant in croisé (to corner 1). Same to L. Repeat entire exercise.

The teacher suggested leading with the back foot in the bourrée, that the feet should "feel" they are touching. There should be no spaces between the feet. The back foot should feel that it is pushing away from the floor with lots of energy instead of "dragging." The dancer should allow the back foot to lead.

Exercise 3

This is done in a circle moving to the R first. Preparation, standing on
                              8   & a
R, L ft tendu croisé devant: Step onto L, glissade précipitée derrière (L
   1   2
ends in frt) R, développé à la seconde R (going into the circle), R crosses
                                        & a   3   4 & a
in front of body and does chassé croisé en avant, same with L with the
                        5 6   &   7 8   1 2
développé going out of the circle, again with R, coupé under, piqué turn
               3   4   5 & a   6   7 & a 8
R 4xs moving in a circle, double piqué turn, chassé pas de bourrée dessous 2xs. Continue to R. Exercise moves only in one direction. When all have done it, start to the L.

The teacher's correction was to be more explicit with the feet after the 3rd développé in the chassé, not just to fall onto the R foot.

Advanced Pointe Class (Level VIII), Houston Ballet School

This class was inspired by Rosemary Miles, principal of the Houston Ballet School.

BARRE

Exercise 1

                              1   2
L hand on barre, 5th position, R ft frt: Tendu devant with R ft, roll thru
                        3   4   5
foot to 4th position with straight legs, tendu close to 5th. Tendu devant,

6   7   8

close 5th with plié, tendu devant, close 5th with straight legs. En croix. Same other side.

Exercise 2

Facing barre, feet in parallel position: Standing on L, R leg crosses over L and places ft en pointe beside the heel of the L ft. Demi-plié on the L and push over the pt of the R ft. The L knee bends and pushes into the

              1   &   2   &

R knee which is bent. Push into the pt, release back, into the pt, release,

3   &   4   &   5   &   6   &

into the pt, release, into the pt, release, into the pt, release, push, release,

7   &

push, release, step on R in parallel position. Same with L ft crossed over. Repeat both sides.

Exercise 3

                                      1   2

Facing barre, feet in 1st position: Tendu R ft à la seconde, roll through

             3   4   5 6

foot to 2d position, roll through L ft to tendu, close L ft to 1st. Same

7 8   1   2 3 4

starting with L ft. Rise up onto pointe with straight legs, hold, roll down

           &   5   &   6   &

with straight legs, press up, lower down, press up, lower down, press up,

7   &   8

lower down, press up, lower down to 1st. Repeat.

Exercise 4

                                  &   1   2

Facing barre, 5th position, R ft frt: Plié, sous-sus onto pt in 5th, spring

             3   4

down into plié, échappé to 2d, spring down to 5th with L ft frt,

5   6   7   8

sous-sus, spring down, échappé to 2d, spring down to 5th with R ft

                             5   6   7   8

frt, repeat counts 1, 2, 3, 4, and sous-sus and hold and hold, spring down in plié to 5th with L ft frt. Repeat with L ft frt.

The relevés are executed with a spring, but the teacher reminded dancers that this exercise must be smooth and not bouncey, in spite of the spring. The exercise is repeated to capture this quality.

Exercise 5

                                1   2   3

Facing barre, 5th position, L ft frt: Jeté R, spring into relevé, spring

       4   5   6   7   8   &   1   2   3

down into plié, relevé, plié, relevé, plié, relevé, plié, jeté L, relevé, plié,

    4   5   6   7   8   &

relevé, plié, relevé, plié , relevé, plié. Repeat R and L.

CENTER

Exercise 1

5th position, R ft in frt, en face: Tendu R ft à la seconde, demi-rond de [1/&] jambe to 4th position derrière, plié (preparation for pirouette), double [a/2/3] pirouette en dehors, close R ft in 5th derrière. Sous-sus, demi-détourné, [4/5/&6] chassé pas de bourrée dessous upstage toward wall 7 (Cecchetti) or wall [7/and/a] 5 (Vaganova), 4th position plié with L ft frt. Double pirouette en [8/1] dehors, close R ft in 5th derrière, sous-sus, demi-détourné, roll down, [2/3/4] tendu R ft à la seconde, demi-rond de jambe to 4th position derrière, plié, [5/&/a/6] pirouette en dehors, closing R ft derrière. Same starting with L ft. [7/8]

Exercise 2

5th position, R ft frt, en face: Plié, pirouette en dehors with a développé [&/1] à la quatrième devant demi-hauteur, close 5th, R ft frt after one revolution. [2] Port de bras: the arms go into Cecchetti 4th position en avant on the plié, the L arm comes in to meet the R as the turn starts, and the R arm goes (French 4th position) overhead as the body & head incline to the L and the dancer looks under the R arm. Landing in 5th, straighten the body and return arms to the preparation position. Do this pirouette [1 2 3 4 5 6] 3 times, and then one double en dehors normally closing the R leg [7 &/8] derrière in 5th. Repeat the pirouettes to the L. Repeat entire exercise.

The remainder of the class is spent with two groups dancing the Black Swan variation from *Swan Lake,* after watching it several times on the VCR and discussing its execution.

Advanced Pointe Class, Ruth Page Foundation School

This class was inspired by Larry Long, director of the Ruth Page Foundation School. The class starts in the center after an hour-and-a-half ballet class.

Exercise 1

R ft in frt in 5th: Tendu with R devant, close 5th, tendu à la seconde,
close 5th derrière, tendu derrière, close 5th derrière, sous-sus, demi-plié.
Same with L. Tendu L à la seconde, push into the pointe, straighten to
tendu, close 5th devant. Same with R. Tendu R devant close 5th 2xs,
tendu L derrière 2xs, fondu to the tendu à la seconde with L, soutenu
with L ft frt, demi-plié. Repeat last 8 counts starting with R to back.

This exercise is repeated after a lecture by the teacher that students must
really "work" the foot inside the pointe shoe.

Exercise 2

5th position, R ft frt: Échappé to second 4xs. Sous-sus, plié, sous-sus,
plié, relevé on L with R sur le cou-de-pied pointed devant, plié in 5th,
relevé passé with R passing to the back at the ankle, close 5th derrière.
Same with L ft frt. This exercise is repeated 3 more times.

Exercise 3

5th position, R ft frt: Échappé to 2d making quarter turn to R (ending with L ft 5th frt), bring L to retiré devant and demi-plié in 5th
with L ft frt. Continue with another quarter turn and retiré R, to 5th
plié (facing bk), another quarter turn (facing wall 6) and retiré L, to
5th plié, another quarter turn (now facing front) and passé R ft bk
ending in demi-plié L ft frt in 5th. Same going other way with L ft frt.
Repeat exercise.

Exercise 4

Exercise 3 is repeated except there is a half turn on the 3 retirés and 1
passé. That is, quarter turn échappé (facing wall 8), half turn retiré (facing wall 6), quarter turn échappé (facing frt), half turn retiré (facing bk
or wall 7), quarter turn échappé (facing wall 6), half turn retiré (facing

5 6　　　　　　　　　7 8

wall 8), quarter turn échappé (facing bk), half turn passé (facing front). Repeat going in other direction with L ft frt to start.

Exercise 5

1 2 3 4

5th position, R ft frt: Échappé to second, but don't change feet, 2xs,

5　　　　　　6　　　　　　7　　　　　　8

relevé retiré devant, demi-plié in 5th R ft frt, pirouette en dehors close

R ft in 5th derrière. Same with L foot. Repeat 3xs.

Exercise 6

1　　　　　　　　　　2

Effacé devant, R ft pointing to corner 1: Piqué on R en avant, step

3

back on L, piqué R en avant, as body turns to effacé facing corner 2

&　　　　　　　　　4

the L does petit battement derrière and petit battement devant as R

5 6　　7 & 8　　　　　&　　　　1 2 3 &

rolls down to fondu. Same to the L. Step onto R and coupé L. Do last

4 5 6 7 & 8　　　　　1 2 3　　　　　4

8 counts moving en arrière. Pas de bourrée dessous, coupé under,

5 6　　　　　　　　　7 8

bourrée en avant leading with L ft, bring R ft forward in 4th position

1 2

preparation (en face), pirouette en dehors finishing with L ft bk in 4th

3 4　　　5 6　　　　7　　　　　8

demi-plié, temps lié onto L with R ft tendu croisé devant. Step onto R

1–8 1–8 1–8 1–8

and execute exercise starting to the L. Repeat both sides.

Exercise 7

1　　　　　　　　2

Moving across the floor to the R en diagonale: Piqué arabesque R, step

& a　　　　3

on L, glissade précipitée derrière, piqué to attitude derrière on R croisé

4　　　　5 & a

derrière (facing corner 2), roll down to 4th with R ft frt. Relevé arabesque turn on R en dedans, remaining en pointe place L ft down

6

as R lifts for one half turn en dehors and R does développé à la demi-

& 7 &　　a 8

hauteur effacé, chainé turn R. Repeat to the R across floor. When complete, do exercise moving across the floor to the L.

It is easier to do a chassé pas de bourrée before stepping into the piqué arabesque for the flow of the step. The teacher said to get the attitude "up" immediately. He also wanted a high arabesque since in modern times "long skirts and lilies don't work anymore." Also he wanted the dancer to be on the leg in the arabesque. The "rump" must be right up on top of the leg. Coming out of the arabesque—as the L leg comes through, the R one rolls down—it doesn't all collapse at once.

Exercise 8

Moving across the floor to the R en diagonale: Piqué turn R 3xs, relevé
123456
&78
attitude croisé devant. Continue across floor to R. Then L.

Exercise 9

Preparation, standing on L, R ft tendu devant: Piqué turn R, piqué
12   3
arabesque R, step on L with R sur le cou-de-pied derrière, coupé
4   5
dessous. Same to L. Same to R. Same to L except go into sous-sus
678 12   34567   8123   4
instead of the sur le cou-de-pied and the coupé. Chainé turn R coming
hold 5 6 7 8   1 2 3 4 5 6
out of it with a quick pas de chat R. This exercise is easier to count as
78
12345 12345 12345 123 sous-sus 4 hold 5678.

Exercise 10

5th position, R ft frt: Demi-plié, releve retiré devant with R, demi-plié,
&   1   2
relevé passé with R, plié. Same with L. Again with R and L. On the last
3   4   5678   1234   567
count of 8 coupé dessous. Turning effacé, ballonné en relevé devant sur
12345678 1234
la pointe 7xs. On the 7th one, do a slight fouetté to turn the body en
5
face and leg à la seconde. Close R leg in 5th derrière in demi-plié, sous-
6   7
sus, demi plié. Same starting with L ft frt. Repeat both sides.
8   1–8 1–8 1–8   1–8

On the ballonné devant sur la pointe, the teacher wanted the dancer to arrive in the relevé immediately.

Exercise 11

Repeat the 1st two counts of 8 in exercise 10. Turning écarté, ballonné
12345678 1   hold 2
devant sur la pointe 5xs moving downstage on the diagonal. Step onto
345
R and double piqué tour on L en dehors (lame duck), close R ft der-
6   7   8
rière in 5th, demi-plié, sous-sus, demi-plié. Same starting with L. Repeat both sides.

Advanced Pointe Class, American Ballet Theatre School

This class was inspired by Marina Stavitskaya. It follows an hour-and-a-half technique class. There is no barre.

Exercise I

1st position, en face: Échappé to 2d [1], plié in 1st [&], échappé to 2d [2], plié in 1st [&], échappé to 2d [3], hold [&4], plié in 1st [&]; échappé to 2d [5], plié in 2d [&], rise in 2d [6], plié in 2d [&], rise in 2d [7], hold [&8], plié in 5th, R ft frt [&]. Échappé to 2d [1], plié in 2d [&], relevé on R with L in retiré devant [2], plié in 5th L ft frt [&], échappé to 2d [3], plié in 2d [&], relevé on L with R in retiré devant [4], plié in 5th with R ft frt [&], échappé to 2d [5], plié in 5th L ft frt [&], échappé to 2d [6], plié in 5th R ft frt [&], échappé to 2d hold [7], plié in 5th L ft frt [&8]. Same starting with L ft frt. Repeat R and L 4xs. [1–8 1–8]

The teacher's corrections were that the movement should be more "special"—more exciting and lighter.

Exercise 2

Preparation, standing on L, R ft tendu à la quatrième derrière: Piqué on R sur la pointe [1], ballonné with L de côté, ending sur le cou-de-pied derrière in plié [&]; same with R [2 &], same with L [3 &], same with R [4], but with R ending sur le cou-de-pied devant [&]. 4xs ballonné devant sur la pointe effacé moving toward corner 2 [5 & 6 & 7 & 8], tombé on R with L sur le cou-de-pied derrière [&], ballonné derrière sur la pointe effacé moving toward corner 6 2xs [1 & 2], tombé on L with R sur le cou-de-pied devant [&], ballonné devant sur la pointe 2xs [3 & 4], close R ft frt in 5th plié [&], échappé to 2d [5], plié in 4th L ft frt [6], double pirouette en dehors [7 &], close R ft 5th derrière [8]. Same starting with piqué onto pt with R. Repeat both sides. [1–8 1–8]

The teacher's corrections were that the leg should not be thrown away; it should feel as if it is being pulled.

Exercise 3

Preparation, standing on L, R ft tendu à la quatrième derrière: Turn body to face Vaganova corner 2, croisé derrière, piqué arabesque R (1st arabesque), failli L as R rolls off pointe and arms change to Russian 4th arabesque (now in a lunge in 4th position, L ft frt facing corner 2). En face glissade précipitée derrière R, piqué R attitude croisé derrière (arms Vaganova 3rd), roll off pointe to 4th position as arms open to 2d. Piqué L 1st arabesque, chassé with R to corner 8, step R, from écarté derrière, grand rond de jambe en l'air relevé en dedans (arms do a reverse circle from 2d to Vaganova 3rd), finishing with L ft tendu croisé devant and R fondu (wrists are crossed in front of body). Contretemps and repeat starting to the L. Repeat both sides.

This is executed very slowly to gain strength and control. The teacher's corrections were that the back must be very expressive; it must be a "talking back." Also, stepping into the piqué arabesque, the foot must be *completely* stretched.

Exercise 4

Preparation, standing on L, R ft tendu croisé derrière: Moving on the diagonal toward corner 2 pas marché (or in Vaganova, pas jeté fondu) sur la pointe with petit battement sur le cou-de-pied beating derrière and then devant—step R, L, same pas marché on R, but turning body to face corner 4 with L leg extending to corner 2, turn again and step on L with the R leg beating and extending to écarté devant. Piqué retiré devant en avant stepping toward corner 2 with body facing corner 8 2xs. Close 5th R ft frt, plié. Relevé double rond de jambe en l'air écarté devant, close R ft frt in 5th, plié. Moving backward toward corner 6, pas jeté fondu sur la pointe with petit battement sur le cou-de-pied beating devant and then derrière—step L, R, L. Piqué arabesque on R, close L devant in 5th plié. Assemblé soutenu sur les pointes en tournant en

210

456 123   456

dehors, chaîné turns on the diagonal toward corner 1. Finish in big posé effacé derrière. Step is executed moving L.

The teacher's corrections were that dancers must be careful not to drop from the toe to the heel on the pas jeté fondu, but roll very carefully—lower gently through the foot. The feet must be very beautiful on the petit battement.

Exercise 5

&

Preparation, croisé, R ft frt in 5th facing corner 8: Fondu on L and
a 1   2   &
développé croisé devant with R, close 5th plié, fondu on R and
a   3   4
développé croisé derrière with L, close 5th plié, turning en face, dou-
5 & a   6
ble rond de jambe en l'air relevé en dehors on L, close 5th derrière plié,
7 & a   8
double rond de jambe en l'air relevé en dehors on R, close 5th derrière
1   & 2   & 3
plié. Piqué on R to lst arabesque, plié, relevé, plié, relevé to attitude
&
derrière (changing to attitude arms), passer la jambe fondu on R with
4
L in tendu croisé devant and wrists crossed in front of body. Moving
5 6 7   8
to the L, bourrée in circle around self to finish facing corner 2 L ft frt
1–8 1–8
in 5th, croisé devant. Same starting with L ft frt. Repeat both sides.

The teacher stated she did not want the circle to be a tight one—it should be a full circle with the front leg straighter than the back one to make it easier to get around in the circle. She also wanted the dancers to move very fast, "pushing" the back foot to allow for quick movement.

Exercise 6

Moving across the floor to the R. Preparation, standing on L, R ft tendu
1 2 3
croisé devant: Emboîté en tournant en dedans sur les pointes, R L R,
4   5 6 7 8   1 2 3 4
plié on L, piqué tour en dedans 2xs on R, repeat the emboîté (R L R plié
5 6 7   8
on L), piqué into chaîné turns to the R, plié on L. Continue across the floor to the R. Same to the L across floor.

The teacher's corrections were that she wants very strong and sharp feet; dancers should not get up to pointe slowly.

211

Exercise 7

Preparation, R ft frt in 5th, croisé devant: Entrechat quatre, passé R ft closing 5th derrière as body turns to face corner 2. Same with L ft starting front and turning on the passé to face corner 8. En face, 4 passés; closing derrière. Turning en dehors in one complete revolution, passé R, close bk, passé R, close frt, passé R close bk, passé R close frt (now directly en face). En face retiré R devant, close 5th devant in plié, double pirouette en dehors, close 5th derrière plié. Same starting with L ft frt in 5th.

The teacher's corrections were that on the pirouette, dancers should bring the arms in to be smaller; if the arms are big, they make it difficult to turn. She wants them to stay for a moment in every relevé so she can see the position.

Every exercise in this class was extremely slow, which demanded tremendous strength and control. Following these 7 exercises, the class worked on two variations from *Sleeping Beauty*. The entire class lasted one hour.

ADULT CLASSES

Adult Pointe Class, Ruth Page Foundation School

This class was inspired by Patricia Klekovic.

BARRE

Exercise 1 (Plié)

L hand on barre, demi-plié, straighten legs, tendu à la seconde close 5th back, tendu à la seconde close 5th front. Demi-plié, straighten knees, rise to pointe, roll down. Demi-plié and relevé, push out in plié en pointe over the pointes, straighten knees. Demi-plié, relevé en pointe,

6 7 8
lower heels through plié, relevé and lower on straight legs. Repeat to other side.

Exercise 2 (Dégagé or battement jeté)

& 1 & 2 & 3 & 4
L hand on barre, 5th position, R ft frt: Dégagé devant 2xs, dégagé der-
5 6 7 8
rière 2xs, échappé to 4th, plié in 5th 2xs. Repeat starting to the back.
& 1 & 2 &
Dégagé à la seconde with R, close bk, same close frt, dégagé à la seconde
3 & 4 5 6 7 8
with L, close frt, same close bk, échappé to 2d, plié in 5th 2xs. Repeat except starting with inside leg for dégagé à la seconde. Repeat to other side.

Exercise 3 (Tendu)

1
1st position, facing barre, both hands on barre: Tendu R à la seconde,
2 3 4 5 6
flex ft, inside circle with ankle, touch floor, push over pointe to R (lung-
7 8
ing to R), straighten up, close to 1st. Repeat L, R, L.

Exercise 4 (Rond de jambe)

1 &
L hand on barre, 5th position, R ft frt: Tendu R devant, plié in 4th,
2 & 3 & 4 &
relevé in 4th, plié, relevé in 4th, plié, straighten L pt frt, R close 5th.
5 & 6 & 7 & 8
Tendu L derrière, plié, relevé in 4th, plié, relevé in 4th, plié, straighten
& 1
R pt back, L close 5th. Rond de jambe en dehors with R, finishing with
2 & 3 & 4
R frt tendu devant, plié in 4th, relevé, plié, straighten L and pt frt with
5 6 7 8 1 2
R. Repeat en dedans. Rond de jambe en dehors 2½xs finishing with R
3 & 4 & 5 6 7 8
ft tendu devant, plié in 4th, relevé, lower L heel, cambré forward with
1–8
R ft still in tendu devant and both legs straight. Repeat en dedans. Close 5th. Repeat to other side.

Exercise 5 (Développé)

& 1 2
L hand on barre, 5th position, R ft frt: Demi-plié, sous-sus, retiré R leg
3 4 5 6 7 8
to knee, then développé devant, close 5th. Same with inside leg to
1 2 3 4 5
arabesque, same with R à la seconde, hold in 2nd. Fouetté to face barre,
6 7 8
balance in arabesque, close to 5th and turn to begin other side.

213

Exercise 6 (Rond de jambe en l'air en dedans)

Facing barre, R ft behind in 5th: $\overset{1\,2}{}$ Glissade derrière R, $\overset{3}{}$ rond de jambe en l'air $\overset{4}{}$ en relevé en dedans with R, close 5th frt. $\overset{1}{}$ Same L. Passé R ft, $\overset{2}{}$ close 5th frt. $\overset{3}{}$ Passé R ft to 4th. $\overset{4}{}$ Pirouette en dedans, $\overset{5\,6\,7}{}$ close to 5th frt. $\overset{8}{}$ Repeat to L.

Exercise 7 (Glissade précipitée with relevé)

Facing barre, R ft frt in 5th. $\overset{\&\,a\,1}{}$ Glissade précipitée devant 2xs R, relevé on $\overset{\&}{}$ R with L in $\overset{2}{}$ retiré derrière, plié on R and $\overset{\&}{}$ relevé, $\overset{3}{}$ plié passé $\overset{\&}{}$ with L end-$\overset{4}{}$ ing in 5th in frt. Repeat to L. Repeat exercise except instead of 2 relevé and 1 passé, do 4 $\overset{5\,6\,7}{}$ relevés, hold a balance and then $\overset{8}{}$ close L in 5th in front. Repeat to L.

Exercise 8 (Grand battement)

L hand on barre, R ft in 5th frt. Preparation, sous-sus: $\overset{\&}{}$ Grand battement $\overset{1\,2}{}\ \overset{3\,4}{}$ devant 4xs. $\overset{5}{}$ Développé R devant, $\overset{6}{}$ fouetté to $\overset{7}{}$ arabesque putting R hand on barre, $\overset{\&}{}$ close R in 5th bk and $\overset{8}{}$ roll down. $\overset{\&}{}$ Sous-sus. Grand battement à la seconde 4xs $\overset{1}{}$ closing $\overset{2}{}$ bk, $\overset{3}{}$ frt, $\overset{4}{}$ bk, $\overset{5}{}$ frt, développé L à la seconde, $\overset{6}{}$ retiré $\overset{7}{}$ derrière and $\overset{8}{}$ close bk. $\overset{\&}{}$ Sous-sus. Grand battement derrière with L 4xs, $\overset{1\,2\,3\,4}{}$ développé L leg to $\overset{5}{}$ arabesque, $\overset{6}{}$ fouetté away from the barre, $\overset{7}{}$ close 5th, roll $\overset{\&}{}$ down with L ft frt in 5th. $\overset{8}{}$ Sous-sus. Grand battement à la seconde with R $\overset{1}{}$ closing $\overset{2}{}$ frt, $\overset{3}{}$ bk, $\overset{4}{}$ frt, $\overset{5}{}$ bk, développé R à la seconde, $\overset{6}{}$ retiré devant, $\overset{7}{}$ close 5th in frt and $\overset{\&}{}$ roll down. $\overset{8}{}$ Sous-sus. Grand battement derrière with inside $\overset{1\,2\,3\,4}{}$ leg (L) 4xs. Développé derrière to $\overset{5}{}$ arabesque, $\overset{6}{}$ fouetté $\overset{7}{}$ toward the barre, $\overset{\&}{}$ close 5th and roll $\overset{8}{}$ down with L ft in 5th frt. Repeat to Lt.

Although it is atypical to have five sets of 8 counts, we feel this exercise is more complete with the five sets.

CENTER

Exercise 1

R ft in 5th frt: Relevé, plié, 3xs, hold the balance, roll down to 5th, 2xs. *(counts: 1 2, 3, 4 5, 6, 7, 8)* Repeat except in 4th position. Repeat to L.

Exercise 2

Moving across floor, R ft in 5th position frt: Chasé, pas de bourrée *(counts: & 1, &, a, 2)* dessous (under) to R (or tombé instead of chassé), to 4th position facing directly front (à la quatriéme). Pirouette on L en dehors. *(counts: 3, 4)* Repeat across floor. Same to L.

Exercise 3

R ft in 5th back: Glissade derrière R, rond de jambe en l'air en relevé *(counts: & 1, & 2)* en dedans with R. Same L. Pas de bourrée dessous en tournant to R, *(counts: & 3 & 4, 5 & 6)* finish in 4th position, R ft frt, facing corner 2. Pirouette en dedans *(count: &)* finishing with L in 4th facing corner 1. Pirouette en dedans ending *(counts: 7, &)* with R ft in 5th frt facing directly front. *(count: 8)* Repeat to L.

215

Pointe-related Injuries and Their Remedies

Prevention of Injury

The following is a list of ways to help prevent *unnecessary* pointe-related physical problems:

Do not wear ribbons that are too tight. Tight ribbons cut off circulation and mask shoe-fitting problems.

Do not allow ribbon knots or tight elastic to apply undue pressure to the Achilles tendon.

Do not blame foot problems on pointe shoes if they are being caused by a poor choice of street shoes. When walking on concrete, wear well-cushioned athletic shoes, not skimpy sneakers or shoes.

Be aware of how feet are used when they are not dancing. A habit like wrapping feet around the legs of a couch while watching television can be the actual cause of what appears to be a dance-induced injury.

When starting to "knuckle forward," look for weaknesses in muscles. Hip alignment could be off, or an arabesque could be too far forward. If the problem is not a technical fault, try changing to a pointe shoe with a square box instead of a round one.

Look at the whole body on pointe when trying on shoes. Do not buy a shoe that changes the center of gravity. Observe how the shoe affects the rest of the body. Beware of shoes that thrust the hips forward.

Never skimp on warming up and stretching. When the body is not warm enough, or does not have enough range of motion to fit into a particular stance or position, something is going to strain or pull. Warming up and cooling down are crucial to the longevity of a dance career, no matter how limber or resilient the dancer thinks he or she is.

Whenever possible, take a regular technique class before a full pointe class. Do not dance on pointe without first warming up, since this is a frequent cause of tendinitis.

Check the wear pattern on the heel of pointe shoes. If there is evidence of foot contact a half inch or longer on the satin at the heel of the shoe, the size may be too short.

Remember that leg warmers warm from the outside and not the inside. So it is a good idea to put them on after warming up to preserve the warmth, rather than wearing them to warm up and then removing them.

Wear tights in natural fibers like cotton that allow legs to breathe. Lycra tights and plastic pants may be bad for circulation. These fabrics encourage "cold perspiration" and make it difficult for perspiration to evaporate. As one dance teacher commented, "If you put plastic pants over your head and try to breathe, you'll get a good idea of what you're doing to your lower extremities by wearing them."

A shorter shoe may create a better line and make the instep look higher, but it can also cause tendinitis or a bone spur on the back of the foot. Wearing shoes too short prevents the arch from expanding. Once the elasticity of the arch is lost, the ability to jump is lost. Short shoes can also lessen a dancer's plié.

Shoes that are too big lessen control over movements. A shoe that fits correctly allows full flexion and full ability to spread the arch, as well as control of the foot and ankle. Stuffing a large shoe with lamb's wool or a toe pad to "make it fit" will not allow adequate control. A large shoe can cause sprained ankles, overstretched tendons, and overdevelopment of muscles that are straining to hang on to the shoe. Rigidity may also be created in the back, shoulders, and neck, when the body tries to compensate for the loss of range of motion experienced when control of the foot is lost.

Think in terms of strengthening joints to accomplish the maximum possible for your range of motion. Do not risk injury by imitating someone else. Each body has its own range of motion; each body can do some things better than others.

Stretching and working on the instep and forefoot will lessen the chances of ankle problems.

John Gossett at the Houston Body Conditioning Studio suggests thinking of the feet and toes as hands and fingers as they are exercised. Open the toes to strengthen all the small muscles. Work to articulate the foot.

Gossett also recommends icing the feet at the end of the day. Muscles swell as the dancer works, and although applying heat to them may feel good, ice is a better idea. After a heat application, the muscles tighten up. After an ice treatment, the blood vessels are constricted and the body temperature is lowered. Swelling and aching are lessened after icing. Use ice water or ice water with ice cubes.

Keep the skin on the feet dry and pliant at all times. Do not let it dry out so that it cracks or becomes moist and tender, allowing it to rub off and form blisters or soft corns between the toes. Do this by massaging Vaseline into the skin of the toes each night; push Vaseline into the space around the toenails and rub it on the heels. Massage each toe and knead the metatarsal arch with the thumbs.

Be particularly careful when fatigue sets in. Medical specialists have noted that the majority of ballet injuries happen between four and six in the afternoon, when physical and mental fatigue appear after a long day of class and/or rehearsal.

Pointe Dancing and Injury

In addition to natural ability, motivation, and dedication, a dancer must have a supple body and feet, natural turnout, healthy knees, and excellent training geared to developing proper technique in order to survive the rigors of pointe work.

As Dr. Justin Howse, former orthopedic surgeon to the Royal Ballet School, explains in his book *Dance Technique and Injury Prevention,* no dance-related injury is an "act of God."[1] Variables such as the time spent dancing per day, week, or month; experience level; anatomical limitations; technical knowledge; quality of teaching and shoe fitting; history of previous injury; surfaces on which dancing is performed; and strength and conditioning level are among the factors that determine the likelihood of sustaining a pointe-related injury.

In his book *Dancer's Guide to Injuries of the Lower Extremities,* Stuart Wright, who has worked with students at the North Carolina School of the Arts as well as with many professional dancers, states, "Virtually all dance injuries result from faulty technique."[2] Wright feels that incorrect line and improper weight-bearing are the principal factors that lead to injury, and suggests that technical correction is the best means of prevention and treatment.

Even with optimum technique, dancers who wear pointe shoes are bound to experience wear and tear on their feet. Structural problems in pointe shoes, long strenuous classes and rehearsals, or poor placement caused by tired or weak muscles incapable of holding the feet in proper alignment may cause a variety of physical stresses and strains.

Injuries can also be the result of oversights by teachers or choreographers. Doctors expect a sharp increase in the number of ballet injuries each winter and spring during *Nutcracker* and concert and recital seasons. Rehearsal schedules suddenly multiply, resulting in overuse injuries. These could be avoided by beginning rehearsals sooner and increasing them gradually.

Dr. Louis Galli, a New York City podiatrist who works with many New York City Ballet dancers, says that one of the things that makes a successful dancer is knowing when to say no—when to back off. A young dancer has the lung capacity and heart rate to dance for ten hours a day, but mechanically may not be suited for it. Also, young dancers are so eager to work that they may be taken advantage of by choreographers who are more concerned with their work than with their health.

Dr. William Hamilton notes that the injuries of professional and nonprofessional dancers are quite different. He finds "tremendous Darwinism at work in ballet, or survival of the fittest." Most of the "wrong" bodies, and less talented children, are weeded out in the training process, leaving the "thoroughbred racehorses" to enter the profession. Many of the injuries he sees in nonprofessional patients occur because their body types are not suited to ballet.

A major consideration in many injuries is that the average dancer often lacks even the most basic knowledge of the anatomy, kinesiology, and biomechanics of her own body. To meet the physical as well as the artistic demands of pointe dancing, such knowledge is vital.

Finding Medical Care

Good medical care for pointe-related injuries should be sought from a caregiver who has as much knowledge of dance as medicine. Needless to say, this remains a rare commodity. With the exception of the medical specialists who work with major dance companies, there are still few doctors who know much about dance injuries. Many dancers have to settle for a competent doctor who has little experience dealing with dancers or even athletes.

There are some muscular disorders unique to dancers, which the average doctor may not know how to treat effectively. As chiropractor Janiz A. Minshew explains, the fact that dancers are so far beyond the norm, in terms of physical conditioning, makes them a mystery to "lay" doctors. A dancer can be out of commission professionally, and still appear to be healthy by normal (nondance) standards. Doctors who treat dancers quickly learn that what may be normal on a dancer's X-ray may not be normal for a nondancer.

Since dancers have a large range of motion, they must maintain exceptionally strong muscles and cannot be treated in the same manner as nondancers. Taking time off can lead to pain in noninjured areas, where there was none before. The better physical condition a dancer is in, the faster she loses that condition without exercise.

Often a dancer seeking care for a routine injury is told to stop dancing until it heals. This is usually not the correct advice for a dancer who knows she must make every effort to keep up her training level. In the time it takes for an injury to heal, the dancer can get out of shape. When she returns to dancing, she could reinjure herself as a result of the layoff. Realizing that she must stay active, she ignores the advice of doctors who try to tell her otherwise.

It is rare to find specialists like New York chiropractor Dr. Nathan Novick, who says, "When a dancer tells me 'I've got to go on!' and I know they shouldn't, I just say good luck and I'll see you tomorrow! Dancers' emotional and mental health is just as important as their physical health. If you take away dance, they'll suffer in other ways."

Dr. Lillie Rosenthal, director of Physical Medicine and Rehabilitation at the Miller Institute for Performing Artists, says she focuses on the dancer's emotional as well as physical state. She says, "I look at the whole picture;

it's not just about the foot. If a dancer can't perform, there is a huge emotional impact. The situation has to be addressed on many levels. It's important to read between the lines to know what is going on with the dancer emotionally as well as physically. Therefore, it's very important for dancers to see somebody who understands them."

While the fields of sports medicine and dance medicine are beginning to attract more interest, the simple economic fact is that few doctors can afford to specialize in the treatment of dancers. In many places there are few dancers to treat, and gaining the specific skill and background needed to deal with their special problems requires a great deal of time, and of course a knowledge of dance. Dance injuries are frequently far more subtle than sports injuries, and they demand an awareness of the intricate movement patterns that may have caused them. In addition, dancers often have limited incomes and no medical insurance.

Fortunately, a few health-care professionals have shown their passion and commitment to dance and the performing arts. Facilities like the Harkness Center for Dance Injuries and the Miller Institute for Performing Artists, both located in New York City, will treat dancers and artists for free, if necessary. Recognizing the need for more physicians who understand the special needs of dancers, Dr. Donald Rose, director of the Harkness Center, says that they have developed a training program that has attracted doctors and physical therapists from around the world. Many of these health-care specialists are involved in sports medicine and want to improve their expertise by developing an understanding of dance technique and dance medicine. This interest usually stems from a commitment to the arts, since remuneration in this field is usually meager.

Still, it is important for an injured dancer to do anything and everything possible to see a doctor with dance-injury expertise. She or he should seek out sports medicine specialists to discover if they might also be familiar with dance, call the nearest ballet company or college dance department head for a suggestion, and ask other dancers. In the event of serious injury, a dancer might have to travel a great distance to reach the right doctor. The inconvenience and expense of travel to find skilled care have to be weighed against the possibility of ending a career in dance.

Dr. James G. Garrick of the Center for Sports Medicine in San Francisco urges dancers to "shop" until they find someone who listens to their needs, and offers informed help. He adds that it is important to avoid "quick and dirty one-shot treatments"; someone who will inject a dancer with cortisone on request to keep her dancing today may not care what happens to her two years from now.

The adage "no pain, no gain" can be a dangerous one for a dancer to follow. Although there is a certain degree of healthy "feel-good" discomfort that comes from a well-stretched muscle, there is a fine line between that and the kind of pain resulting from incorrect stretching. Learning to differentiate between "good" pain and "bad" pain is vital if a dancer wants to avoid permanent damage to her or his body.

Dancers often wait too long to address an injury; they try to ignore small things that unnecessarily turn into major problems. This is a basic human tendency, but it is sometimes encouraged in dancers by unsympathetic responses from teachers, directors, and choreographers, and by pressure to keep dancing.

Dr. Garrick notes that professional dancers often have medical problems on the road, when local medical personnel may feel pressured to get them back on stage at the expense of their long-term well-being. He advises dancers to call for advice from a care center they trust, and not to make a bad or unwise decision under management pressure.

This problem is related to the fact that, unlike dancers in other parts of the world, American dancers have no job security. Members of major European companies often have their job guaranteed by contract for twenty years. They are on salary during periods of medical injury, their medical expenses are covered, and helping them maintain their health and productivity is a direct concern of their employers. This is a far cry from the typical American dancer who is terrified of becoming injured because she cannot afford to pay the medical bills, fears losing her job, and cannot find a qualified specialist to treat her.

A dance specialist will approach a dancer's injury as a medical detective. As podiatrist Dr. Tom Novella explains, a dance specialist must look at everything in the dancer's history rather than at a single injury. Everything is linked. The doctor needs to identify the original injury in a chain. He or she needs to treat the cause of a specific injury, as well as cure it. Otherwise there is a strong possibility the injury will return.

Many female dancers' problems stem from the lack of mobility caused by pointe shoes, yet some problems that appear to be caused by shoes are actually technical or structural problems. On the other hand, sometimes what appears to be technical or structural could be the result of the shoe. Again, the doctor must be a sleuth.

In recent years dance medical specialists have noticed a disturbing trend among pointe dancers toward elective cosmetic surgery. For instance, a dancer might want to have her arches made higher. Dr. Tom Novella had an inquiry from a dancer whose choreographer wanted her foot to have a more winged look; she wanted a surgically induced bunion. Noting that even the best surgeons have failure rates of one out of forty cases, Dr. Novella suggests that if a dancer is active and healthy, she should hold on to what she has, and work with it. In other words, if it does not hurt, leave it alone.

Chiropractor Janiz A. Minshew reminds dancers of another vital reason to pay careful attention to the treatment of any injuries they sustain. She says, "Age alone will not significantly alter performance and physical ability. However, age combined with injury, combined with years of compensation cause ability to diminish rapidly. If you can fix problems rather than compensate for them throughout your dance life, this attrition will not be as sharp or as fast."

Dr. Lillie Rosenthal adds that a dancer wants his or her body to work long-term. She recognizes that dance is a passion "that dancers eat and drink; it's a part of their identity. Ideally, they should have long, healthy careers that do not burn out like a bright star."

Medical Specialists: Who Does What?

When starting to look for medical assistance, it helps to have a clear idea of the role of each specialist.[3]

First, the words "medical doctor" must be defined. There are parallel, but separate, medical schools in the United States. The M.D., described as allopathic, and D.O., described as osteopathic, are both fully licensed physicians and generally have the same skills, ability, and go through similar training. After graduating, they both can choose any specialty. What sets the D.O. apart from the M.D. is that the D.O. has additional training in the musculoskeletal system and in manual healing techniques.

The D.O.'s general approach is a bit more holistic than what is thought of as the traditional M.D. A doctor can be a D.O. or an M.D. and still be an orthopedic surgeon or another kind of specialist. The public is less familiar with the work of osteopaths. There are only eighteen osteopathic schools in the United States as opposed to the many schools where one can obtain an M.D. In the following list orthopedists, osteopaths, and physiatrists are fully licensed physicians. Podiatrists, chiropractors, and physical therapists are not. That means they cannot prescribe medication and cannot do surgery. This rule varies from state to state for podiatrists; in some locations they can operate only on the foot or on the foot and leg—in other words, some do surgery and some do not.

Orthopedists are physicians who specialize in bones and muscles. After medical school, they complete a five- or six-year residency in orthopedic surgery. Although they are trained to treat any area of the body, a small but ever-growing number specialize in foot and ankle problems, and many have completed postresidency fellowships in this field.

Osteopaths are physicians who diagnose, prescribe for, and treat bodily diseases and injuries. They are concerned with research into the causes, transmission, and control of disease and other ailments attributable to impairments in the musculoskeletal system and disorders of bones, muscles, nerves, and other body systems. They use X-ray, drugs, and other accepted methods of medical and surgical care. When deemed beneficial, they use manipulative therapy to treat and correct body impairments.

Physiatrists are M.D.s or osteopaths who take care of any disability, be it an acute injury like an ankle sprain or more severe disabilities. A physiatrist is a blend of nonoperating orthopedist, neurologist, family practitioner, and physical therapist.

Podiatrists, or Doctors of Podiatric Medicine (D.P.M.s), treat feet exclusively. Podiatry school requires four years of training beyond college, and some podiatrists take additional training. Those certified by the American Board of Podiatric Surgery have additional practical experience.

Chiropractors adjust the spinal column and other joints of the body to prevent disease and to correct abnormalities believed to be caused by interference with the nervous system. Using X-ray and other instruments and equipment, they examine patients to determine the nature and extent of the disorder present. Chiropractors do not have medical degrees.

Physical therapists plan and administer medically prescribed physical therapy treatment programs that restore function, relieve pain, and prevent disability after disease or bodily injury. Physical therapists may work in private practice or be employed in hospitals and rehabilitation centers.

Levels of Injury

There are three major levels of dance-related injuries. First are acute injuries, which are injuries at the time they occur, such as a sprained ankle. Whether acute injuries are mild, moderate, or severe, they usually produce bleeding or hemorrhage into the surrounding soft-tissue structures. Treatment of these injuries is designed to lessen the initial injury to soft tissues, since recovery is directly tied to the degree of original trauma and bleeding.

Dr. Hamilton suggests dancers remember the acronym RICE when confronting an acute injury: Rest, Immobilization, Cold, and Elevation. Rest means getting weight off the injury to avoid stirring up more bleeding and swelling. Immobilization means splinting. In the case of a mild injury, the splint might be a simple Ace bandage applied loosely enough to avoid impairing circulation, but tightly enough to restrict swelling. Elevation and ice also help keep swelling down. Ice should be wrapped in an ice bag or towel and not applied directly to the skin. An injury should be iced intermittently over the first twelve to twenty-four hours. Heat should not be applied during this period because it dilates the blood vessels and can cause excessive bleeding. Bleeding is no longer a factor after twenty-four to thirty-six hours, and heat can then increase circulation, and has a positive impact on the healing process.

For acute injury of the leg, Dr. Hamilton tells his patients to get off the injured leg, elevate it, and ice it for twenty-four hours. Then they should keep weight off the leg as much as possible, keep it elevated for the next twenty-four hours, and start warm soaks after thirty-six hours.

Chronic injuries—the second level of dance-related injury—are those that have never healed, or from which the patient has not completely recovered. If an acute injury is incorrectly treated or receives inadequate rest, it may develop into a chronic injury. Tendinitis, overuse strains, stress fractures that have never healed owing to lack of rest, or pulled hamstring muscles that have become chronically tight and developed painful scar tissue are examples. Chronic problems require prolonged activity reduction in order to heal, and can limit the dancer for as long as several months.

A type of chronic injury is overuse, which can be the result of faulty technique, says Dr. Galli. Traumatic injuries, such as being dropped by your partner, have a beginning and end, but overuse injuries have a beginning and no end.

Third are recurring injuries—those that do heal but return again. For instance, a sprained ankle may heal but still be weak. Therefore it may be reinjured a month later. This cycle can only be broken through strengthening and rehabilitation. Dr. Galli suggests that when a dancer finds that injuries continue to recur, she might need to increase her range of motion, increase her strength or wear a different shoe. Some of these injuries may be cuased by such external factors as hard floors or errors in technique, placement, or alignment.

Dr. Hamilton observes that chronic injuries are the most common among dancers, and that the specific injuries differ in frequency from company to company. This is the result of different choreographic styles as well as the difference in the floors they dance on, how much they travel, and the body types the company seeks.

Pointe-related Injuries of the Foot and Ankle

In 1986, Dr. James Garrick reported the results of a five-year study in which he analyzed 1,055 injuries to dancers from two professional ballet companies and a large professional school. The dancers studied ranged in age from five to over forty. He observed that nine percent of these injuries occurred to the spine, 3.8 percent to the upper extremities, 9.7 percent to the hip, 22.3 percent to the knee, 11.4 percent to the leg, 16.6 percent to the ankle, and 21.6 percent to the feet.[4]

While pointe shoes and pointe work have implications for a variety of injuries to the knee, leg, hip, and spine, we have chosen to stress the sites where the strain of dancing on pointe has the most immediate impact: the foot and ankle. Most injuries start from the bottom up, with problems such as feet that sickle or roll in or out, weak ankles, lax ligaments, and exceedingly high or low arches that are aggravated by flawed technique. On the other hand, Dr. Novella suggests that if a dancer is prone

226

to foot injuries, the cause could be weakness in the hips or back, which brings stress to the feet. Without adequate strength in the upper torso, the dancer can land too hard and injure her feet.

The following review of foot and ankle injuries and conditions is a compilation of information and suggestions received from the medical personnel we interviewed. These brief summaries should help the dancer identify an injury. They are not intended to supplant the advice of a properly qualified medical specialist. Diabetics should not self-treat even the most minor foot problems without the supervision of a physician.

The Foot

In Dr. Garrick's study of ballet injuries, foot injuries were the second most often seen injury. Dancing on pointe adds a new list of demands to an already challenged foot. Not only does the dancer have to bear her weight on the tips of the toes, but also she has to adjust to the non-anatomically designed aspects of pointe shoes.

When injuries of the foot and ankle force the dancer to keep weight off her lower extremities, Dr. Novella suggests doing floor barres and other exercises not involving the feet, to keep the rest of the body stretched.

Problems on the External Surface of the Foot

Athlete's Foot. Athlete's foot is a fungal infection that thrives in a moist, dark environment. Tight, closed shoes and perspiring feet provide the ideal environment for Athlete's foot. To prevent Athlete's foot, the dancer should wash her feet at least once a day, being careful to dry the skin between her toes. If she develops the condition, over-the-counter remedies should cure it, or a doctor can prescribe a strong antifungal drug. She needs to continue preventive steps once the condition clears up since it can readily return. Athlete's foot is contagious and can be contracted by not wearing shoes in the dressing room or shower room.

Blisters. Blisters are caused by continuous friction when tender skin is rubbed back and forth against the inside of the shoe. This friction separates skin layers, and one layer slides over the other. The resulting pocket fills up with fluid that is either clear or contains blood. Many blisters caused by pointe shoes are blood blisters. Blisters may result from shoes that fit incorrectly, or they may develop during the breaking-in process. Seams in tights or socks that are too snug, or wrinkles in those that are too loose can be responsible.

Using a drying powder can reduce moisture and the chances of getting blisters. Blister-prone dancers sometimes routinely tape their problem toes or lubricate them with petroleum jelly and wrap them in lamb's wool. In the days of czarist Russia, ballerinas reportedly put thin slices of veal in their shoes to prevent blisters.

It is best to catch blisters before they form. The warning sign is a warm red "hot spot." As soon as the dancer sees the skin is irritated, she should use a friction-proof substance such as petroleum jelly, or cover the spot with a Band-Aid or moleskin. There are numerous new products on the market that are geared especially for the pointe dancer to protect the skin on the foot from blisters.

Once caused, a blister can be a small annoyance or a serious infection. The dancer needs to deal with blisters before they pop open and bleed. Once the blister opens, the dancer must find a way to prevent infection from occurring while she continues to dance. When the raw skin is exposed, the pain of dancing with a large blister can be extreme. In such cases it may be necessary to give the blister time to heal, rather than risk deepening or infecting the area by applying more friction. The exposed skin can be treated with merthiolate.

A blood blister requires immediate consultation with a medical specialist since there is a greater risk of infection, but a dancer can treat an unpopped blister with clear fluid herself. First, sterilize the blistered area with alcohol and then sterilize a needle with alcohol or flame. Using the needle, puncture the blister in several spots around the edge. Carefully push on the blister with a sterile pad to release the fluid.

Dancers used to be told to cut away the dead skin, but they are now advised to allow it to remain, to cut down the risk of infection. Then apply an over-the-counter antibiotic ointment to the blister and cover it with moleskin. Repeat this complete procedure three more times within twenty-four hours. After three or four days, the dead skin comes off naturally. Try covering the tender new skin with a product like Spenco's Second Skin or New Skin, until it has time to toughen up.

Expose the blister to fresh air whenever possible, being careful to keep it sterilized. If dancing on pointe is painful before the blister has healed, try surrounding it with several circular layers of moleskin, or some other new cushioning product.

Calluses. Calluses are thick, hard mounds of skin that appear on the bottom or side of the foot. They are caused by the friction and pressure of rubbing the skin of the feet against supportive surfaces. They usually occur on the knuckles and tops of the toes, and on the Achilles tendon where the shoe rubs the heel. Dancers with flat feet or exceptionally high arches tend to develop a lot of calluses. Excessive callus also frequently forms on one side of a tilted heel or imbalanced big toe.

Calluses appear as reddened areas that may be tender following pointe work, but will harden later. While some callus formation is useful for dancers in toughening the feet, a lot of callus may also indicate poor posture and weight-bearing, or poorly fitted pointe shoes.

Callus that has grown too thick can produce pain and a burning sensation. It can also crack and bleed, and infections can result. Thickened callus that has lost its elasticity tends to move as a mass, and can actually tear.

A painful blister can form under a callus. If such a blister breaks, the callus may fall off, resulting in a very sore foot and a long, painful healing process. A callus under the second metatarsal sometimes forms a hard core, another source of considerable pain. Calluses under the second metatarsal are a common problem for dancers with bunions.

To keep callus under control, soak the feet in a bowl of warm water and several tablespoons of mild soap for ten to fifteen minutes. Then gently file off excess callus accumulation with an emery file, and massage the area with a small amount of olive oil. Do not try to remove the entire callus build-up in one treatment, but be sure to keep any remaining callus level with the skin around it. Finally, smooth the area with the finer side of the emery board. Repeat this procedure after bathing or showering, being careful never to file away too much callus. The area can be protected by applying moleskin, or another type of cushion, before dancing.

Corns. Corns are the result of abnormal pressure from incorrectly fitted shoes, and can be quite painful. Unlike calluses, corns form in places that do not bear weight, or they develop between the toes. Dancers with high arches are susceptible to corns because their toes tend to buckle.

There are two kinds of corns—hard and soft. Both types result from shoes pressing on the top layer of tissue, causing the tissue to be pressed inward. Since corns press on nerve endings and cause inflammation, they can be painful and incapacitating.

A hard corn is most often found on the side or the top of the little toe, and can be caused by short pointe shoes. The most logical way to get rid of a hard corn is to remove the friction that is causing it. In other words, pad the spots where corns are forming and look closely at the way the fit of the pointe shoes may be causing the problem.

Surgically removing corns is not an option open to dancers. Chemical corn pads should also be avoided because of the risk of infection from a burn to the skin. If a dancer insists on using such pads, he or she should read the directions with care, and be aware of any signs of infection, such as redness (particularly red streaks running up the leg), heat, pain, or swelling. She should seek medical care immediately if these signs persist, because he or she could have blood poisoning and might need antibiotics.

To safely reduce the size of hard corns, soak the feet in warm, soapy water for five or ten minutes. Dry the feet and massage the toes with olive oil. Carefully rub the corn with the coarse side of an emery board and smooth the area with the finer side of the emery board. Do not go too far with this first effort. Repeat this routine whenever corns are softened with a shower or bath, until the corn is even with the skin. Only a podiatrist should cut away a corn.

Soft corns, which develop in the moist environment between the toes, have a mushier appearance than hard corns. They are gray-white in color and often appear between the fourth and fifth toes, resulting from pointe shoes that are too tight across the metatarsal area. Soft corns may signal the need to wear a pointe shoe with a broader box. Soft corns thrive in warm, wet conditions, so feet must be kept as dry as possible with an antiseptic powder.

To treat soft corns, the dancer must separate the toes involved to eliminate the pressure point. Once the pressure is gone, and the area is kept dry, soft corns should disappear. The toes can be separated with lamb's wool, cotton, or a commercial toe spacer. Without this cushioning, bone spurs can rub away the tissue and cause an ulcer, which is very painful and can become dangerously infected. If this separating strategy is unsuccessful, consult a doctor about the possibility of removing the blisterlike covering over the corn. Again, surgical removal of soft corns is not an alternative for dancers, and the use of medicated corn pads with soft corns should be avoided.

Dr. Novella warns that a thick soft corn can almost become an abscess, without the dancer's feeling it, if it is masking a pinched nerve. Novella often sees this happen between the third and fourth toes. A doctor should check to see if the sensitivity in the area of the soft corn is the same as it is in the rest of the foot. If not, he or she can try to discover the cause before it leads to infection.

Dermatitis. Dermatitis is a skin irritation that occurs in reaction to something—usually an allergen or stress. The feet are often afflicted with itching, burning, or reddened areas. Reddish bumps or blisters may appear. Contact dermatitis usually results from skin contact with a substance to which one is allergic. Sometimes shoe leathers are processed with strong chemicals that are highly allergenic. If necessary, a test can be performed to determine the nature of the allergy. Neurodermatis is stress-related.

Problems With Toenails

Toenails are far more complicated structures than they appear to be. Each nail has six parts, starting from the inside and working to the tip—the matrix, the lunula, the cuticle, the root, the nail bed, and the tip. Toenails are made of protein keratin, similar to the protein that makes up hair. To avoid problems, nails should be kept properly trimmed and cleaned.

Ingrown Toenails. Ingrown toenails occur when the side edge of the toenail curls and pushes down into the soft skin of the toe, causing irritation or infection. Ingrown nails can be caused by abnormal pressure from pointe shoes that are too short or narrow, by incorrectly trimmed toenails, and by thickened nails caused by pointe work.

Redness is the first sign of an ingrown toenail. Sharp pain and swelling can follow. If any pus or infection is present, see a doctor immediately. If pain occurs, soak the foot in hot water and antibacterial soap several times a day, and place a bit of thin, alcohol-soaked cotton under the edge of the nail to push the skin away while the nail grows. By lifting the nail away from the nail bed, the cotton should provide relief from pain.

If the ingrown nail has reached a point where it must be clipped away, it is wise to see a doctor. Podiatrist Dr. Steven Baff treats serious cases by cutting away the ingrown nail so the tissue around the nail does not become inflamed, or by permanently removing the ingrown portion of the nail down to the root using a chemical or a laser beam.

Dancers can help avoid the problem by trimming the toenail straight, with only a slight rounding at the corners. The nail should never be rounded enough to come into contact with the skin on either side of the nail bed. Some dancers cut the nail a little shorter in the middle, giving the nail the shape of a letter U or V, and then pack a tiny bit of lamb's wool in the corners of the nail plate. Investing in a good pair of nail clippers is an essential for toenail maintenance.

Bruised Toenails. The toes take a beating every day in pointe shoes, and may show evidence of bruises and bleeding under the nails. This is particularly true if pointe shoes are too short or too narrow, as well as if the toenails are too long. When the blood vessels under the toes rupture, this blood cannot escape, causing a clot under the nail. This condition can also be caused by dropping on the toe an object heavy enough to bruise.

If the nail is iced as soon as the trauma has happened and kept iced periodically, the blood clot may be kept from forming. If the clot does form, the toenail can be saved if it is treated within two days after the blood has entered the space between the nail and the nail bed.

To treat the nail, Dr. James Garrick suggests heating a paper clip in a flame until it is red hot and pushing it through the nail to release the blood. The clip may have to be reheated a few times to complete the procedure, and additional pressure may have to be applied

232

to the sides of the nail as well. This method should bring instant relief. After performing this procedure, soak the foot three times a day in warm water and Epsom salts, and keep the nail painted with merthiolate. Keep the nail covered with a Band-Aid.

If not treated soon enough, the nail will probably be lost within a month. If the nail does start to detach itself and there is no sign of infection, secure the nail in place with adhesive tape to protect the tissue underneath. It will take the new toenail about six months to grow back.

Thickened Toenails. A thickened toenail is grayish-black or brown in color and occurs when the toe is constantly jammed by a pointe shoe. The pressure produces an additional layer of nail that in turn creates more pressure against the bed of the nail. Consult a podiatrist for treatment of thickened toenails.

Fungus Nails. A thick nail that becomes yellow-brown and has spongy growths underneath might be a sign of a fungus infection. A fungus infection can be a very serious condition and may spread to other toes. See a doctor immediately for a suspected fungus infection.

Problems With Toes

Toes of Various Lengths. Dr. Richard Braver estimates that one-third of the population has a second toe longer than the first toe, one third has a first toe longer than the second, and one-third has both toes the same length. A second or third toe is not meant to function as the pressure-taking toe, so pain in the ball of the foot as well as stress fractures can result in pointe dancers who have longer second or third toes. While feet with longer second or third toes are not designed to be subjected to pointe shoes, recently introduced orthotic devices may help by elevating or repositioning the toes to avoid undue pressure.

Bunions (Hallux Valgus). Dr. Novella feels that almost all dancers have a bunion or bunions at some stage of development. A bunion is a bony knob on the outside of the big toe, which forms when the toe is forced to angle inward toward the smaller ones. The projection is caused by the deviation or drifting out of joint of one of the bones of the big toe. Pressure on the projection causes the skin around it to thicken, adding to the pressure. A portion of the bunion is made up of a bursa between the skin and the bone. This fluid-filled sac may feel bone-hard. A red, swollen bunion is the result of an inflamed bursa.

This condition is often inherited and is usually seen on feet where the second toe is longer than the first, the first metatarsal is short, and the ball of the foot is over-flexible. Dancing on pointe and rolling in to increase turnout can cause a mild case of hallux valgus (bunion) from stretching the ligaments on the inside of the foot.

While some bunions do not produce pain while dancing, in some cases shoe pressure on the jutting joint can cause bursitis or inflammation of the joint, causing it to become painful, swollen, and tender. A bunion can be caused by the stress and friction of tight pointe shoes. When bunions are painful, a toe spacer can be worn between the big and second toes properly positioning the big toe and preventing it from being crushed into the other toes at an angle. A toe spacer can be made of lamb's wool or a one-inch strip of paper towel folded into a small rectangle and placed between the toes. Moleskin pads and commercially made bunion cushions can also be used.

Care should be taken to see that pointe shoes (and street shoes) are wide enough across the metatarsal joints to avoid undue pressure, and that the foot is placed properly on pointe. Padding around the bunion is helpful, and latex bunion shields or Dr. Scholl's Bunion Splints may provide relief from pressure. Try cutting slits in the side or back of pointe shoes to cut down on pressure, or cut wedges out of these areas and fill them in with elastic or moleskin.

When the bunion projections are sore and inflamed, treat them with ice and contrast (hot and cold) baths (see p. 251). Anti-inflammatories may also be helpful. Often, as the result of a bunion, other parts of the foot may start to hurt. The dancer might have pain under a second toe or develop a hammertoe. A soft corn could form between the first and second toe.

Most doctors agree that the hazards of bunion surgery outweigh the benefits for dancers. While the cosmetic result may be more attractive, such surgery may result in limited motion of the joint, sharply reduced technique range on *demi-pointe*, and chronic pain.

Bunionette. A bunionette (sometimes called a tailor's bunion) is an enlargement of the head of the fifth metatarsal. This congenital condition causes the foot to be exposed to abnormal pressure, so a bursa may form over the joint to protect it. When this bursa fills with fluid and becomes inflamed, a burning sensation, swelling, and pain can result. Taking anti-inflammatories and applying ice help reduce the pain and swelling. The bunionette should be padded with felt or moleskin, or covered with a commercially produced bunion shield to protect it from the pressure of the pointe shoe.

Hammertoes. Hammertoes are those that curl or hook downward. The condition can be either inherited or aggravated by wearing shoes that are too tight and too short, thus forcing toe joints and the extensor tendon to contract. Eventually the toes become locked and the tendon is permanently shortened. Hammertoes may accompany a bunion. They frequently occur in individuals whose second toes are longer than the first or who have a high arch.

Protective U-shaped pads can keep bent-up hammertoes from rubbing against the inside of the shoe and causing corns. These corns on the tip of the toes, or the spot where the joints buckle, are the actual source of pain from hammertoes. Treat a hard corn on a hammertoe as if it were a hard corn in any other location. A podiatrist can cut off a portion of the corn if it becomes excessive.

A hammertoe can be strapped with half-inch adhesive tape to the toes on either side during rehearsal or performance to take weight off it. A podiatrist can guide you in strapping the toe. A hammertoe can only be corrected by surgery, an option not suggested for dancers.

Hallux Limitus and Rigidus. Stiffness of the big toe joint is common among teenage dancers and comes from shock and forceful pressure on the joint. Repeated strain causes the toe joint to become inflamed and stiff in the hallus limitus phase. Since the range of motion in the big toe is limited, body weight shifts to the outside of the foot when the dancer is on *demi-pointe*, which may cause outer ankle strain, weak foot muscles, and pain in the outer leg. Unless the causes are controlled, the toe can become totally rigid, at which point the condition is call hallux rigidus. The key symptom is extreme pain in the joint of the first metatarsal when the dancer goes from *demi-pointe* to full pointe. The tendency is to shift weight to the outside of the foot to avoid this pain in the big toe.

The dancer should take anti-inflammatories, should cushion street shoes, and pad the area under and immediately behind the joint. Several weeks of rest may be required. Consult a doctor for advice on this condition since, in its extreme form, hallux rigidus may require surgery to restore movement, leading to permanent weakening of this important joint.

Jammed Big Toes. As a result of many consecutive hours of pointe work, the ligaments of the toe joint may be sprained, the cartilage may be bruised, or the joint capsule may be stretched and torn. Any of these injuries can be extremely limiting. Treat them by taking anti-inflammatories and massaging with ice three times a day for fifteen minutes.

Neuromas. Morton's neuroma is a knotting of nerve fibers marked by shooting pains extending from the ball of the foot between the metatarsals into the toes. These enlarged, inflamed nerves in the ball of the foot usually occur between the third and fourth toes, but sometimes between the fourth and the fifth.

At first a Morton's neuroma may appear as a burning feeling that spreads from the heads of the metatarsals toward the heel, initially noticed when weight is borne on the foot. Eventually, the feeling is present at other times too. Then it begins to resemble an electric shock that shoots from the ball of the foot into the toes. Numbness and cramping may be present as well. The pain usually goes away when shoes are removed. If ignored, the involved nerve may become more swollen and permanently scarred. The condition is usually caused by excessively tight pointe shoes, jamming the heads of the metatarsals together.

The nerve returns to normal if the pressure is eliminated. Treat it with ice three times a day for twenty minutes, and take anti-inflammatories. Be sure to ice after class, rehearsal, or performance. Also look in drugstores for special toe pads that separate the affected toes. Keep a pad behind the area that hurts to reduce pressure on the nerve. With luck, relief will arrive in several weeks. Before returning to pointe, see a shoe-fitting expert and experiment with shoes that have wider boxes. If these efforts fail to provide relief, see an orthopedist for advice. Since surgical removal of neuromas involves no joints or bones, this procedure is not out of the question for dancers.

Problems on the Top and Bottom of the Foot

Extensor Tendinitis. This injury involves pain on the top of the foot, accompanied by swelling and redness that can be caused when pointe shoes are too tight and do not allow enough room over this area. As a result of pressure and friction, the extensor tendons are inflamed. The top of the foot appears puffy, and lifting the toes causes discomfort.

Protect tendons by covering the foot or the inside of the pointe shoe with moleskin. As soon as possible, work with a skilled shoe fitter to find a style of pointe shoe that allows more room over the top of the foot.

Dorsal Exostosis. This bony bump on the top of the foot may be congenital or caused by constant jamming of the big toe. The friction caused by pointe shoes aggravates the bump, making it inflamed and swollen. Flat or pronated feet are particularly liable to experience these bumps. Treat a swollen, aggravated bony bump by icing it several times a day for twenty minutes, and take anti-inflammatories. Surround the bump with moleskin to relieve pressure.

Plantar Fascitis. The plantar fascia is a dense bundle of fibrous tissue strands that starts at the heel and connects with the metatarsal bones at the base of the toes. It stretches and contracts each time the foot is used. If it stretches so far that it loses its flexibility, it tears and causes an overuse condition called plantar fascitis. The key symptom is pain in the bottom of the foot, which may become bruised or swollen. Dancers with high arches and tight fasciae are prime candidates for this injury.

Treat the injury with rest from those movements that cause pain, and with anti-inflammatories, ice, and contrast baths. Visit a podiatrist to discuss ways to reduce the pressure on the fascia.

Plantar Warts. These virus-caused growths on the soles of the feet can make a dancer feel as if there is something in her shoe. Plantar warts grow in, rather than out, and appear under the heel, on the ball of the foot, or on the side of the big toe. Normal skin ridges, which continue across the surface of a callus, encircle a plantar wart, leaving only the growth surface smooth. Sometimes the warts appear in groups. If left alone, plantar warts eventually leave on their own. If they grow larger or cause discomfort, see a podiatrist about removing them.

Plantar warts are contagious, so wear shoes in the dressing room and shower room. If a classmate or fellow company member who shares such facilities discovers a plantar wart, disinfect the area with undiluted Clorox.

Sesamoiditis. If pain is experienced at the base of the big toe where it joins the ball of the foot when pushing off the toe, the sesamoid bones may be irritated. The sesamoids are very small bones in the tendons connected to the big toe. They serve a pulleylike function and can be strained or even fractured. Sesamoids are particularly vulnerable when a bunion is present. Bony feet and working on a hard dancing surface are also risk factors. Sesamoid trouble is recognized as pain experienced under the metatarsal in the *demi-pointe* position. Swelling will also be present.

Rest, ice, and anti-inflammatories should be used as treatment. Continue resting until the area is pain-free; then slowly resume activity. Padding beneath the sesamoids can reduce the impact of pounding. If pain is still fairly intense after two weeks, see an orthopedist to determine if there has been a fracture of a sesamoid and a cast is needed.

Stress Fractures. Stress fractures, which can occur in any bone, are ranked by Dr. James Garrick as the fifth most frequent dancer's injury. They usually result from big changes in activity levels. Stress fractures can happen in any area of the foot that contacts the ground in a stressful way. They can happen in the sesamoids under the ball of the foot or in the metatarsal shafts. In experienced dancers, stress fractures are common in the base of the second metatarsal. The bone may thicken like the bark of a tree, from work and exercise. In novice dancers they are common in the middle of the second metatarsal.

A stress fracture is evidence of the body's attempt to become stronger by removing calcium from one area and laying it down in another area. The stress fracture is a "too much, too soon" injury that happens during this process of removing and laying down calcium. A stress fracture occurs when a bone bends almost to the breaking point. The physical evidence appears in the form of a hairline crack that may not show up on an X-ray. As a result, with rest, a stress fracture may heal before it is diagnosed. Dr. Garrick uses radioisotope bone scans to confirm the diagnosis of a stress fracture early in its history.

Since a stress fracture develops over a period of time, the area around it usually feels tender before any pain is present. This area may not be any larger than the diameter of a penny. Eventually the pain becomes more intense and a burning sensation surrounds the fracture. The area involved becomes very painful to touch and will probably be swollen. Bearing weight often become excruciating when a stress fracture is present.

When treating stress fractures at an early stage, a pain-free state can often be reached after a day or two of complete rest. Anti-inflammatories may be useful during this period, and ice can be applied if there is swelling. Resting a more serious stress fracture might require as long as a week on crutches.

When it is possible to resume dancing, find a level of activity that stops short of causing pain. Wear a thin layer of absorbent padding in the pointe shoe at this stage of the process. When discomfort is experienced, drop back to a lighter activity level. Keep increasing and decreasing the activity level until normalcy returns. Then watch for the warning sign of a tender area the size of a penny, to avoid future fractures. Dr. Galli says that stress fractures develop because dancers ignore the early signs of foot pain. Do not ignore pain!

It is important to identify stress fractures as early as possible, because if ignored, they can work all the way through the bone, actually causing it to snap in two. The resulting advanced fracture can require splints or casts, immobilization, and a long recovery period. Dr. Steven Baff uses a surgical shoe, which is a compression type of bandage, when treating advanced stress fractures. This is an anti-inflammatory, wet type of bandage that hardens on the foot, contouring it to the shape of the foot and locking it into a normal position for function.

Stress fractures may be avoided if the dancer is sensitive to the possibility of developing them during increased periods of activity. The body is most vulnerable to stress fractures about three weeks into an intensified activity period; therefore, it is a good idea, if possible, to pull back for eight or ten days during this period when bone removal is at its peak.

Dr. Tom Novella has a theory that adolescent dancers who are extremely active with a heavy class load, and who start their menstrual periods late in their teen years, may be prone to stress fractures because they have a lack of circulating estrogen needed to make strong bones. If a young, very active dancer has not had her period yet and is getting stress fractures, a medical specialist should be asked about the possible need to take extra calcium. This connection between injury, menstrual function, and nutrient intake was the subject of a research study reported in an article in the *Journal of the American Dietetic Association* in 1989.[5] Since then, many articles have been written in the *Journal of Dance Medicine and Science* exploring this subject.

Some stress fractures are caused when a dancer works for speed and, to accomplish this, does not put the heels down between steps. Since the calf muscle is a spring, without a *plié* it does not open completely. Then it retains shock instead of absorbing it. Making the heels touch the ground uses muscular energy and takes the stress off the ball of the foot. Stress fractures can also be caused by the impact of repeated jumps and leaps. The lack of shock-absorbing materials in most pointe shoes, and unresilient dance floors are also factors. In recent years, some pointe shoe manufacturers have completely changed the pointe shoemaking process by introducing shock-absorbing materials, which they claim will reduce injury and add to comfort.

A dancer can also develop a stress fracture when she works in soft shoes or bare feet, if she is used to working in a rigid pointe shoe. The toes may not be able to withstand contact with the floor after being shielded in a hard block. On the other hand, a pointe shoe that is too short can cause the toes to curl under, compress, or knuckle forward; as a result, the toes do not work properly when a dancer lands from *relevés* and jumps, thus developing stress fractures on the ball of the foot.

Problems with the Heel

Bursitis. A bursa is a pocket of fluid wrapped in fibrous tissue that is found in areas of the body exposed to friction. A bursa's walls are moist and lubricated so that they can slide. By easing friction where ligaments and tendons cross over bones, bursae make it possible for us to move. When too much pressure irritates a bursa, it can develop thickened walls and become inflamed. Fluid forms, making the bursal sac larger and causing more irritation. An inflamed bursa may be spongy at first, but it gradually hardens as it grows, causing more pain. Bursitis can also be caused by a direct blow to the foot, which ruptures tiny blood vessels in the bursae.

Bursitis can occur in a number of locations on the foot as a result of shoes that are too narrow, too pointed, or too tight. Dancers who roll in may irritate the bursae on the inside of the foot. Pointe dancers often suffer from either a metatarsal bursitis or a bursitis of the heel. In the case of metatarsal bursitis, tight pointe shoes and jumping or leaping on hard, uneven surfaces can cause pain to streak across the ball of the foot, particularly during *pliés*, jumps, and leaps, because the bursae at the heads of the metatarsals are bruised and inflamed.

The inflammation of metatarsal bursitis can be helped by taking anti-inflammatories and by icing the area three times a day for three days, followed by warm soaks or contrast baths. This problem, however, is best solved with a period of complete rest from weight-bearing; recovery can take from one to three months. High heels should be avoided, and extra cushioning should be added to street shoes. This pain can also be confused with other problems that plague the metatarsals, such as stress fractures, and should be reported to a medical specialist.

Bursitis at the heel can be either congenital or caused by pressure on the heel from a tight drawstring or a too-stiff shoe back. Posterior calcaneal bursitis is found at the center of the heel and is an inflammation of a bursa between the tendon and the skin. Another type of bursitis, Haglund's deformity, is located to the side of the heel and takes the form of a raised, hard formation. Bursitis of the heel is often seen in dancers with very low or high arches.

Skin blisters are a warning sign that too much shoe pressure is present. A burning or aching sensation may precede intense pain. Once pressure is removed from the area, swelling can be reduced in several weeks by icing the heels for twenty minutes twice a day and taking anti-inflammatories. Avoid shoes with closed heels, or pad the backs of shoes with moleskin and elevate the heel with a lift. Some dancers cut the heel of their pointe shoes and sew in an elastic insert to get relief.

Contusions. Contusions are bruises that often occur in the foot region; the skin or heel of the foot is especially sensitive to contusions. A contusion produces a pool of blood that has nowhere to go, so remains trapped under the skin. Mild contusions produce little inflammation, and most of the discomfort comes from muscle spasms. Apply cold and pressure to avoid swelling, followed by a gradual stretch to relieve muscle spasms. If discomfort persists for more than five or ten minutes, wear an elastic bandage for the rest of the day. If symptoms are present the second day, try contrast baths. More serious contusions result from a hard blow to a muscle or bone and produce a great deal of pain and tenderness when touched. Ice the area and apply an elastic wrap intermittently for twenty-four hours. Elevate the injury. Following a serious contusion, it is wise to see a medical specialist to discount the possibility of fracture.

Dancer's Heel. Sometimes too much pointe work on nonresilient floor surfaces creates inflammation in the dancer's foot above the heel bone. It seems to be a reaction to an injury to the joint where the ankle is connected to the foot. Pain is experienced deep in the area of the Achilles tendon each time the foot is pointed.

Treatment should include icing three times a day for three days, and taking anti-inflammatories. Pointe work will be very uncomfortable, so the dancer should try to limit her time on pointe until the pain has subsided, or she should flex the knee slightly while working on the injured pointe. If the pain does not diminish greatly in ten days, the dancer should see an orthopedist, since the symptoms of dancer's heel can also signal the presence of an extra bone, the os trigonum, in the back of the foot.

Heel Bruises. Calcaneal periostitis is one of the worst acute injuries a dancer can experience. It is caused by repeated compression of the tissue covering the bottom of the heel bone or its bursa. Dancers with bony feet or irregularly shaped heel bones are particularly subject to this injury, which can be induced by coming down incorrectly from a jump, or by overuse. It can also be caused by stepping on a small object. The injury intensifies after leaping or jumping. This injury also makes it extremely painful for the heel to make contact with the floor.

Ice should be applied at once, and icing should continue three times a day; an anti-inflammatory should also be taken. Dr. Garrick suggests wearing a rigid heel cup in street shoes to cup the heel and re-form it to its original shape. A dancer can also strap and pad the heel to take painful pressure off the bruise.

Heel Spurs. Heel spurs are bony growths on the bottom of the heel bone; dancers with flat feet are prone to develop them. Plantar fascitis can also cause heel spurs by pulling a piece of bone loose at the heel. Upon rising in the morning, and after extended periods of weight-bearing, pain is felt when pressure is applied to the front of the heel bone. Treatment involves removing the pressure and reducing inflammation. Anti-inflammatories can be helpful, and an application of ice for fifteen or twenty minutes at a time is suggested. Rest, contrast baths, and added support in street shoes may also be useful. If the symptoms do not ease after a few days, see a podiatrist for help.

The Ankle

In Dr. Garrick's study of ballet injuries, he found that the ankle was the third most involved anatomical region. Acute injuries in this area were more common than overuse injuries. Sprains involved the ankle more than any other joint. Many of these sprains result from missteps and faulty landings during the acquisition of technical skills in dancers thirteen to eighteen years of age. A dancer with a hyperflexible high instep, whose muscles, tendons, and cartilage are stretched beyond their maximum capacity, often lacks the strength in her ligaments to prevent ankle strains and fractures.

Achilles Tendinitis. The Achilles tendon, the largest tendon in the body, extends down the back of the leg, connecting the muscles of the calf to the heel bone. The Achilles tendon allows the dancer to rise onto pointe. Achilles tendinitis can be caused by overwork or bruised heels. Some dancers try to protect their heels by not putting them down, and as a result strain the Achilles tendon. Pressure from the back of an incorrectly fitted shoe, the elastic, or a ribbon knot can cause problems with the Achilles tendon.

In Dr. Garrick's study of ballet injuries, most instances of Achilles tendinitis beyond the mid-teen years were the result of overuse or inadequate rehabilitation of calf muscles after an ankle or foot injury. In older dancers he found that the problem could result from microscopic tears from repeated injuries over the years.

Symptoms of Achilles tendinitis include soreness along the length of the tendon, swelling, and severe pain, particularly in *relevé*. A slight noise may be heard in the rear of the heel when the ankle is moved. The pain is usually at its worst upon rising in the morning.

Tendinitis starts as tears in the individual tiny fibers that make up the Achilles tendon rub against the sheath that surrounds it, causing the sheath to swell as well. At the first signs of Achilles tendinitis, it is wise to consult a medical specialist to determine a proper course of action. The specialist might suggest a combination of stretches, anti-inflammatories, and ice therapy for a mild case, or complete cessation of dance activity for as long as three weeks in more serious cases.

When advised that it is safe to return to dancing, the dancer should begin barre work cautiously, stretching the tendon carefully. At first, all *relevés*, pointe work, and jumps should be avoided. Add only a few exercises at a time if no pain is present. If any pain develops, the dancer needs to stop immediately and give the area more rest, elevation, and ice. If allowed to persist, Achilles tendinitis can become very difficult to cure. Strengthening the calf muscles is a good insurance policy against Achilles tendinitis.

Sprained Ankle. Dr. Novella finds that sprained ankles are the most common injury he sees in pointe dancers. The anklebone is able to roll toward the inside of the joint more easily than it is able to roll to the outside. If a traumatic event forces it to roll too far to the inside, the ligaments on the outside of the ankle bear the brunt of the sudden movement and can stretch, strain, or tear. This type of sprain is called a lateral sprain, and results in pain and swelling on the outside of the ankle. Medial ankle sprains, which are much less common, occur when the foot rolls away from the body and causes pain to the inside of the ankle. Sprains can occur because of ankle muscle weaknesses or a structural problem such as a short fifth metatarsal. If the midfoot is loose, it can sickle in the center and give way during *demi-pointe* or *relevé*.

When testing an injured ankle to determine the extent of damage, the dancer will find that she can put weight on a sprain and twist it with some pain. However, if she feels anything grinding in the ankle, experiences numbness or a sensation of cold, or is concerned that the injury might be more than a sprain, she should see a medical specialist right away. If the pain is on the inside of the ankle, indicating a medial fracture, it is especially important to seek medical advice.

The initial swelling of a sprained ankle stems from internal bleeding resulting from torn ligaments and the surrounding soft tissues. This swelling makes the ankle stiff. To control swelling, wrap a sock around the injured ankle bone and then wrap the ankle area with an Ace bandage. Keep the area wrapped for twenty-four hours, and intermittently apply ice over a layer of bandage. Do not use heat immediately after sustaining a sprained ankle. If swelling remains after the first day and/or if any discoloration is present, see a medical specialist to be X-rayed and checked for fractures.

After the swelling has subsided, try contrast baths, alternating between warm and cold soaks to increase circulation. Also begin moving the ankle to keep the muscle from wasting. Increase the ankle's range of motion and the overall activity level, with pain as a guide. Do as much as you can as soon as you can do it without pain. At night, keep the injured leg elevated on several pillows, and use an Ace bandage if swelling intermittently returns.

Dr. Hamilton suggests that swimming can be helpful as a form of substitute conditioning until a dancer can resume dancing. As ankle motion returns, he suggests doing a barre in chest-deep water after swimming twenty-five laps. Working on *relevé, plié, tendu,* and *frappé* in the buoyancy of the water helps restore strength and motion. When the dancer is ready to try a barre in the studio, at first it should be a "flat-footed" barre on both feet, and without *relevé.*

A dancer working to avoid future sprains needs to think in terms of building strength and balance in both the ankle and midfoot. Sometimes balance training that makes use of such devices as balance boards and tennis balls can help.

Most experts in dance medicine agree that a dancer's sprained ankle should be healed with exercise and treatment, rather than a cast, since when it is removed, the dancer is weaker, causing her to be more susceptible to future injury. If the nature of a sprain demands a cast, an air cast might be useful. This type of cast allows the foot to pointe and flex, but not roll in and out. It can be taken on and off with a Velcro fastener. In the instance of severe sprains, an air cast can reduce healing time from the usual three to six months to six to eight weeks.

Posterior Impingement Syndrome. Dr. Garrick's study found that working on pointe is often responsible for this common overuse problem. Impingement is a condition of the ankle that results from pressure applied while the dancer is in *plié*. The skin and soft tissue surrounding the bones of the ankle compress and wrinkle like an accordion. Some anklebones react by developing ridges that cause the tissue to swell, reducing flexibility. As a result of this build-up of soft tissue and bone in the front or back of the ankle, *plié* or rising to pointe become impossible. Temporary relief is obtained by reducing the swelling and inflammation of soft tissues. But when a serious dance student spends more and more time dancing, with fewer opportunities for rest, the soft tissues stay swollen and permanently thicken. This adds another obstruction to an already crowded rear ankle.

Strong calf muscles can help ward off this problem, and dancers can attempt to take pressure off the ankle by technique adjustments. Surgery to remove the extra tissue and bone is the only cure for the problem. However, some dancers have had to repeat the surgery several times, since the tissue and bone may thicken again. In Dr. Garrick's study, dancers undergoing this surgery were most often in their late teens.[6]

Tools for Treating and Preventing Pointe-related Injuries

Remedies

(Listed in chapter 6 are companies that carry a variety of tapes, bandages, blister kits, and other accessories to assist the pointe dancer.)

Adhesive Tape. Use special lightweight cloth athletic tape, or any of the new tapes that serve the same purpose. Prepare the skin before applying the tape by removing perspiration, dirt, and hair. Commercial tape adherents can be sprayed onto the skin to help the tape stick. Use one-half-inch to one-inch tape in short strips, instead of one long piece, to avoid wrapping it too tightly.

Antiseptic liquid bandages. Commercial preparations such as New Skin (there are several others) put a protective coating over a raw spot until the skin can grow back over it. They are waterproof, but allow the skin to breathe. Liquid bandages dry rapidly to form tough-but-flexible coverings to screen wounds from dirt and germs. They are used to prevent and protect blisters, protect cuts and scrapes, and help prevent callus formation. To use it, clean and dry the broken skin area and spray from six inches away until coated. Allow the preparation to dry, and apply a second coat for added protection. Keep the knuckles bent when applying and drying. A liquid bandage can be removed by applying a fresh coat of the product and rubbing it off quickly with a disposable wipe. Read the cautions on the package before using the product, which is available in pharmacies.

Anti-inflammatories. Nonprescription pain relievers containing ibuprofen, such as Advil or Nuprin, and pure unbuffered aspirins are anti-inflammatories. Buffered aspirin and aspirin substitutes like Tylenol provide relief from pain, but do not act to reduce inflammation. To reduce the inflammation of a tendon or joint, two five-grain unbuffered aspirins every four hours for up to seventy-two hours is considered a maximum dose. During this critical period immediately after an injury, some experts suggest taking this increased dosage and also to determine if any other currently prescribed medications should not be taken with aspirin. Take anti-inflammatories with a full eight-ounce glass of water to reduce the risk of side effects, such as gastrointestinal problems and dizziness. While standard ibuprofen-containing anti-inflammatories and aspirin are available over the counter, stronger anti-inflammatories are only available by prescription.

Blister kits. Spenco as well as other companies (refer to chapter 6) offer a convenient mix of products to help protect against blisters.

Call Spenco's toll-free number (1-800-433-3334) for the name of a local dealer.

Blister, corn, and callous padding. Commercial pads designed to help protect against corns, calluses, and blisters are available in pharmacies and through dance-oriented companies (refer to chapter 6). Avoid using medicated pads because of the danger of infection.

Exercise bands. These rubber devices are six inches wide, vary in length from two to three-and-a-half feet, and come in a variety of colors that represent different tensions. They are excellent for strengthening or warming up the feet and are easy to transport. A dancer with calf problems puts the center of an exercise band over the ball of the foot, flexes the foot, and pulls on the band by holding both ends. The band can also be used to warm up and strengthen the feet when a dancer pulls on it for resistance while pointing her feet. Overuse of exercise bands can lead to tendinitis, so it is best to have specific exercises. They are available under the brand names Thera-Band® and Stretch-Ease Band, and may be found at dance shops and sporting goods stores. They are also dispensed by physical therapists, as well as through some of the companies mentioned in chapter 6.

Pointe shoe manufacturers also sell many of the products mentioned above.

Foot soaks. Burrow's Solution is a popular foot soak. It acts as an antiseptic and anesthetic as it gives off a sensation of heat. Since overuse of such solutions can cause the skin to crack, Burrow's Solution should be diluted and used in a footbath. Hot-water soaks with soap flakes can also be soothing and effective.

Hydrogel dressings. Dressings such as Spenco Second Skin are helpful for covering abrasions and blisters. They help to reduce friction on the skin.

Moleskin or molefoam. This felt or foam has an adhesive backing that can be used as padding on the foot and ankle.

Heat rubs. Heat rubs or analgesic balms, such as Ben-Gay and Tiger Balm, work by irritating the skin and causing a dilation of the small blood vessels, thus bringing a flood of blood and a feeling of warmth to the area. Once the acute phase of an injury is over, heat rubs are useful to provide relief from discomfort while a dancer is in motion. Heat rubs can be applied directly to the skin or to a cloth that is covered with plastic wrap and secured with an Ace bandage.

Heat rubs can burn if overused or used with strong heat from a lamp or electric heating pad. Avoid rubbing the eyes when heat rub is on the fingers. Some of the ingredients used in heat rubs are oil of wintergreen, red pepper, and menthol.

Orthotics. Orthotics are custom-made devices created with negative plaster casts, which work to counteract the impact of structural limitations and injury on the foot. Often the materials used in making orthotics are similar to those employed to support the frame of an aircraft. In an orthotic, these materials support the frame of the foot. Orthotics tend to be extremely long-wearing.

An orthotic locks the foot in normal position so it can function optimally. Whatever the foot's predisposition, the orthotic is made to hold it in a way that avoids the development of what would otherwise become a definite problem. Dr. Steven Baff believes that orthotics can slow down the advent of such problems by as much as ninety-five percent. In other words, if a dancer has a predisposition for a bunion, wearing an orthotic can slow down its development to that extent.

Orthotics absorb a tremendous amount of shock, and extend from the heel to the end of the metatarsal heads, but not the length of the toes. While there are many such devices on the market for foot problems related to walking, until recently there have been few designed for dancers. Orthotics are not yet widely embraced as an effective tool for dancers, but they have enthusiastic supporters who claim they help the feet function properly with less trauma, just as glasses make the eyes function properly.

Surgical or metholated spirit. This product is popular in Great Britain for deadening the top layers of epidermis on the foot, which helps dancers with tender feet to toughen their skin and get used to wearing pointe shoes. Surgical spirit must not be used if a dancer develops blisters.

Toe caps. Dancers have tried to correct for toes of differing lengths by adding various types of padding material, such as cardboard, wadded-up tissue paper, and lamb's wool, to the boxes of their pointe shoes. We spoke to one dancer in Dallas, Texas, who, out of desperation, had created her own toe cap. By a lengthy process of experimentation, Alicia Hicks, a hand therapist, fashioned a toe cap from materials used in her profession to compensate for the fact that her second toe is almost two joints longer than her first. This device made it possible for her to dance with less pain.

While a dancer without Hicks's therapy background would find it difficult to make a safe and effective device for herself, we have learned about custom-made toe caps that are now available for dancers. These toe caps are made to fit each dancer's foot and can be worn with pointe shoes. They are created by a podiatrist, Allan S. Woodle, D.P.M., a specialist in sports medicine and company podiatrist for the Pacific Northwest Ballet in Seattle, Washington. Dr. Woodle's toe caps are molded to the dancer's foot while she alternates standing on pointe and flat in her pointe shoes under Dr. Woodle's supervision.

Dr. Woodle works with the dancer to make numerous finely-crafted adjustments in the toe cap for maximum comfort and effectiveness. When the toe cap is worn, it is placed on the foot first; then the shoe is put on. A change to another brand or style of pointe shoe may require modifications to the toe cap. Dr. Woodle reports that after the toe cap has been "tuned" to the dancer's specific needs, it assists weight-bearing balance as well as reducing pain. It also makes unnecessary the incorrect physical adjustments, sometimes called compensating mechanisms, that a dancer sometimes makes just to hold a balance. Dancers who have problems with toes that are much shorter or longer than other toes, have painful bunions, sickle in or out, or place excessive stress on one or two toes on pointe may be interested in contacting Dr. Woodle about his toe caps. He can be reached at Greenwood Foot and Ankle Center, 8111 Greenwood Avenue N., Seattle, WA 98103; telephone: (206) 784-3144.

Therapies

Elevation. When elevating an injured foot or ankle, keep it above the level of the heart. If you lie down and prop up the injured foot or ankle on several plump pillows, it should be at the right height.

Heat. Heat speeds up circulation and metabolism, and encourages drainage. Superficial heating works on the skin's surface; deep heating acts within body tissues. The dancer herself can apply superficial heat, but deep heat treatments must be taken under the supervision of a professional therapist or other medical specialist.

Heat is never applied immediately after an acute injury, and is often not prescribed for as long as three days after an injury. When superficial heat is used, it should be applied to the injured area when getting up in the morning and before starting an activity. Superficial heat can take the form of an electric heating pad, or a shower or bath. Moist heating pads are a popular option. An electric heating pad should not be applied for longer than twenty minutes.

Warm-water baths can be started at a lower temperature and gradually made hotter, depending on the skin's tolerance. A good starting temperature is ninety degrees. Warm-water baths should last from ten to twenty minutes, and be repeated several times a day. Hot wraps, such as the Spenco Hot Wrap, are reusable sources of soothing moist heat. They come in sizes ranging from small to extra large.

Contrast baths. Alternating hot- and cold-water soaks relieve swelling and muscle spasm. For a contrast bath, prepare two tubs of water—one with a temperature of one hundred and five degrees and one with a temperature of sixty degrees. Soak in hot water for four minutes and then in cold water for two minutes; then in hot water for four minutes and then in cold water for two minutes. Repeat the four-minute (hot) and two-minute (cold) cycles for sixteen more minutes, ending in the hot water. In a pinch, Dr. James Garrick suggests running hot water in the tub for the hot soak, and sticking the foot in the toilet for the cold.

Cold. When cold is indicated as a therapy, it must be applied immediately after an injury. However, it should be used only for as long a period of time as advised by your medical specialist: usually twenty-four to forty hours. Later, cold may be part of longer-term therapy.

Cold works by restricting blood vessels and reducing spasms. After twenty minutes of cold application, an increase of circulation in the deeper tissues results. Stick the foot in a basin of cold water with ice cubes, or ice an injury by using a plastic bag filled with ice held in place by an Ace bandage. (A cloth that has been soaked in water can be frozen and placed in a plastic bag to use in the same fashion.) If no ice is available, a chemical cold pack can be purchased that will become cold when mixed with water and lasts for about thirty minutes. Reusable cold wraps such as Spenco Cold Wrap are available in pharmacies. These stay soft and flexible for greater comfort and come in small, medium, and large sizes.

Ice massage is often used in treating muscle injuries. The following regimen is repeated several times a day: freeze water in a paper or styrofoam cup, and tear off the paper to produce a cylinder of ice. Wrap a cloth around the ice, and rub the injured area with small circular movements until the skin feels cold and numb. Then stretch the injured area gradually, maintaining the stretch for one to two minutes.

Pilates mat and apparatus work. Developed in the early 1900s by exercise expert Joseph Pilates, the Pilates technique of body conditioning has been a dancer's tool for many years. Pilates brought the technique to the United States in the 1930s, and operated a studio in New York for more than forty years. The Pilates technique has been integrated into dance training by George Balanchine and other major figures in the world of ballet.

The technique revolves around a series of exercises done on a mat, in conjunction with related exercises done on various types of apparatus. The key piece of equipment is the *Reformer*, a horizontal platform with a moveable carriage, on which the dancer reclines, sits, or stands. Apparatus work and mat work educate the dancer in the "recentering" of body alignment.

Environmental Causes of Injury

Temperature

Temperatures in which dancers take class, rehearse, or perform can have an impact on injury. Muscle injuries in particular are far more likely to occur when a dancer is not adequately warmed up. Therefore temperatures should not be allowed to fall below sixty-eight to seventy degrees.

On the other hand, overly high temperatures can induce excessive sweating, leading to loss of water and electrolytes like salt. Inadequate replacement of lost fluid can result in muscle cramps and spasms.

Floor Construction

Floors are an extremely important factor in environmentally caused injuries. The problems encountered with floors fall into three areas—the actual construction of the floor, the angle of the floor, and its surface.

The actual construction of the floor is of the greatest importance to the dancer. Chiropractor Dr. Nathan Novick feels that dance floors that do not breathe and rebound are responsible for many dance injuries. An ideal floor surface for dance must be resilient and nonslip; it must also absorb significant impact and provide lateral foot support. Unfortunately, the floors on which dancers often take class, rehearse, and perform were often not constructed for dance, and have reinforced concrete as their underlying foundation. The ideal dance floor is a sprung or "floating" wooden floor. Such a floor features crossbars, padded sleepers, slats, and runners or risers placed at intervals under the subfloor and flooring to provide air pockets.

As chairperson of the Dance Department at Towson State University in Maryland, Helene Braezeale designed and supervised the installation of new studio floors at her institution. Working with Jay Seals (now retired) of Robbins Sports Surfaces, she designed a floor featuring spring coils measuring one-and-three-quarter inches in height, mounted on wood blocks at one end and fastened to two-by-four inch sleepers at the other end. The sleepers are covered with a three-quarter-inch plywood subfloor, and the floor surface is T&G Northern Hard Maple flooring. Each studio has fifteen hundred coil springs under the 1,870 square foot surface.

Towson State faculty member Edward Stewart, who taught advanced ballet students, observed that the number of major and minor injuries normally attributed to poor surfaces, such as sprains, tears, tendinitis, shin splints, back problems, and knee problems have come to a halt. Braezeale says, "The hefty price tag of $25,000 for each floor is a small price to pay for the years of pain-free productive work for any dancer who is fortunate enough to study in such a facility." (The price varies greatly depending on the cost of local labor.)

253

Robbins Sports Surfaces, (4777 Eastern Avenue, Cincinnati, OH 45226; telephone: 800-543-1913 or 513-619-5932; www.robbins-floor.com) offers a host of user friendly wooden floor products, as well as dance floors, to the dance community.

A wooden floor surface should not mislead a dancer into assuming the wood has been sprung. It may have been placed directly over concrete or rolled steel joists. The resulting lack of spring can cause many injuries. To determine whether a wooden floor is sprung, rap on it with your knuckles or the heel of a shoe. A resilient sprung floor will sound a hollow drumlike retort, since the sound of your rapping will be amplified by the air space. A sharp click will be heard when you tap a floor with a concrete base since there is no air space to create resonance.

While nothing can take the place of a properly sprung floor, the strain of dancing on a concrete floor appears to be lessened when it is covered with layers of special cushioned vinyl. Although this is a possible alternative for occasional performances, the dancer should do everything within her power to find a situation that offers a resilient well-sprung floor for class and rehearsal, avoiding tile and cement.[8]

Since wooden floors and the construction of permanent sprung floors (also referred to as subfloor or floating floor) can be prohibitively expensive, manufacturers have been working on less expensive, portable alternatives. These subfloors must be distinguished from the vinyl floors that are rolled and taped on top to prevent slipping. These nonslippery surfaces have been referred to as *Marley* floors, but Marley is merely the name of one of the earliest types of floors; it is no longer produced. Dance floor surfaces made from vinyl and linoleum, similar to Marley, which are put down on sprung floors, have become almost standard in recent years. Rosin must not be used on these surfaces.

Floor Angle

The problem of floor angle refers to the fact that many performing surfaces around the world are *raked*, or slightly slanted down toward the audience. A raked stage gives the audience a better view, but can both cause dance injuries and prolong them. Dancing on even a slight incline puts a severe strain on the body, because the dancer has to readjust throughout the entire dance or performance. A raked stage forces a dancer to throw his or her weight back, and is also difficult to move across.

Floor Surface

Finally, the actual surface is important. Rosin overuse can be a problem. Floors that are heavily rosined must be cleaned regularly to prevent build-up in irregular and uneven patches; otherwise a dancer may find his or her foot sticking to the floor, with potentially disastrous consequences to the ankle or knee.

Margret Kaufmann, who has danced in the United States, Great Britain, Germany, Holland, Sweden, and Finland, found that the raked stages of Europe were not only difficult to dance on, but also that the painted floor carpets were extremely slippery and unsuitable for *pirouettes*.

Deborah Allton, who danced with the Metropolitan Opera Ballet, says that the members of that company endure a variety of floor problems. The stage is wood over cement and equipped with multiple hydraulic devices, turntables, and elevators. Consequently, there are high ridges in the surface, places where the floor sections do not meet, and even trap doors. Since the floor is covered with a floor cloth, these hazards are masked from the dancers' view. She recalled dancing in the opera *Macbeth*, which had a forty-five-degree raked stage and a floor covering hiding numerous holes and uneven seams. She had to do hops on pointe in front *attitude* going downhill on a raked floor, and hopped into a pothole!

When American Ballet Theatre performs at the Met, it brings its own floor to surmount these problems. Before New York City Ballet acquired its portable floor, the dancers could only perform at the Kennedy Center in Washington for two weeks at a time, to prevent their legs from becoming "hamburger" from the knee down.

Rosin and Slip NoMor concentrate are two very good solutions to slip-proofing dance surfaces. Rosin is the brittle resin left after distilling turpentine from pine pitch. It is also used in the manufacture of varnish and ink, and for rubbing on violin bows. Rosin can be purchased in rock and powdered form. Rock rosin, which is placed in a container large enough for a dancer to step into is preferable.

The new, improved SlipNoMor 2000 adds a slip-resistant surface to all floor surfaces including wood, vinyl, and linoleum for up to one week. It is a good substitute for rosin and does not damage floor surfaces. At one time it was unavailable for shipment in the winter, but now the products are available in specially insulated heat packing. SlipNoMor

2000C is a new concentrated formula, which means only half as much is needed. One gallon, when diluted, makes fourteen to twenty gallons of the product. There is also a Slip NoMor Cleaner guaranteed to make any surface twenty percent more slip-resistant while cleaning wood, vinyl, linoleum, and stone surfaces. It can all be ordered from Stagestep in Philadelphia, or contact Sam Jamison at (800) 523-0960, or e-mail sam@stagestep.com. Neither rosin nor Slip NoMor is appropriate for the new vinyl nonslip dance floors.

Special Care Facilities

Although medical care specifically tailored for dancers is still in dramatically short supply across the country, there are now several excellent facilities specializing in this field. Hopefully, they will serve as models for more centers that emphasize dance medicine.

Dance Medicine Division

Center for Sports Medicine
St. Francis Memorial Hospital
900 Hyde Street
San Francisco, CA 94109

The Center for Sports Medicine is headed by Dr. James G. Garrick, an orthopedic surgeon who specializes in working with skaters, dancers, and gymnasts. The Dance Medicine Division, specializing in dance injury rehabilitation and general conditioning, offers Pilates-based apparatus and mat techniques, and affords the dancer an opportunity to refine strength, flexibility, centering, and quality of coordination.

While many of the same injuries are seen on a daily basis, each dancer's specific problems in dealing with his or her injuries are unique. As the result of evaluation at the Dance Medicine Division, a physician or therapist may detect a dancer's technical error that is contributing to, if not causing, an injury.

After a client receives a preliminary physical examination, Garrick's assistant watches the individual go through a simulated class at the barre, from both a lateral and a forward view, and notes technical flaws. Dr. Garrick says that this level of symptom evaluation cannot be accomplished by a doctor or by a teacher who is trying to watch an entire class or rehearsal. He feels it is safe to assume that the dancer is unaware of the usage problems, or the injury might not have happened. Armed with the knowledge gained by the team at Dance Medicine, a dancer may be able to prevent the injury from recurring.

The rehabilitation work at Dance Medicine is then structured to adapt to each dancer's particular needs. Often, after the rehabilitation process is complete, dancers continue with the program for general conditioning and centering work, in conjunction with their training or performing. Clients of Dance Medicine also have access to the Physical Therapy Division, where whirlpools, friction massage, ultrasound, EGS bikes, weights, and Thera-Bands are available. Universal reformers or *plié* machines, and trap tables for Pilates work, are also available at the center.

Dr. Garrick believes that it is possible to do the best job for the dancer when the entire treatment process is under one roof. Doctors, trainers, and physical therapists are able to look at the patient together, and practice more effective medicine as a result, since they do not have to communicate by telephone or in writing. He mentions that there is "no hiding from the patients" in this kind of environment. Contact is maintained with members of the team, and feedback is much more efficient. He feels that patients often get lost in the shuffle when they have to be sent to several different locations, from physician to physical therapist to conditioning studio. The cost of multilocation treatment is also often greater than "one-stop" medicine. Dr. Garrick feels that the division must help each dancer find a way to be rehabilitated to dancing "full steam." He finds that of the dancers he sees, fully eighty percent of their problems are fairly common complaints, while the remaining twenty percent are unusual instances. When treating those, he frequently consults Dr. Justin Howse in London and Dr. William Hamilton.

The Dance Medicine Division treats all kinds of dancers, from recreational enthusiasts to professionals and from any dance discipline. The income from recreational dancers helps support the costs of treating professionals. Many company-affiliated dancers are treated under worker's compensation plans.

Westside Dance Physical Therapy

53 Columbus Avenue/ 62nd Street
New York, NY 10023
Telephone: (212) 541-8450
Fax: (212) 541-8582

Administered by Director Marika Molnar and Assistant Director Liz Henry, and assisted by staff member Katy Keller, Westside Dance Physical Therapy specializes in preventing and rehabilitating the injuries of performing artists. Treatment incorporates evaluation of the neuro-musculoskeletal system and development of individualized rehabilitation programs.

Services include evaluation of alignment, flexibility, strength, and proprioception; manual therapy technique, including soft tissue and joint mobilization, myofascial release, and neuromuscular reeducation; craniosacral therapy; biomechanical assessment of the spine and lower extremities; dance technique analysis and modification; and instruction in home exercise programs and preventive measures.

Marika Molnar has worked with New York City Ballet as a physical therapist since 1980. She was a dance teacher and has a master's degree in Dance Education and an MS in Physical Therapy.

The majority of pointe shoe–related problems seen at the center are foot and ankle injuries, and some back injuries. Many problems experienced by professional dancers are related to the choreography they are working on at any given moment. Since learning a new role, or rehearsing intensively, involves repeating the same movement over and over, injuries are often the result of overuse. They can be a direct result of cooling down while standing around waiting for a choreographer to make a decision. Also, the type of dance movement required by the choreography may not be in the dancer's repertoire. If a modern dance choreographer creates a piece for a ballet company, there should be a few classes of modern to introduce that type of movement to the dancers.

Molnar finds it particularly challenging to work with professional dancers to find a way to help them go on performing within the framework of their physical problems. This often involves helping them find a new way of moving.

258

Irene Dowd

Neuro-Muscular Therapist
14 East 4th Street, Suite 606
New York, NY 10012
Telephone: (212) 420-8782

Irene Dowd takes a functional approach to treating dance injuries. She observes the dancer in action to determine the minimal technical corrections that can correct problems. She was the protégée and assistant of Dr. Lulu Sweigard, who taught Anatomy for Dancers at Juilliard in New York. Dowd has been a member of the faculty at Teachers College at Columbia University, and is now teaching in the Dance Program at Juilliard and at Canada's National Ballet School in Toronto. In addition to treating individual neuromuscular problems, she teaches anatomy classes at her studio.

Pilates Studio

2121 Broadway, 2nd Floor
New York, NY 10023
Telephone: (212) 875-0819
www.pilatesguild.com

The studio, founded by Joseph Pilates, also the founder of the Pilates method, offers individually supervised programs administered by instructors who have trained in this system of body conditioning. Since 1990, the Pilates Guild™ has been an international organization dedicated to the preservation of Authentic Pilates™, passed on to Pilates' protégée, Romana Kryzanowska, in 1967. Under the direct tutelage of Romana, and with the most comprehensive archival documentation available, the Guild™ seeks to maintain Pilates in its purest form.

After a four-year court battle over the trademark "Pilates," which the disciples of Joseph Pilates lost in 2000, anyone can now use the word or name "Pilates" in any type of exercise program. This New York studio, now run by Sean Gallagher, uses "Pilates Guild," "Authentic Pilates," or "New York Pilates Studio" to distinguish itself from others.

The key aspects of the Pilates method are control and centering of the body, precision movement, flow of motion, proper breathing, and relaxation. This work is concerned with both adjusting the entire body and training the muscles to support the correction. All Pilates exercises start on a flat back and gradually change positions. The body is toned without pressure on the ankles, legs, and lower back.

The studio offers a training program to develop Pilates instructors, which entails up to a year of work, although some people do it much faster. The student must first take seventy-five private sessions just to be able to apply to the program. The sessions usually last fifty minutes. Once the seventy-five sessions are completed, the student may apply for admission to the program. The application is reviewed, and an interview is required before acceptance. The training program consists of both classroom work and apprenticeship. Basically, there are twelve days of training, and it is usually broken up into three sections: the basic system, the intermediate, and then the advanced systems. There is a manual to study and discussions are held about the system and how to teach it.

Next come the apprenticeships. The students spend the first two hundred hours in observation; after that, they are tested. They have both a written and a practical exam, in which they have to guide someone through a workout. After the test, they move on and do the next two hundred hours, which is assistant teaching. In the last two hundred hours, the students actually teach. They have their own clients, but they are under supervision.

This program is offered in New York and all around the world. Students can do their required hours in any certified center; they do not have to be done in New York. Although some centers have abbreviated courses, there is no short cut to "Authentic Pilates."

In addition to this certification program, classes are offered for alignment and corrective work. After an injury, dancers work out there to reestablish alignment before returning to class. They also use the Pilates method to help prevent injury. Gallagher provides physical therapy backstage for thirteen Broadway shows. He also takes care of Paul Taylor Company and David Parsons Company, and sometimes goes on tour with Hubbard Street Dance Company. Many of the studio's clients dance with New York City Ballet and American Ballet Theatre. The Pilates method is of particular benefit to the pointe dancer because it strengthens the back and stomach, keeping weight off the feet and knees. Foot problems are often solved by working on the body at a Pilates studio.

Houston Body Conditioning Studio

1916 West Gray Street
Houston, TX 77019

The Houston Body Conditioning Studio has a thirty-year association with the Houston Ballet—testimony to the Houston Ballet's philosophy of responsiveness to their dancers' physical needs, and its interest in making them "last." It was established initially as an aid to dancers recovering from injuries, or for dancers working to prevent injuries.

The Pilates-based method used at the studio seeks to balance the body for any physical activity. Once imbalances are detected, weaker areas can be strengthened through isolation. The staff closely supervises a general program of stretching and strengthening and seeks to identify potential problems, arresting them before they can cause injuries. The studio's body conditioning retrains the body. Muscles elongate, and joints are freed to achieve natural alignment. By conditioning muscles to support the spine's natural curve, lower-back pain is alleviated, and shoulders relax and fall into place.

Professional Division students and company members use the studio for warm-up and rehabilitation at no cost. Students in Ballet 4-8 are greatly encouraged to utilize the program, but they must pay a fee.

Kathryn and Gilbert Miller Health Care Institute for Performing Artists

425 West 59th Street
New York, NY 10019
Telephone: (212) 523-6200

The Miller Health Care Institute is a multispecialty ambulatory care center associated with St. Luke's–Roosevelt Hospital Center. Founded in 1985 with a grant from the Kathryn and Gilbert Miller Fund, this unique institute offers general and specialized health care for performers and those in associated trades, such as teachers, production crews, designers, directors, and choreographers. It occupies custom-designed facilities that include a performance-evaluation studio with a sprung floor, barre and mirrors, and video equipment.

The professional team at the institute is headed by Mitchell Kahn, M.D., Director (Primary Care), Philip Bauman, M.D. (Orthopedic Surgery),

261

Anthony Jahn, M.D. (Otolaryngology), and Lillie Rosenthal, D.O. (Physical Medicine and Rehabilitation). These dedicated professionals understand that dancers' livelihoods depend on their ability to perform.

In the primary care area, the institute's physicians perform check-ups, physicals, and women's health examinations. They administer diagnostic tests and treat illness and injury. In addition, specialists treat injuries and disorders that result from rehearsal and performance. Fees are competitive, but these specialists understand the performance environment, and their diagnostic skills are fine-tuned to the exacting standards required by top professionals.

Artists can find treatment at the institute for everything from sprained ankles to chronic tendinitis, and from colds and flu to performance-related problems and injuries. While ballet presents special problems because of turnout and pointe shoes, Broadway dancers also have specific issues. Many of these injuries are caused by things most people would never think of, such as costuming. For instance, in *The Lion King*, injuries and strains in the neck and shoulders are caused by the puppetry; in shows like *42nd Street*, the mike pad that is worn on the head pushes the head forward, causing problems.

The institute's Three-Stage Preparation Program involves a physical examination to determine state of health and muscle condition, a video-tape analysis of performance technique, and a graduated series of muscle strengthening and conditioning under the guidance of a physical therapist, while institute doctors monitor the performer anatomically.

Treatment is offered for illnesses such as anorexia and bulimia. Both mental and physical health are addressed. There are very specific dance injuries that occur over and over again—and focusing only on the physical needs without looking at the emotional and nutritional needs would be a mistake, says Lillie Rosenthal. She feels it is necessary to address not only the acute injury, but also to prevent reinjury, which involves treating emotional problems, as well as physical ones.

Under the Michael Fokine Fund, administered by the New York Community Trust, low or no-cost care may be available for serious students or professional dancers with demonstrable financial need who are ill or injured and need medical care in order to dance.

BalleCore Body Shaping

23 Canton Ave
Milton, MA 02186
Telephone: (617) 698-CORE
Fax: (617) 696-3277
E-Mail: ballecore@ballecore.com
www.ballecore.com

Molly Weeks is the developer of the *BalleCore® Body Shaping Program.* Her teaching is enriched by twenty years of practice and formal study of Pilates, ballet, and Hatha Yoga. She is currently on the faculty of the Boston Ballet.

This fifty-minute workout is a combination of physical and mental conditioning and balletic moves, designed to develop strength and dynamic power in the body's core muscles. The class begins with stretches, moves on to mat-work, and ends with a free-standing *BalleCore®* Barre. The *BalleCore® One to One* is a fifty-minute class that allows the student to develop a strong base created especially for him or her. Exercises are performed on the floor and standing.

BalleCore® has a *Prenatal/Postnatal Program* to prepare the body for pregnancy and help it remain flexible and strong. Class focuses on toning specific areas that help with the rigors of labor and delivery, while stretching tight areas.

Gyrotonic®

134 Dingman Court
Dingmans Ferry, PA 18328
Telephone: (570) 828-0003
Fax: (570) 828-0005
E-mail: info@gyrotonic.com
www.gyrotonic.com

Gyrotonic® and *Gyrokinesis*™ are the names of the therapeutic movement system invented by former dancer and healing guru Julio Horvath. His dream of a machine that would help a dancer achieve a better turnout or *pirouette* resulted in the development of the *Gyrotonic® Expansion System.* It was developed for anyone wishing to gain strength, flexibility, and coordination, and was conceived using principles of gymnastics, swimming, ballet, and yoga. It is a general conditioning system for dancers as well as people from all walks of life, from children to senior citizens.

The fundamentals of the system consist of an exercise system using *Gyrokinesis*™ as the basis to exercise the musculature while mobilizing and articulating the joints. It simultaneously stretches and strengthens the body with minimal effort, while increasing range of motion and developing coordination. The system is largely machine-based with one hundred fifty exercises on four different machines that are designed to build core strength along with muscular flexibility, joint suppleness, and fitness. The motion patterns are natural, with repetitive cycles of circling movement and rhythmic breathing creating a bridge between contraction and extension through the rotating movement of the joints.

Harkness Center for Dance Injuries

Hospital for Joint Diseases
301 East 17th Street
New York, NY 10003
Telephone: 212-598-6022
E-mail: Harkness@med.nyu.edu
www.danceinjury.com

The Harkness Center for Dance Injuries (HCDI) was founded as a program of the Hospital for Joint Diseases Orthopedic Institute (HJDOI) in 1989, in response to the New York dance community's critical need for specialized and affordable health care. HCDI offers a full variety of health care programs from preventative screenings through acute care injury management.

Now headed by Dr. Donald Rose, HJDOI has been specializing in the treatment of patients with various orthopedic, rheumatologic, and neurologic ailments since it was founded in 1906. HCDI also provides care for a specialty population—that of the student, amateur, and professional dancer. Through a process of comprehensive medical evaluations with physicians and therapists, factors contributing to the dancer's dysfunction are discovered and discussed with the dancer. Treatment programs are tailored to each individual dancer's needs.

The Harkness Center offers an extensive variety of patient services, special programs, and conferences. One of the most interesting is the *One-on-One Injury Prevention Assessment Program*. It is a program that offers two all-day, free-of-charge injury prevention assessments for dancers each month. The purpose is to assess risk, and discuss dancers' concerns with it, before an injury occurs. Senior dance physical therapists staff this first and only-of-its-kind clinic. Each dancer is seen individually for an hour by a therapist who reviews the dancer's training, medical and nutritional histories, hears his or her complaints, and puts the dancer through a battery of appropriate screening tests. They are then given an individually tailored injury prevention exercise regime, with recommendations for modification of their technique, training strategies, footwear, and/or dance environment to maximize their potential for good health and well-being.

PT Plus

Dance, Orthopedic & Sports Physical Therapy
City Center
130 West 56th Street, Suite 6M
New York, NY 10019
Telephone: (212) 246-3700
Fax: (212) 246-3701
E-mail: mj@pt-plus.org

Housed in one of New York City's historical landmark buildings and most treasured dance theaters, PT Plus is a highly specialized physical therapy practice for dancers, athletes, and individuals with neuromusculoskeletal injuries and/or occupational health concerns. PT Plus Director Marijeanne Liederbach is a licensed physical therapist, certified athletic trainer, certified strength and conditioning specialist who holds two master of science degrees (Sports Medicine and Physical Therapy), and is a Ph.D. candidate in Biomechanics at New York University.

Throughout the 1980s, Liederbach was the supervisor of physical therapy at Lenox Hill Hospital's Nicholas Institute of Sports Medicine and was director of Dance Medicine Services for the Joffrey Ballet. In addition, she has provided backstage physical therapy for the English National Ballet, American Dance Festival, Alvin Ailey American Dance Theater, Merce Cunningham Dance Company, and Ben Vereen's various Broadway shows.

The director and staff are all former professional dancers with expertise in osteopathic manual medicine and Pilates training, and are all current affiliates of the Harkness Center for Dance Injuries at the Hospital for

Joint Diseases. Liederbach is responsible for developing the center's many clinical and educational outreach programs, including its free injury-prevention clinic, its off-site centers at Dance Theatre of Harlem, SUNY Purchase, and numerous Broadway shows. The center has a state-of-the-art biomechanics research laboratory that houses the same real-time digital technology as the Olympic Training Center; this one, however, is devoted solely to the study of dancers, their unique movement capabilities, and their injuries.

Department of Physical Therapy and Occupation Therapy Services

Children's Hospital
300 Longwood Avenue, FA 123
Boston, MA 02115
Telephone: (617) 355-7223, main number (617) 355-6000
Fax: (617) 730-0151
E-mail: michelina.cassella@tch.harvard.edu
Division of Sports Medicine Clinic
Department of Orthopedics

The Division of Sports Medicine in the Department of Orthopedics at Children's Hospital has been providing evaluation and treatment for dance-related injuries since the early 1980s. In 1991, a physical therapy satellite clinic was established on-site in the new Boston Ballet Studio at 19 Clarendon Street in Boston. The physical therapy staff works under the medical direction of Lyle J. Micheli, M.D.

In addition to providing direct services for professional company dancers, the physical therapy staff, directed by Michelina C. Cassella, provides evaluation, treatment, and injury prevention and lectures to students enrolled in Boston Ballet's Center for Dance Education.

Stage and Studio Flooring

There are now a number of alternatives to the ultra-expensive, custom-built, permanent sprung hardwood floors necessary to protect a dancer from injury because of unyielding and slippery floors. Listed below are several companies specializing in stage and studio flooring.

Choice Floors

510 South 46th Street
Philadelphia, PA 19143
Telephone: (800) 720-8099
Fax: (215) 386-5585
E-mail: ChoiceFloors@aol.com

Choice Floors manufactures ten nonslip dance floors for ballet, modern dance, jazz, tap, and more. The company sells vinyl and linoleum, as well as wooden sprung floors. These floors can be portable, permanent, and semipermanent.

EFS Entertainment Flooring Systems

River Road, #319
Wilton, CT 06897
Telephone: (866) 616-3375
E-mail: www.info@flooradvice.com
www.flooradvice.com

Not only does EFS offer four different dance surfaces, but will also answer any question concerning dance floors. Michael Sean Graves has answers to questions such as, "What is that black goo on the floor?" or "What is a floating floor?"

Duofloor is the only reversible dance floor that will accommodate all styles of dance. It is durable yet lightweight, and will lie flat quickly, making it appropriate for touring as well as for stage and studio installations where the floor may have to be moved.

Mezzafloor is an inexpensive multipurpose dance floor for studios and stages. It is heavy-duty contract quality vinyl designed for permanent and semipermanent installations, designed to last for many years. It is available in twenty marbled colors and solid gray or black.

Primafloor is EFS's premier ballet and modern dance floor, providing "perfect controlled slip," designed to serve equally well for most other styles of dance. It is the most durable dance vinyl available (often referred to as Marley). It has a woven mesh backing, making it a good choice for permanent installations. In addition, it is UV-resistant, which is ideal for outdoor venues and studios with nat-

267

ural light. *Primafloor* is also tear-resistant, which makes it an ideal touring floor. It has a nonreflective matte finish.

Timberfloor has the traditional look of a wood floor with the low maintenance of vinyl flooring. Its danceability is suitable for most kinds of dance including ballet, pointe, jazz, and tap. It provides slip control without the use of rosin.

Stagefloor is extremely durable; made of heavy-duty industrial-strength vinyl, it is designed for concerts and special events. Stage and music equipment can move freely and easily over this floor while still providing protection for an existing floor underneath.

Studiofloor was designed for the multipurpose studio and facility. It offers excellent resistance to ballet, pointe, modern, and jazz dancers. Additional styles like tap, Irish, or ballroom can be performed without worry of damaging the floor—and it is durable enough to stand up to the abuse of any heavily used floor space.

Tour de Force is a unique floor that is two-sided with a slightly different floor speed on each side. This design offers a choice of surface so that tappers will get a crisp, clean sound while ballet dancers will have more slip control.

EFS Sprung Floor is an "install it yourself" floating floor. Constructed from eleven-layer beech and alder plywood, it comes with a patented resilient foam channel understructure. The 5-3/8" wide and 7'-11" long planks easily fit together and are held in place with a special adhesive that is provided. This resilient floor is built with the safety of the performers in mind. Topped with a vinyl surface floor, the overall height of this flooring system will be 1" or less.

EFS Spring Pads are made from recycled rubber making them tough and resilient as well as environmentally friendly. These shock-absorbing pads are for use with spring floor systems. They are fatigue-reducing and provide support and spring which help prevent injuries. They come in two sizes: the 1/2" size is for aerobics and athletics, while the 1" spring pads are designed for dance floors.

En Pointe Enterprises Ltd.

282C Campion Street
Kelowna, BC, Canada V1X 758
Toll free telephone in North America: (866) 491-9019
Telephone: (250) 491-9019
Fax: (250) 491-9014
E-mail: enpointe@telus.net
www.en-pointe.com

One of the ventures of En Pointe Enterprises Ltd. was a tour of "The Stars of Canadian Ballet"—professional ballet dancers from three major Canadian ballet companies. While on tour, David Lucas and his wife, Lissette Salgado, dancers with the Royal Winnipeg Ballet Company, recognized the need for portable dance barres. This idea led to the development not only of portable barres, but also portable mirrors, stages, dance floors, and accessories. Along with Marley floors and sprung panel floors (both permanent and for touring). En Pointe makes an unusual *Porta Floor*—a practice floor with a durable laminate surface and a cushioned underpad of high density foam. It is available in 3' x 4' or 6' x 4', or in custom sizes on request. It comes with a tote bag that has a shoulder strap and carrying handle.

Gerstung

1400 Coppermine Terrace
Baltimore, MD 21209-2012
Telephone: (410) 337-7781
Fax: (410) 337-0471
E-mail: info@gerstung.com

Subfloors

Gerstung **AirBase®** floors are known in the dance industry for their resiliency, stability, and shock absorbency. This floor is a flat, sturdy subfloor supported by Energy Blocks™, trapping air and providing a base for a safe landing.

The **AirBase® 100** permanently installed subfloor consists of a double layer of imported plywood over 1.5-inch Energy Blocks™, with a choice of *Dance* or *Studio Vinyl* top surface. It is a very tough floor, firmer than *AirBase® 200*. The *AirBase® 200*, on the other hand, has a single layer for permanent or removable installations. It has more spring than *Airbase 100* and is recommended when wood is the top surface. (It is not removable if wood is used.)

The **Airbase® 300** floor system is ideal for quick set-ups and take-downs. It is a portable system with interlocking edge connectors, ideal for theaters, dance studios, and performance and competition stages, where the quick assembly of a resilient floor is required.

Hardwood floors

The **Dance Parquet** floor is for aerobics, ballet, modern dance, and tap. It is to be used with *Airbase® 100, 200,* and *300*. This sanded parquet floor is a maple hardwood surface.

Vinyl floors

These floors can all be used with any *Airbase®*, or alone.

Dance Vinyl is a lightweight sheet vinyl, which is simply rolled out and taped in place. It is an inexpensive solution for ballet, modern dance, and general stage use. It also serves as a protective cover for wood floors.

Studio Vinyl is a three-layer construction from France, primarily used for permanent glue-down installations. A center layer of woven fiberglass reinforces the vinyl wear surface and provides dimensional stability. It can also be taped in place for removable application.

Performance Vinyl is a special PVC vinyl formulated by Gerstung especially for the dance industry. It is suitable for both permanent and temporary installations. The top features a tough wearing, matte finish, slip-resistant PVC layer. Below the wear surface is a stabilizing scrim to reduce shrinking and stretching.

Reversible Dance Vinyl, an intermediately priced vinyl, is perfect for temporary, tape-down situations. It is a reversible, doubled-sided, two color PVC sheet vinyl. It is easy to maintain and good for touring or studio use.

Harlequin

American Harlequin Corporation
1531 Glen Avenue
Moorestown, NJ 08057
Telephone: (856) 234-5505
Fax: (856) 231-4403
Toll Free Telephone: (800) 642-6440

British Harlequin plc
Bankside House, Vale Road
Tonbridge, Kent, England TN9 1SJ
Telephone: (44) 1732 367666
Fax: (44) 1732 367755

Harlequin International Sarl
29 rue Notre-Dame
L-2240 Luxembourg, Belgium
Telephone: (352) 46 44 22
Fax: (352) 46 44 40
E-mail: dance@harlequinfloors.com
www.harlequinfloors.com

Harlequin Floors is a worldwide source of dance floors and dance floor systems, with offices in London, Luxembourg, Philadelphia, Los Angeles, Fort Worth, and Sydney. The company offers three different sprung floors and four choices of vinyl overlay floors, which are appropriate for ballet. The company's permanent floors are vinyl, which may be installed using vinyl adhesive; the seams would be sealed with either vinyl hot weld or chemical weld. The floor cannot be removed.

Portable floors are described as follows: (1) roll-out floors that may be rerolled and stored for future use; (2) roll-out floors that may be *loose-laid* (secured by top seam tape only); (3) very heavy vinyl roll-out floors that may not be suitable for daily removal and relaying but are not installed permanently (the *Allegro*); (4) roll-out floors that may be loose-laid only (the *Reversible*).

The four vinyl overlay floors appropriate for ballet are:

> **Harlequin Studio** is ideally suited for either loose-lay or semipermanent lay on a hard subfloor, and the firm foam backing gives resilient support. *Studio* also has a glass-fiber interply, which makes

it roll out on the floor fast, flat, and in a straight line. Many dance studios use this floor, including the Royal Academy of Dancing in London, Pacific Northwest Ballet in Seattle, Canada's Royal Winnipeg Ballet, San Francisco Ballet, Ballet West in Utah, Joffrey Ballet in Chicago, Dance Theatre of Harlem, and well-known modern dance companies.

Harlequin Reversible is a two-sided stage flooring with a different color on each side. It may be used either side up, rolling it out as often as necessary. There are three color combinations: black/white, black/gray, and gray/T.V. white (a very pale gray). This enables decor to be switched between performances.

Harlequin Cascade is a heavy-duty sheet flooring produced from a homogeneous (solid) vinyl. It has proved to be ideal for use by large dance/opera companies, rock groups, and any company needing a rugged floor for its stage or touring schedule. Although it is hard-wearing, it has a soft construction that is popular with dancers. *Cascade* may be used for portable, permanent, or semi-permanent installations

Harlequin Allegro is a new roll-out flooring aimed at dance/aerobic/gymnastic studios and at professional touring dance companies who need a floor with a high degree of resilient protection from hard subfloors. *Allegro* is 3/8" thick and is constructed with a deep backing of PVC foam reinforced with a strong mineral fiber scrim. This construction gives a considerable cushioning effect, and yet is firm. It is the equivalent of a roll-out sprung floor, and for many companies it ends the need for a full joinery-constructed sprung floor. It may be loose-laid or installed in the regular fashion, like a conventional sheet vinyl floor. It combines the advantage of a loose-lay vinyl and a shock-absorbent sprung floor.

The three choices of sprung floors are:

Harlequin Activity Floor is a complete, permanently installed sprung floor system, which has a triple "sandwich" composite structure. There are no metal springs or rubber pads, and no fixings to the existing floor. It can be laid on almost any surface without preparation. This floor has been installed in the studios of the English National Ballet School in London.

Harlequin Sprung Panels are premanufactured panels for permanent or stage use. The panels are joined by a pivot join with elastomer blocks at regular centers on the underside to give uniform and consistent shock damping. Panels are laid in brickwork fashion so the cross-joins do not coincide.

Harlequin Basketweave is a traditional-construction sprung wooden floor. This construction was developed in the nineteenth century, and there are some professionals still wedded to the idea of a basketweave floor. This traditional construction consists of a triple layer of wooden bearers laid at right angles to one another onto neoprene pads and screwed together. The bearers are then covered with a layer of plywood or hardwood, and finally with a vinyl covering.

Rosco Laboratories, Inc.

52 Harbor View Avenue
Stamford, CT 06902
Telephone: (203) 708-8900, ext. 234
Fax: (203) 708-8919
E-mail: tracey@rosco.com

Besides the branch in Stamford, Rosco Laboratories, Inc., is located in Hollywood, London, Toronto, Madrid, Sao Paulo, and Sydney. The company sells dance floors, floor tapes, and floor cleaners, as well as many products for the theater, such as lighting.

The newest floor is the *Rosco Subfloor.* It was developed and tested by dancers to insure a perfect combination of spring or bounce with stability. It is flexible enough to absorb the energy from a dancer's impact, and provides resistance for dance movements ranging from ballet to tap, modern dance, flamenco, and Irish dancing. The 42" x 42" panels lock into each other, while perimeter pieces, 4-3/8" wide, lock the entire floor together. The *SubFloor* can be bolted to concrete or wooden floors, and can also be removed and reused. Panels weigh forty pounds each.

Rosco makes eight other floors, ranging from floors hard enough for tap and other hard-shoe dance styles (as well as being suitable for ballet), to styles that are highly portable, permanent, semipermanent, and foam-cushioned. The floors come in a broad range of prices.

The names of these floors are *Adagio, Cabriole, Dance Floor, Royale Floor, Studio Floor, Apprentice Floor, Performance Floor, and Show Floor.*

Stagestep, Inc.

2000 Hamilton Street
Suite C200
Philadelphia, PA 19130
Telephone: (800) 523-0960
E-mail: Stagestep@stagestep.com
www.stagestep.com

Stagestep has been making products for the dancer for more than thirty years. The company produces portable barres, mirrors, and floor-care products, as well as floors for all types of dance. These are the floors available at the time of publication of this book:

Dancestep is a heavy-duty permanent or semipermanent floor for concrete subfloors that feels like a resilient wood floor at half the price and one-tenth of the maintenance cost. High-density foam backing reduces noise and creates an insulation barrier keeping the floor warm to the touch. It is good for ballet, modern, or jazz, but not for tap or clogging—*Dancestep* absorbs sound.

BravoB and **Classic Bravo** are two professional floors that offer light weight, many uses, and low cost. They are designed primarily for touring but are good choices for studios working with tight budgets.

Super Bravo has a fiberglass lining that allows it to lie flat. Designed for touring, it is a good budget choice for the studio.

Timestep is described as the ultimate multipurpose floor. It is portable or permanent and can handle heavy scenery and props. It comes in 6'6" widths.

Timestep5 is another multipurpose floor suited for any movement activity. It is heavy duty and portable for touring or can be used as permanent flooring in the studio. It comes in 5' widths.

Woodstep and **Woodstep Plus** have a realistic wood design. *Woodstep* is slightly textured and has a heavy-duty surface ideal for ballet, jazz, modern dance, and tap. (Defective taps can cause scratches that will show on the wood grain.) *Woodstep Plus* will reduce the sound of tap and clogging. Its five layers provide a seven-year surface guarantee, a fiberglass layer for stability, and a high-density foam underlayer to absorb shock. Both floors are excellent for home use.

Quietstep and **Quietstep5** are portable or permanent resilient floorings for studio, stage, and touring. There is an additional cushion for wood subflooring which reduces noise. The floor surfaces are warmer because of additional insulation. *Quietstep* comes in 6'6" widths in marbleized gray. *Quietstep5* comes in 5' widths in solid colors.

Tourflor is an interlocking portable floating wood subfloor that provides all the absorption and resilience of a permanent floating floor. No tools are needed for installation. It can be covered with any performance floor surface and is available for use outdoors.

Encore is a new hardwood portable or permanent wood floor with an attached floating wood subfloor. This low-cost floor can be do-it-yourself and put together without any tools. It is suitable for home or studio.

NOTES

1. Howse, Justin. *Dance Technique and Injury Prevention* (New York: Theatre Arts Books, 1988), p. 59.

2. Wright, Stuart. *Dancer's Guide to Injuries of the Lower Extremities: Diagnosis, Treatment, and Care* (Cranbury, NJ: Cornwall Books, 1985), p. 14.

3. Much of the information included in this chapter was gathered through interviews with medical professionals who specialize in the treatment of dancers. These professionals are the following:

Orthopedists

Dr. James G. Garrick currently heads the Center for Sports Medicine at St. Francis Hospital in San Francisco, a facility that includes a unique Dance Medicine Division.

Dr. William G. Hamilton has been the orthopedic consultant for the New York City Ballet since 1973; he has also been affiliated with American Ballet Theatre since 1979 and School of American Ballet since 1975. He is an attending surgeon at St. Luke's-Roosevelt Hospital Center.

As the director of the Harkness Center for Dance Injury at New York University Hospital for Joint Disease, Dr. Donald Rose cares for many professional dancers and also trains medical personnel who come from all over the world to study at the Harkness Center.

Podiatrists/Podiatric Surgeons

Dr. Steven Baff, Diplomate with the American Board of Podiatric Foot Surgery Ambulatory Division, the International Society of Podiatric Laser Surgery, the National Board of Podiatry, and the Academy of Ambulatory Foot Surgery, has a practice that includes many professional dancers.

Dr. Richard T. Braver, a podiatrist specializing in dance and sports medicine and foot and ankle surgery, is affiliated with the physical therapists for the New York City Ballet.

Dr. Tom Novella, who works with many patients who are members of major dance companies in New York City, has been treating dancers since 1978 and often lectures on dancers' foot problems.

Dr. Louis Galli, D.P.M., F.A.C.F.A.S., practices sports and dance medicine, working very closely with the New York City Ballet as well as with modern and Broadway dancers.

Physical Medicine and Rehabilitation

Dr. Lillie Rosenthal, D.O., practices physical medicine and rehabilitation at the Miller Health Care Institute for Performing Artists in New York City.

Physical Therapists

Marika Molnar is director of Westside Dance Physical Therapy in New York City and holds an M.A.P.T.

Shirley Hancock was principal physiotherapist to the Royal Ballet Schools, the Royal Academy of Dancing, and the Remedial Dance Clinic, London, England.

Chiropractors

Dr. Nathan Novick, a favorite of many professional dancers and teachers, retired after practicing for fifty-two years in New York. He is president emeritus of the American College of Chiropractors. Dr. Janiz A. Minshew is a chiropractor whose New York City practice includes many performing arts professionals.

4. Garrick, James G. "Ballet Injuries," in *Medical Problems of Performing Artists* (Philadelphia: Hanley and Belfus, Inc., 1986), pp. 123-127.

5. Benson, Joan. "Relationship of Nutrient Intake, Body Mass Index, Menstrual Function, and Ballet Injury," *Journal of the American Dietetic Association,* vol. 89 (January 1989), p. 58.

6. Garrick, James G. op. cit., p. 125.

7. For further guidance in identifying, understanding, and treating dance injuries, we recommend James G. Garrick and Peter Radetsky, *Peak Condition* (Crown, 1986); Celia Sparger, *Anatomy and Ballet* (Theatre Arts, 1970); Justin Howse and Shirley Hancock, *Dance Technique and Injury Prevention* (Theatre Arts, 1988); Daniel Arnheim, M.D., *Dance Injuries* (Princeton Book Company, 1991); and Stuart Wright, *Dancer's Guide to Injuries of the Lower Extremity* (Cornwall Books, 1985).

8. An introduction to resilient flooring can be found in G. James Sammarco, ed., *Clinics in Sports Medicine: Symposium on Injuries to Dancers* (Philadelphia: W. B. Saunders Company, 1983).

# Conversations on Pointe

After the various theories about dancing on pointe have been debated, and the facts relating to pointe shoes have been clearly defined, the true nature of the experience of dancing on pointe remains elusive. A deeper understanding of the relationship between a ballerina and her blocked satin slippers can be gained only by listening to dancers speak about their shoes.

As we traveled around the country gathering information for this book, we spent many hours talking to dancers about pointe shoes. They shared their professional secrets about selecting shoes, preparing them, and working in them. Perhaps more importantly, they revealed how they feel about these unique instruments that are so much a part of their ability to create magic on stage. In closing this book, we would like to share some of these conversations. What follows are reflections on pointe by some of the great contemporary dancers.

Adrienne Canterna

Even as a young student, Adrienne Canterna was well known as a brilliant technician and performer. When she first went on pointe, her feet were so small that she could only wear whatever shoes would fit her. Then, like most other dancers, she kept changing shoes until she found those that worked. When she was about twelve years old, she tried Grishko's shoes, and they were the answer.

Since winning the Gold Medal at the Jackson Competition in 1998, Adrienne has danced with the Universal Ballet in Seoul, Korea, has been a freelance artist, and is starting her own traveling performing arts company. This exceptional dancer says that she does not have good feet. She feels that the Grishko *Elite* makes them look better and it also has a flat box that she likes very much.

She prepares her shoes by cutting the satin off the tip. Then, she sews on elastic for rehearsal shoes, and ribbon for performances. "I can't wear elastic and ribbons because my foot tends to fall asleep when I wear both. I can't have those restrictions on my ankles." Even though the shoes are really hard, she makes them harder by using Jet Glue inside and sometimes even on the outside of the box. She also puts it on the inside and the outside of the shank. Adrienne does not feel the need to "beat up" her shoes. She feels lucky because she finds that the shoes really work for her.

Ashley Tuttle

Dancing on Broadway in *Movin' Out* (Twyla Tharp's choreography and Billy Joel's music) and performing as a principal dancer with American Ballet Theatre, almost simultaneously, keeps Ashley Tuttle extraordinarily busy. In the ABT spring 2003 season at the Metropolitan Opera House, she danced in *Swan Lake* in the afternoon, performed in *Movin' Out* in the evening, and even danced in the Tony Awards show the next day. It really keeps her busy! She did take the week off from the Broadway show before *Swan Lake*, because it is more technically demanding and she wanted to focus on it. But normally she just goes back and forth. In the fall of 2003, she took six weeks off from the show so that she could rehearse and perform in ABT's fall season at City Center (New York). Then she went back into *Movin' Out*.

Ashley has found that dancing in the show is a little different from being in the ballet world. First of all, she said that the staff wants to sew her ribbons for her, not realizing that ballet dancers always sew their own. Also, even though the floor was sprung, she found it slightly slippery. When Marley was put down, it remained slippery. Ashley feels that it is because of the nature of the choreography: "There's a lot of sliding that people do on their bodies, and they do not wear a lot of clothes. The crew is very nice and is always washing [the floor] for me." She is the only dancer who wears pointe shoes in the show, which means that it is more a problem for her than for anyone else. Tharp thought about putting rubber on her shoes, but then realized it would not work because of the slides on pointe that Ashley must do several times.

Capezios are the shoes she has worn since she was thirteen years old. When she was a student at the School of American Ballet, she discovered that the shoes of a dancer in the New York City Ballet fit her perfectly. She then went to Capezio, and Judith Weiss custom-designed pointe shoes using the shoes she had been wearing as a guide. She says that, obviously, the size is a little bigger, but basically the shoes are the same she has always worn. She wears a 3¾ D width in the metatarsal, and C width in the back. The shank is extra thick and is ¾.

Ashley prefers her shoes to be soft and pliable, and tries to make them last a long time. She cuts the satin off the tip for a better grip on the floor. The shoes she wears in the show are black, so she then colors in the platform with a black magic marker. They are ordered from the factory in black. After the spring season with ABT, she found that she had shoes she had worn in *Swan Lake* that still had life in them. She dyed them black and could wear them in the show. She likes the softer shoes because when the floor is slightly slippery, soft shoes give her more control. When Ashley dances with ABT, she sews her ribbons to be sure that they will not come out. Nevertheless, she has to change from pointe shoes to character shoes so quickly in *Movin' Out* that sewing is impossible. She uses tape to hold her ribbons in place—the type of Scotch Tape used to wrap packages.

Jenifer Ringer

When Jenifer Ringer was a student, she wore Capezio pointe shoes. Later she tried both Bloch and Capezio. When she was taken into New York City Ballet, she switched to Freed, mainly because the company preferred them.

Jenny says that while she has good feet, they are not the extraordinarily arched ones that all dancers love. Her ankles have always pointed well, but her toe strength is something she has always had to work on. She has to work very hard to get the bottom of the shoe to bend and her toes to point.

When she was first in the company, she found a shoe that she loved. Her best friend, Yvonne Borree, was wearing it. At the time, when she did not have a very developed sense of what she wanted, she felt fortunate that what her friend wore was perfect for her. The Freed E has a very light box, but the shank is fairly hard. What she really likes about it is that it makes no noise. Jenifer says that early in her career she worked a lot with Jerome Robbins—and he did not like noisy pointe shoes. All she has to do is bang it on the wall a couple of times and it makes no noise. The soft box also makes the transition from pointe to *demi-pointe* smoother.

One of the recent changes she has made in her shoe is that she went to a ¾ shank; in fact, it is almost a half shank. Prior to this, she would physically break her shoe on purpose, at the point where her arch bends the shoe. She did this so that she could better articulate her feet and curve the shape of her shoe more easily with her toes. Now she has the company cut the shank for her.

Recently, she developed plantar fascitis. It became so painful to stand that she had to find a way to ease the discomfort. She bought Dr. Scholl's gel heel pads, and taped them into the heel of her pointe shoe with masking tape, so that the shank does not push into her foot. Even though her left foot is worse than her right, she puts them into both shoes so that they feel even. She says it works very well.

Earlier in her career, Jenifer found that the fabric was bagging around her arch when she was on pointe. Therefore, she has it cut down on the sides, with the heel a little higher, to insure the shoe stays on. Her vamp is square cut. In the past she painstakingly sewed elastic into her ribbons to prevent tendinitis, but now she buys the ribbon, already prepared, from Bunheads. She wears elastic around her ankle in the typical way, and always sews the ends of her ribbons under the knot for performance. Last, she cuts the satin off the tip of her shoes for better traction.

Rather than using Jet Glue or shellac to make her shoes last longer when they get too soft, Jenifer prefers to put another paper towel inside the box if her feet are not too swollen. Many members of New York City Ballet use the type of paper towel she prefers; they are so popular that they are kept backstage in a paper towel rack. She says that a couple of times the attempt was made to change the type of towels, but the dancers caused an uproar! They are very particular about the kind they like to use for padding inside their shoes. She says that they hoard them and take them on tour.

Jenifer uses rosin in two ways. To keep her shoes on, she dips her tights-clad heel in the bucket of water that is kept backstage, and then into rosin before she slips on her shoes. She does not feel the need to do it if she is not wearing tights, since a bare foot holds more securely to the sole of the shoe. Her second use for rosin is for covering dark smudges. She says she just rubs it on the dark spot and it lightens up a bit.

Her latest trauma, one she shares with many other dancers, is that her maker has stopped working. Freed keeps sending shoes for her to try out, hoping she will find something that works for her. She says, "We wear a lot of shoes, and if we're happy, then they're happy."

Larissa Ponomarenko

Larissa Ponomarenko, principal dancer with the Boston Ballet since 1993, has been in the United States since 1991. Her parents still live in Odessa.

Ponomarenko was born in Ukraine and studied in St. Petersburg. She worked for a year in Ukraine after graduation and then came directly to the United States. Larissa joined the Boston Ballet after dancing in Jackson, Mississippi, and Tulsa, Oklahoma.

Even though dancing on pointe is not easy for anyone, Ponomarenko feels the Vaganova School in St. Petersburg made it much easier because there were so many teachers who helped young students. In addition, she lived in a dormitory where the older girls came to the little girls' rooms, showed them how to sew the shoes, how to make them more comfortable, and to share their own experiences.

When she was in the fourth grade, she was lucky enough to have an incredible teacher who would bring the students pointe shoes from the theater. Even then, she had to wear shoes that were about one size too big, since the shoes were made for professional dancers. Later, her teacher, Ninel Kurgapkina, brought her shoes made for the famous star Ludmilla Semeniaka. "Even though those shoes were made for the Bolshoi and Kirov, they were damaging to our little feet. They were very hard at the tip, but the box was just very soft cloth that did not support the joint of the big toe or the metatarsals. In most cases my foot would sink onto the knuckles (which developed bunions and joint problems), and my ankle had to be clenched in order to stay on pointe. Because of that, my calf muscles were constantly overworked and I was doomed to chronic tendinitis."

When Ponomarenko first came to the United States, she wore Grishko shoes, but now wears Russian Pointe. When she started wearing Russian Pointe, the tendinitis began to disappear. They give her foot the support she needs to be able to pull up on her arch rather than sink into it. The shoes have a special extra low cut on the sides, and they fit her like a glove.

After wearing size 34, model E, for two years, she recently switched to a 34.5, saying she thinks her foot has gotten wider. Now she is thinking about switching to a model F because it has a wider tip. The width and the vamp are size 3, and she uses a Medium Flexible shank.

Like most Russian dancers, Larissa sews above the vamp with cotton thread. When asked where she buys it, she laughs and says that she found it in the popular Boston supermarket Stop n' Shop, next to the garlic and onions. Even though she started to do this because everyone else did, now that she can compare Russian shoes with American and English ones, she believes sewing helps to strengthen the softer Russian box. Also, when she goes onto *demi-pointe*, the shoe makes what she calls "ears" if she does not sew the front. When sewn, the shoe feels like a glove.

Ponomarenko explains that the elastic she wears around her ankle is not really to hold the shoe on her foot. For her it is only mentally (not physically) helpful, and only for performance. When preparing her shoes, Larissa opens the binding that encloses the drawstring on the area that touches her heel. This makes the shoe higher on the back, and the shoe stays on her foot perfectly. "I never wear elastic for rehearsals—it never comes down. Sometimes I put a little bit of rosin on my heels, but when I go on stage, I do not want an accident to happen. Sometimes one heel can hit the other, which would knock the shoe off." Larissa sews her ribbons and elastic with the same cotton thread used to sew up the vamp.

When asked if she wears different strength shoes for different performances, Ponomarenko described her experience in *Swan Lake*. She wears the newest shoe for the Black Swan. They are then ready for her next performance as the White Swan, which calls for softer shoes. Since Larissa does not have much time between performances, she does not really break in her shoes. She thinks Russian shoes are softer than American ones, allowing her to wear them for only one rehearsal before performing in them.

Unlike most dancers, Larissa ties her ribbons on the outside of her ankle. She feels the indentation on the foot is the perfect place to tuck the ribbons. She does not ever sew them to hold them intact because sometimes she has to change shoes too quickly. Instead, she puts a little bit of rosin on her tights and on the end of the ribbons, and checks them after each variation.

Nicole Rhodes

After only two years in the company's school, Nicole Rhodes was taken into the Australian Ballet Company in 1991. Following her debut in 1999 as Kitri in *Don Quixote*, she was promoted to principal artist.

Nicole was only ten years old when she first went on pointe. When she went to buy her first shoes, she simply did not find any that were small enough. Just as she and her mother were leaving the store, disappointed, they spotted a huge basket full of shoes. They searched through and were delighted when they found a tiny pair. Nicole wore them for an entire year.

Nicole says that she has always felt comfortable on pointe; it just feels natural to her. When she was a child she took to it like a duck to water, and when she found *Symphony* by Bloch, she felt she was "really home."

It is unusual for a ballerina to have a narrow foot. Therefore Nicole feels especially fortunate that her size 3B is tapered and fits so well. Dancers in the company cannot believe that she wears nothing inside her shoes. While others wear lamb's wool or padding, she is happy just to put her shoes on and dance.

Nina Ananiashvili

When American Ballet Theatre principal and international guest artist Nina Ananiashvili first went on pointe, she found it was painful and very uncomfortable. The students at the school of the Bolshoi Ballet wore hand-me-down shoes made for the professional dancers in the company. Later, she still found that even when the shoes were made for her, they were inconsistent. Sometimes they were too dry; sometimes they had too much glue. She was always fixing them with needle and thread.

She changed from Russian shoes before she came to ABT. "I switched to Freeds because Kenneth MacMillan made me," she said, with her voice rising. "I was working with the Royal Ballet in London. Kenneth asked if I was wearing Russian shoes. When I said yes, he suggested that I try 'our' shoes, meaning Freeds. I told Michele Attfield, the main fitter, exactly what I wanted, and after several tries, my maker came up with a shoe that was perfect for me."

Nina said that Russian shoes are very narrow and pointy because the Russians feel it looks much better when the foot is pointed. When she came to the West she was shocked to see bigger, squarer-shaped shoes. She particularly likes Freed shoes because they make it easy to roll through her foot. Also, they are more available in the West, where she works most.

She has a narrow foot, so has the sides cut down and a V shape in the vamp. She does not need to sew up the vamp, as is the custom of many Russians, but does darn around the edge of the tip or platform so the satin does not fray. She adds that in Russia most of the dancers open the heel to make it more comfortable, but she no longer feels it is necessary to do this.

When she has a lot of rehearsals the shoe gets soft, so she glues the inside of the box and also the shank so it lasts longer. She also special-orders a wing block to make the shoes a bit stronger; to insure they do not get soft too quickly.

Nina finds it very interesting that in Russia dancers always wear tights or socks with the shoes. But in the United States, many like to cut the tights so that the bare foot makes contact with the shoe. She said if she did that, her toes would be bloody; in fact, she has found a Capezio toe pad with a little jelly in it. She says it is perfect because it is not very thick. Thick pads require a bigger shoe, which she thinks makes shoes that should fit like a glove look big and bulky.

Before she wears her shoes, she flattens the box with her hands to make it more comfortable. She never dances on stage in new shoes—she prefers to rehearse in them a little bit first. Then she sews around the platform and puts the shoes aside until they are needed for performance. She always has several pairs of shoes ready. If Nina is dancing a three-act ballet, she always has two pairs of shoes for each act. She explains that sometimes in the first act, she needs shoes that are somewhat soft. By having several pairs ready, in the next act, when she needs harder shoes for *pirouettes*, she is always prepared.

Paloma Herrera

Paloma Herrera, principal dancer with American Ballet Theatre, grew up in Argentina, where it was hard to find pointe shoes. From the very beginning, she wore Argentinian shoes that were custom-ordered.

Paloma remembers, "When I was about ten, we (my class) all went with our teacher and found the right shoes for each of us."

When asked if she had encountered a specific problem in pointe work that she had to overcome, Paloma answered:

"I guess...it was easy for me. I started ballet at seven, and pointe was always my dream—always. When I got pointe shoes, I loved dancing on pointe; my dream had come true. I remember that day well. I know that some people hate their pointe shoes, but I never did. I love them even today.

I think it was easy, but from the very beginning I worked very well in my ballet shoes...even when I was seven, eight, and nine...so when I went into pointe shoes, the transition was easy."

Paloma says that because of her very high instep, she needs "a stronger shank (¾) and a longer vamp. I try to have really strong feet to control my shoes better." She also uses an elastic drawstring to conform to the shape of her foot.

Herrera wears made-to-order Capezio pointe shoes now. On first arriving in New York, she attended the School of American Ballet and tried regular Capezio shoes. When she joined American Ballet Theatre, Freed was the company shoe; but she ended up coming back to Capezio. "One day I went to Capezio, and they said, 'Ask for whatever you want and we'll do it.' And so I said OK! They really did a great job...they did pretty much everything I asked. Since then I have always worn Capezios, and I feel very, very comfortable in them."

While we spoke, Paloma was recycling her ribbons: unstitching them from an old pair of pointe shoes and putting them on a new pair. She does this to "try and save ABT money." She uses Capezio wide pink ribbons in one long piece sewn into the shoe under the heel and from side to side. Herrera does this so she does not lose a ribbon. When she ties her ribbons for a performance, she sews them so that the ends do not come out. Paloma wears elastic only for performances—not for class or rehearsals.

When preparing her pointe shoes, Paloma does not use a hammer. Instead, she bangs them on the floor to take the noise out. She smashes the box in a door at the Metropolitan Opera House, where the doors are big and heavy. "I used to break a lot of doors at home, so that's why I never do it there." Herrera scuffs the sole with a shoe-scuffer for a better grip on the floor. Nothing comes between Paloma's toes and her shoes: "I never wear anything on my foot… nothing in the shoe. No paper towels, no lamb's wool, no Band Aids. Nothing."

Sasha Dmochowski

Sasha Dmochowski (the "D" is silent) danced with the Boston Ballet for eight years before joining American Ballet Theatre. She knows that she is pretty lucky because she has toes that are all the same length. She says she has her parents to thank for that!

Her first shoes were Capezio. Then she tried Freed, but found they got really "mushy." Next she wore Gaynor Minden shoes for a year, before finally discovering that the Chacott *Coppelia II* worked well for her. Later she switched to the Chacott *Veronese* and has been wearing them for about ten years.

Sasha wears stock shoes, but she does many things to customize them. First she cuts the shank to three-quarter with garden sheers borrowed from her father. Then she puts mole foam across the cut part so that it does not dig into her foot. Next she crisscrosses two thin strips of elastic over her ankle to give more support, and, last, she cuts the satin off the tip. The entire process takes about forty minutes. Once in a while she will put a little bit of Super Glue on the shanks, but normally she just wears the shoes until they "die." "Once the shoes have been worn a lot, they start to warp with the glue. That's why I don't usually use it."

Since her feet sweat a lot, she is always rotating three or four pairs of pointe shoes. The rotating allows them to last about two weeks. Wearing ToeFlo pads strikes her as being "Dolly Dinkle," but she does it anyway. She comments that in the past, dancers had to be "martyrs" and wear lamb's wool, paper towels, or even nothing at all, but she likes the pads, saying they make her shoes a perfect fit.

Sherri LeBlanc

Before joining San Francisco Ballet, Sherri LeBlanc was a member of New York City Ballet. When she was a student at the School of American Ballet, she started looking for a pointe shoe that would meet her needs. She says that she does not have very strong ankles or good feet; she has to work them twice as hard as most people, because she doesn't have nice arches and there is not a great deal of movement in the joints. Constantly trying to make them look better brings about over-work. The shoe she was wearing as a student was not supportive, which wreaked havoc on her ankles.

When she found Eva shoes, she found a shoe that gave her feet the need-ed support as well as a longer line. Even though ¾ shanks can be ordered, she still likes to order a regular shank and then use an Exacto knife to cut it herself. Sherri likes the way her arch sits right on the edge because it is very supportive. She rounds off the edge so that it does not dig into her foot. "I like it to be nice and hard so that my foot does not go like a banana and crunch."

To make sure the box does not get soft too fast, she puts glue into the tip to harden it. Sometime she does it when they are brand new, and sometimes after they have begun to break down. "It's really nicer to wear them once, and get them to shape like the foot…to make them more comfortable…and then glue them so that the shoes dry in that shape. The downside is that the shoes might not last quite as long this way."

To cushion the pain of her bunions, she buys a gel pad at the drugstore and puts it between the callous on her big toe and the bunion. It evens out the toe so that she does not develop nerve problems in her bunion. (There is a nerve in the bunion that can get impinged in the shoe. Evening out the area with the gel pads prevents the impingement.) Then she wears a toe spacer, wraps a sock or some type of material around it, and she is ready to go—without having to tape her toes. The material she prefers to use is from old cotton leotards, because it is so soft.

Sherri sews the ribbons almost in the middle of her shoe because she feels that they support her foot better there, where her arch breaks. In this position the ribbons pull the shoe right against her arch. She says, "When you do not have much of an arch, you want to make the most of what you have." She then uses dental floss to sew the ribbons to the shoe because it is so strong. "I use ribbons that the company (San Francisco Ballet) orders that have elastic inserts. This allows the ribbon to give in the back where it crosses the Achilles tendon. Sometimes I even sew the elastic on myself, even though it is a lot of sewing."

Vanessa Palmer

Dancing with the Royal Ballet was Vanessa Palmer's dream. To attain that goal, she had to audition for the Lower School at White Lodge, the English boarding school that trains dancers for the Royal Ballet. When she was eleven, she felt she was not yet ready to leave home, but by age twelve, she auditioned and was surprised when she was selected.

For many years she had worn the same brand of pointe shoes. "It wasn't until God sent Gaynor Mindens to dancers about five years ago that I realized how painful pointe work was getting, and how the shoes were starting to eat my feet. The other insoles used to curl up and cut my soles. I got so many blisters and bruised toenails and just thought it was a part of the job. I liked to wear my pointe shoes for class and it was getting to the stage where I just couldn't." The first time she put on the Gaynor Mindens, they were so comfortable that her feet "purred." She will never forget the feeling.

Changing shoes necessitated a posture realignment. The result of this realignment is that her legs have lengthened in muscle tone and totally changed shape. Vanessa is amazed that she can wear her shoes all day in complete comfort. Another characteristic she likes is the ease of preparation: all she does is sew a little bit of elastic on the heel to make a snug fit and then molds the back under the heat of a hairdryer. This makes the shoe follow her metatarsal as she points. The shoe stays like that until it wears out. They are harder to sew because the consistency of the material is different from other shoes, but she feels it is worth the extra effort. Vanessa literally steps into the new shoes—and they are exactly like the pair that has just been discarded!

Marisa Soltis

Marisa Soltis studied in New York City at Harkness House under the tutelage of Nanci Clement. More recently, she has danced as principal dancer with the Ballet Theatre of Boston and Fort Wayne Ballet.

Soltis has not had much difficulty with pointe shoes because her toes are all very even. She began her career wearing Bloch *Serenade* shoes, but ran out of them in the middle of a long *Nutcracker* season and had to make an emergency switch. The day before dancing the Sugar Plum Fairy, she faced wearing a completely different shoe because her back-order had not yet arrived.

Marisa now wears Gambas, size 4½ XX, and feels completely at home in them. She finds that style *93* is better for performance, but wears *92* for rehearsal. The more lightweight *93* needs very little breaking in. Soltis simply sews on the ribbons and elastic and goes right out on stage. She feels that these shoes have the quality that everyone likes in Freed shoes, but that they last longer. Freeds seem to wear out for her in about half an hour. Unlike many dancers who change shoes for each act of a full-length ballet, Soltis can wear the *93* shoes for an entire *Coppélia*, plus one more act the next day.

When preparing her shoes, Marisa likes wider elastic, and crisscrosses it over her ankle. For rehearsal, she does not go to the trouble of sewing on ribbons, because she feels somewhat freer in the shoe without them. When Soltis does put ribbons on, she sews them directly on top of the elastic on the outside of the shoe. Her high arch feels more comfortable and not as confined as when the ribbon is sewn on the inside. She never cuts the satin off the tip because she does not find it slippery.

While dyeing her shoes and ribbons black for a role, Soltis discovered that Krylon works better than dyes she had used. It dries in about fifteen minutes and the dye never comes off on her foot—even when rehearsing without tights. Nor did it change the texture of the shoe. In the past, dyes occasionally shrank her shoes, as well as making them harder. Krylon did neither.

Lei Zhao

Born in Shanghai and trained at the Shanghai Ballet School and later the Northern Ballet School in England, Lei Zhao is now a member of the Birmingham Royal Ballet in Birmingham, England. She wore Chinese pointe shoes as a student because there were no other options. When Lei participated in an international ballet competition, she discovered Freeds which she thought were very comfortable.

After moving to England, she continued wearing them, but was not totally satisfied because of her particular type of foot. "I have a good arch, but my feet are very thin. I have to point from my ankle because my foot is flat on top. The shoes I had been wearing were too wide so I would put toe pads inside as filler. This made a big bulge and was bulky which made it difficult to do *adagio*. I felt unstable. Also, I am wide in the toe joint but shallow and narrow closer to the back of my foot. It looks like a triangle. They are very difficult feet!"

About three years ago a few girls in the company were trying out a new English shoe called *Workshop 2000* made by Bob Martin. Lei found the *Innovation* solved her problems. She wears a 3XX and uses a Phillips insole. (Light and thin, it is famous because Margot Fonteyn used a Phillips.) Lei says that the lightness makes dancing very nice. Her jumps are easier to control and she feels very steady on the ground. She warns that if a dancer has a big arch, these shoes probably would not give the needed support, and if a too-soft shoe is worn, it really is bad for the ankles. It's difficult to find a happy medium. What is most important to her is, of course, that she feels comfortable.

Because she has such thin feet, she has the sides cut low. "If they are too high, they are like a boat; they cover the foot completely. It's much more beautiful to see more instep instead of more material." On the other hand, she has the shoes cut higher on the heels to be sure the shoes don't come off.

To prepare her shoes, she sews on elastic that is almost transparent. This elastic and the ribbon she uses are supplied by the shoe supervisor to all the dancers in the company. Lei likes this elastic because it is thin and not restrictive. She says sometimes elastic can be so tight that when you stretch your feet, you can overwork your calves. After she ties and knots the drawstring, she cuts off the excess so it won't come out when she is dancing.

Before she wears the shoes, she shellacs the entire insole to extend its life. Lei doesn't like to put shellac in the top because it makes too much noise. Even though the shellac dries in about twenty minutes, she says it is better to wear them the next day because it gives the shoes extra strength. To insure the shoes wear evenly, she alternates the pair with each wearing. She says she used to do a lot to her shoes because they were too big, but once she found those that fit properly, she has to do almost nothing to them.

Bibliography

Adshead-Lansdale, Janet, and June Layson, eds. *Dance History: An Introduction,* 2nd ed. London/New York: Routledge, 1994.

Arnot, Michelle. *Foot Notes.* New York: Doubleday/Dolphin, 1980.

Barnes, Clive. "Barnes On...," *Ballet News* (February 1986) vol. 7.

Beaumont, Cyril W. *The Cecchetti Method of Classical Ballet: Theory and Technique.* Reprint. New York: Dover, 2003.

Benson, Joan. "Relationship of Nutrient Intake, Body Mass Index, Menstrual Function and Ballet Injury," *Journal of the American Dietetic Association* (January 1989) vol. 89.

Bentley, Toni. "The Heart and Sole of a Ballerina's Art: Her Toe Shoes," *Smithsonian* (June 1984) vol. 15.

Berardi, Gigi. *Finding Balance: Fitness and Training for a Lifetime in Dance.* Hightstown, NJ: Princeton Book Company, 1991.

Bowes, Deborah, ed. *The Ballet Book: The Young Performers Guide to Classical Dance.* Richmond Hill, Ontario: Firefly Books, 1999.

Braver, Richard T. "Tendonitis Rond de Ankle," *Kinesiology for Dance* (September 1988) vol.11.

Brinson, Peter, ed. *The Healthier Dancer: Injuries to Dancers, A Worldwide Problem.* London: Laban Centre for Movement and Dance, 1991.

Brody, Jane. "Personal Health: Ankle Injury," *The New York Times* (September 14, 1989) II:15:1.

Buckroyd, Julia. *The Student Dancer: Emotional Aspects of the Teaching and Learning of Dance.* London: Dance Books Ltd., 2000.

Chmelar, Robin D., and Sally S. Fitt. *Diet for Dancers: A Complete Guide to Nutrition and Weight Control.* Hightstown, NJ: Princeton Book Company, 1990.

Chujoy, Anatole, and P.W. Manchester, eds. *The Dance Encyclopedia.* New York: Simon & Schuster, 1967.

Bibliography

Cohen, Selma Jeanne. *Dance as a Theatre Art: Source Readings in Dance History from 1581 to the Present.* Hightstown, NJ: Princeton Book Company, 1992.

Coussins, Craig. *A Fitting Manual for Ballet and Pointe Shoes.* London: Gamba Timestep Ltd., 1988.

Cox, Meg. "If She's on her Toes, a Ballerina Devotes Hours to her Shoes," *Wall Street Journal* (March 11, 1989) 1:1:2.

Dozzi, Paula A. "Biomechanical Analysis of the Foot During Rises to Full Pointe: Implications for Injuries to the Metatarsal-Phalangeal Joints and Shoe Redesign," *Kinesiology and Medicine for Dance* (fall/winter 1993/94) vol. 16, no. 1.

Farrell, Suzanne. *Holding on to the Air: An Autobiography.* New York: Summit Books, 1990.

Fitt, Sally Sevey. *Dance Kinesiology,* 2nd ed. New York: Schirmer Books; London: Prentice Hall International, 1996.

Flint, Vivi, and Knud Arne Jürgensen. *Bournonville Ballet Technique: Fifty Enchaînements.* London: Dance Books Ltd., 1992.

Franklin, Eric N. *Dance Imagery for Technique and Performance.* Champaign, IL: Human Kinetics, 1997.

Freed, Frederick. Folder of clippings in The Dance Collection, Library for the Performing Arts, New York Public Library.

Garrick, James G., M.D. "Ballet Injuries," *Medical Problems of Performing Artists.* Philadelphia, PA: Hanley & Belfus, Inc., 1986.

_____, and Peter Radetsky. *Peak Condition.* New York: Crown, 1986.

Glasstone, Richard. "Some Thoughts on Pointe Work," *The Dancing Times* (London) (October 1979).

Golovkina, Sophia. *Lessons in Classical Dance.* London: Dance Books Ltd., 1991.

Gow, Gordon. "Freed at 80," *The Dancing Times* (London) (October 1979).

Grant, Gail. *Technical Manual and Dictionary of Classical Ballet.* New York: Dover, 1967.

Grieg, Valerie. *Inside Ballet Technique: Separating Fact from Fiction in the Ballet Class.* Hightstown, NJ: Princeton Book Company, 1994.

Hamilton, Linda. *Advice for Dancers: Emotional Counsel and Practical Strategies.* San Francisco: Jossey-Bass, 2002.

293

Bibliography

Hamilton, William G., M.D. "Ballet and Your Body: An Orthopedist's View," *Dance Magazine* (January 1979).

Haskell, Arnold. *The Russian Genius in Ballet.* New York: Pergamon, 1963.

Hill, Lorna. *La Sylphide: The Life of Marie Taglioni.* New York: Evans, 1967.

Howard, Sharma L. "Taking the Pain Out of Pointe," *Dance Teacher Now* (January 1997).

Howse, Justin, and Shirley Hancock. *Dance Technique and Injury Prevention,* rev. ed. London: A. and C. Black; New York: Theatre Arts Books/Routledge, 1992.

Hughes, Rebecca. "Ouch! Rx for Beat Feet," *Family Circle* (August 1988).

Jonas, Gerald. *Dancing: The Pleasure, Power, and Art of Movement.* New York: Abrams, 1992.

Kaye, Elizabeth, with Clive Barnes. *American Ballet Theatre: A 25 Year Retrospective.* Kansas City, MO: Andrews McMeel, 1999.

Kent, Allegra. *Once a Dancer.* New York: St. Martin's Press, 1997.

Kistler, Darci. *Ballerina: My Story.* New York: Pocket Books, 1993.

Kostrovitskaya, Vera S., trans. by Oleg Briansky. *100 Lessons in Classical Ballet.* New York: Doubleday and Company, 1981.

_____, and Alexi Pisarev. *School of Classical Dance.* London: Dance Books, 1995.

Laws, Kenneth, and Cynthia Harvey. *Physics, Dance and the Pas de Deux.* New York: Schirmer Books; Toronto: Maxwell Macmillan Canada.

Lawson, Joan. "Seventy Years of Gamba," *The Dancing Times* (London) (December 1973).

_____. "Shoes and Injuries," *The Dancing Times* (London) (September 1983).

_____. "Shoe Problems," *The Dance Gazette* (July 1982) no. 180.

Leonard, Maurice. *Markova: The Legend.* London: Hodder & Stoughton, 1995.

Levine, Ellen. *Anna Pavlova: Genius of the Dance.* New York: Scholastic, 1995.

Mara, Thalia. *On Your Toes.* New York: Dance Horizons, 1972.

_____. Steps in Ballet. Hightstown, NJ: Princeton Book Company, 2004.

Martins, Peter, and the New York City Ballet. *The New York City Ballet Workout*. New York: William Morrow & Company, 1997.

Menezes, Allan. *The Complete Guide to Joseph A. Pilates' Technique of Physical Conditioning*. Alameda, CA: Hunter House, 2000.

Miller, E., H. Schneider, J. Bronson, and D. McLain. "A New Consideration in Athletic Injuries: The Classical Ballet Dancer," *Clinical Orthopedics* (1975) vol. 111.

Moore, Lillian. *Artists of the Dance*. New York: Blom, 1969.

————, *Images of the Dance: Historical Treasures of The Dance Collection, 1581-1861*. New York: New York Public Library, 1965.

Neale, Wendy. *On Your Toes*. New York: Crown, 1980.

Novella, Thomas M. "Foot Care for Pointe Shoes," *Dance Magazine* (April 1994).

Paskevska, Anna. *Both Sides of the Mirror: The Science and Art of Ballet,* 2nd ed. Hightstown, NJ: Princeton Book Company, 1992.

Quirk, R. "Ballet Injuries: The Australian Experience," *Clinical Sports Medicine* (1983) vol. 2.

Reid, D.C. "Prevention of Hip and Knee Injuries in Ballet Dancers," *Sports Medicine* (November 1988) vol. 6.

Reynolds, Nancy, and Malcolm McCormick. *No Fixed Points: Dance in the Twentieth Century*. New Haven: Yale University Press, 2003.

Roses, Cynthia Ann. "Preparing for Pointe," *Dance Teacher Now* (November/December 1991).

Sachs, Curt. *World History of the Dance*. New York: Norton, 1963.

Schorer, Suki. *Balanchine Pointework*. Society of Dance History Scholars, 1995.

————. *Suki Schorer on Balanchine Technique*. New York: Alfred A. Knopf, 1999.

Selva and Son. Folder of clippings in file of The Dance Collection, Library for the Performing Arts, New York Public Library.

Serebrennikov, Nikolai. *Pas de Deux: A Textbook on Partnering,* 2nd ed. Gainesville, FL: University Press of Florida, 2000.

Smith, Marian. *Ballet and Opera in the Age of Giselle*. Princeton, NJ: Princeton University Press, 2000.

Bibliography

Solomon, Ruth, Sandra C. Minton, and John Solomon, eds. *Preventing Dance Injuries: An Interdisciplinary Perspective*. Reston, VA: American Alliance for Health, Physical Education, Recreation and Dance, 1990.

Sorell, Walter. *The Dance Has Many Faces*. Chicago: A Cappella Books, 1992.

_____, *The Dance Through the Ages*. New York: Grosset, 1967.

Sorine, Daniel and Stephanie. *Dancershoes*. New York: Alfred A. Knopf, 1979.

Sparger, Celia. *Anatomy and Ballet*. New York: Theatre Arts Books, 1970.

Spilken, Terry L. *The Dancer's Foot Book: A Complete Guide to Footcare and Health for People Who Dance*. Hightstown, NJ: Princeton Book Company, 1990.

Taffy's of Cleveland, Ohio. Folder of clippings in file of The Dance Collection, Library for the Performing Arts, New York Public Library.

Tallchief, Maria. *America's Prima Ballerina*. New York: Henry Holt, 1997.

Thomas, Helen. *The Body, Dance and Cultural Theory*. Basingstoke, Hants., England: Palgrave Macmillan, 2003.

Thomasen, Eivind, and Rachel-Anne Rist. *Anatomy and Kinesiology for Ballet Teachers*. London: Dance Books Ltd., 1996.

Tobias, Tobi. "Toe Shoes: Satin Thorns under Every Ballerina's Feet," *The New York Times* (September 21, 1975) III, 26:1.

Trucco, Terry. "To the Pointe," *Ballet News* (March 1982) vol. 3.

Vaganova, Agrippina. *Basic Principles of Classical Ballet: Russian Ballet Techniques*. New York: Dover, 1969; reprint 1995.

Warren, Gretchen Ward. *The Art of Teaching Ballet: Ten Twentieth Century Masters*. Gainesville, FL: University Press of Florida, 1996.

Watkins, Andrea. *Dancing Longer, Dancing Stronger: A Dancer's Guide to Improving Technique and Preventing Injury*. Hightstown, NJ: Princeton Book Company, 1990.

Whitehill, Angela, and William Noble. *The Parents Book of Ballet,* 2nd ed. Hightstown, NJ: Princeton Book Company, 2003.

Woodle, Alan S. *Digital Length Discrepancies in Ballet Pointe Position: Conservative Treatment with Modable Podiatric Compound*. Seattle, WA: Self-published, 1989.

Wright, Stuart. *Dancer's Guide to Injuries of the Lower Extremities: Diagnosis, Treatment and Care*. Cranbury, NJ: Cornwall Books, 1988.

Index

Index